ALWAYS READY

SEMPER PARATUS

ALWAYS READY

SEMPER PARATUS

FROM
COMMUNIST KGB MASTER SPY
TO CIA OPERATIVE AND
AMERICAN CORPORATE EXECUTIVE

ALEXANDER VON LOCKNER, GP

Copyright © 2006 by Alexander von Lockner, GP.

Library of Congress Control Number: 2006902624
ISBN: Hardcover   1-4257-1234-7
                   Softcover   1-4257-1233-9

Library of Congress Cataloging-in-Publication Data
1. von Lockner, Alexander, 1952-
2. Intelligence officers—Biography
3. Espionage, Soviet-History-20th century.
4. Spies-Soviet Union, Eastern Europe.
5. Soviet Union and Bulgaria.

This book was printed in the United States of America.

To order additional copies of this book, contact:
Xlibris Corporation
International Plaza II
Suite 340
Philadelphia, PA 19113
1-888-795-4274
www.Xlibris.com
Orders@Xlibris.com
33881

CONTENTS

SOVIET INDUSTRIAL ESPIONAGE, TECHNOLOGY TRANSFER AND SOCIALIST PROSPERITY

PROVIDENCE

DEMOCRACY OF TOTALITARIANISM

TO MY INSPIRATIONAL FAMILY

The Publications Review Board of the Central Intelligence Agency has reviewed this book manuscript to ensure that it is not revealing or containing classified information pertinent to the national security of the United States of America, or any friendly NATO nations. This review however, does not admit to, nor acknowledge any of the operations or individuals herewith outlined. I would like to emphasize that the review reflects reasonably professional judgment as of what was secret and what was not. I am thankful to the Central Intelligence Agency and the American government for allowing me to serve with integrity and dedication in the thrilling Cold War against the global communist and terrorist malice.

For professional and security reasons many names and specific locations have been listed fictitiously, even as alias, nor are many particular technical, eavesdropping, monitoring, and collection operations described, as such could be still functional and operational around the world.

This book shares a unique perspective on international espionage. It is a rare example of an individual that finds the blunders of the Soviet communist ideology and socio-economics early on and then bravely realizes that rather than rebel; it is his duty to unearth and reveal its faults to the world. Many defectors have lived to escape their systems and then outline the idiosyncrasies, faults, and treacheries therein; however, rarely is an internal mole able to for years provide information and fulfill intricate CIA operations, and then at the last possible moment cunningly escape the clutches of those he fought and deceived.

While professionals have outlined the KGB actions against the west, this book is unique in that it outlines how the CIA fought against the KGB system from the inside. It reveals many of the unique and dangerous operations conducted by the American government to grind away and annihilate the Soviet and East European totalitarian systems.

AUTHOR'S ACKNOWLEDGEMENTS

I should no longer be silent about the permanent scars left on the Soviet and Eastern European Communism by my role in the invisible and perfidious battles of the Cold War.

Neither shall I disregard the truth or withhold particulars about the merciless secret practices of the totalitarian system in which I was expected to be a dyed in-the-wool apparatchik. Soviet communism thoughtlessly abused power, suppressed human liberty and tyrannically violated human rights. This was all in the name of Marxist-Leninist doctrine and the utopian Bolshevik communality predestined to depart the Earth's socio-economic milieu, condemned as a totalitarian malice by the modern narration of history.

Nor should I be silent and recluse about the distinction and pride of becoming a citizen of the world's gratifying and prosperous democracy, the United States of America.

In mid 1970s, with silent revolt, dignity and human determination, I embraced James Joyce's expression:

"I will not serve that in which I no longer believe, whether it call itself my home, my fatherland, or my church: and I will try to express myself . . . as freely as I can and as wholly as I can, using for my defense the only arms I allow myself to use—secrecy, exile and cunning."

Times have changed, the world has evolved and my cause of actions has proven to be correct. My painful sacrifices, mortal fights and inevitable sufferings have been worth living with, for I have helped to chart the world's modern history. I have succeeded by courageously rejecting the malignant existence of the Soviet totalitarian communism, its greatly ubiquitous leftist and sectarian terrorism, and socio-economic primitivisms.

Alex von Lockner, GP—"SPAR"

INTRODUCTION

LIFE IN THE NAME OF DEMOCRACY

For thirty years I fought the proliferation of the Soviet communism and leftist terrorism, eventually aiding in the final annihilation of the Leninist malice. With courageous determination I infiltrated and fatally windswept the utmost powerful arms of the Soviet KGB and the Sixteenth Soviet Socialist Republic's Bulgarian State Security. As a stealthy American intelligence operative, since the mid 1970s I gathered complex East European secret and strategic intelligence and recruited communist politicians, government, military and intelligence officials. I effectively infiltrated the most secretive Soviet institutions; those considered of most vital interest to the United States of America and NATO.

Uniquely staged circumstances in the mid 1980s led to my crafty exfiltration, even then under the vigilant eyes and deadly, suffocating hold of communist security agents. In the United States of America, I continued my work against the totalitarian communist regimes and their menacing security and intelligence directorates. I professionally fought global communist expansion, the proliferation of bio-chemical and nuclear weapons, escalating leftist and religious terrorism, thievery of western Know How and technology, and crimes against humanity. In my work, I consistently consummated astute cross-cultural and business strategies, advanced international finance and trade tools, multinational marketing and global manufacturing concepts, and nonetheless crafty forms of international negotiations. Academic attentiveness and professional experience rallied around my vast business results and covert intelligence triumphs in varying global circumstances. My utmost mind's eye and most far-flung dreams became reality. I traveled all over the world, sensibly conducting business and duly representing specific American government, geo-political and economic interests. Meetings with global leaders, government and corporate executives, religious fanatics and narcotic lords, blue-blooded nobility and renowned entrepreneurs became routine parts of my innate daily milieu.

From a communist, KGB trained master spy, mercilessly indoctrinated into cunningly fighting the western capitalist and democratic values, I emerged as a successful American intelligence operative, corporate executive, a freedom-loving and democracy-cherishing United States citizen, and a truly credible messenger of peace, global cooperation and economic prosperity.

THE CENTRAL INTELLIGENCE AGENCY

"*C IA Next,*" an almost shocking public announcement, is clearly visible on two highway signs on George Washington Memorial parkway and Dolly Madison Boulevard in McLean, Virginia. Today, the Central Intelligence Agency's headquarters is comprised in part of the old building completed in the early 1960s, accommodating in the southwest wing on the seventh floor the Director of Central Intelligence's (DCI) office and his deputies' compartments. The offices of the four major Directorates, the main intelligence library, the National Historical Intelligence Collection and museum, the gym, a barbershop and a cafeteria are also integral parts of the old setting. A grayish-white marble main lobby further contributes to an initially spooky feeling as first time visitors enter the building.

Meticulously maintained flags of the United States of America and the Central Intelligence Agency flank a white marble memorial on the right wall. It commemorates the intelligence agency's operatives fallen in the line of service around the world (most marked solely with a gold star, as they had used undercover names during assignments). On the left is the statue of William Donovan, the first director of the Office of Strategic Services (OSS), the forerunner of the CIA. A darker polished marble eagle on the center floor of the lobby symbolizes the global mission of the agency. Another new building was completed in the late 1980s, accommodating most Langley employees. However, the roots of the institution remain within the hallowed halls of the old. At any given time, employees and visitors use specially encoded photo identity passes to gain access through the strictly guarded turnstiles and designated sections.

During my years in Washington, D.C., working for the American intelligence, I had different offices in Vienna, McLean, Roselyn and Fairfax, Virginia. It was a precautionary standing of the CIA, hereditary to the grim days of James Angleton's "*mole hunt*" that precluded all but a small group of exceptionally trustworthy assets to work at the main HQ. Although I perceived the imposed segregation as an impediment to my professional efficiency, I become unbiased to the operational settings. I had plenty of work to do in combating the totalitarianism and the never-ending intelligence games of the KGB and State Security around the globe.

A few months after my arrival in the United States, the CIA's Office of Security informed me that the DCI, William Casey, would like to meet with me at Langley. An avalanche of hypotheses passed through my mind as I announced the invitation to my boss Milt Bearden. However, he made me aware that it was one of Director Casey's signature public relations acts to express personal gratitude to someone's exceptional work for the United States government. I was sincerely surprised, for it was unexpected attention with strong moral and patriotic implications.

To reach this moment, I did not sell my soul to the highest bidding international merchant, as so many others had done so well. Early in my life, I had discovered that the communist utopia was an ever eluding and unreachable delusion. The imposed Soviet system was ruthlessly fashioned to carry on the grotesque totalitarian interests of Kremlin. For years I had self-sacrificially and effectively fought Moscow's interests, saving the American government substantial funds, efforts and resources. My conscious beliefs in freedom and democracy transformed my life into an astute struggle against the terrors of the totalitarianism.

For years I worked with the CIA in steadily penetrating the Soviet KGB and the Bulgarian State Security's inner sanctum. We identified and in many instances prevented brutal and senseless totalitarian internal repressions, political purges and persecutions, exposed lasting human deprivations, curbed aggressive intelligence gatherings and shrewd industrial espionage, and halted sinister subversive and terrorist activities of leftist, religious and communist agents against the west.

My difficult journey through treacherous labyrinths of intrigue, inevitably facing the gallows if exposed while flying high on the wings of my conscious soul, was perhaps worthy of Casey's acknowledgement. Notwithstanding, my commitments to the United States government had agonizingly separated me from my great family and inspirational children.

On an early afternoon in September 1984, I traveled with Ron McCarty to the main headquarters in Langley. After the traditional ID and security check, we took the executive elevator in the south end of the old building straight to the seventh floor. It was my first visit to the executive floor. We passed through security and a few support offices amid friendly greetings by the staff. Adjacent to the DCI's office, an administrative assistant advised us that Director Casey was tardy from a lunch with President Ronald Reagan. While waiting for his return, he had arranged for us to spend some time with DDO John Stain (Deputy Director of Operations).

In July 1981, John Stain was appointed Chief of Clandestine Services (DDO), by the then First Deputy of the Central Intelligence Agency, Admiral Bobby Inman. Brilliant connoisseur, John was an avid gardener taking extraordinary care of an exotic rose and orchid garden. His knowledge of wines, especially grand cru clase Rothschilds, Sent Emelions and Château Margos was exceptional. He was often seen driving the winding Great Falls countryside roads of Virginia in his topless, almost vintage Austin-Healy on the way to work. He had purchased it from his old friend Dwue (Duane) Clarridge, (the future Assistant DDO and First Chief of the Counter-terrorism Directorate of CIA). John was a Yale graduate and a fluent French language speaker. Originally from Rhode Island, he was an athlete and a skilled baseball player, carrying with him a distinguished and aristocratic demeanor. His last assignment as Chief of Station to Brussels, Belgium was extended twice due to his outstanding work. Granted, he had brilliant capabilities at being able to network between NATO and EEC political leaders, he was definitely recognized and aided in his challenging pursuits and endeavors by his chic and charismatic French born wife. John's personal impact and influence on the intelligence gathering and the political process all over Western Europe and the francophone regions of West Africa was legendary.

Our dialog evolved around the wonderful green fields of dense treetops, waving with the winds outside his office window, spreading far out to the outer banks of Potomac River and into the Maryland hills. He shifted our discussion to the professionalism that was required by the agency's operational officers, all the while cross-referenced the talk with the educational and professional training and motivational reasoning of the communist officials, diplomats and intelligence officers. *"Big John"*, as Stain was well known, outlined the new changing global environment for the intelligence community. Bluntly making comparisons between his generation's idealistic egalitarian sentiments and convictions, he was critical of the new *"yuppie"* interests. Concisely and semi-critically Stain summarized that the creative and challenging environment of the Agency's Clandestine Services operations (changed to Directorate of Operations) had changed and politically evolved in to a mundane job of primary concerns about monthly checks and job benefits coverage. John Stain then stoically referred to zingers and failures of the Agency, actions blown out of proportion and hideously distorted by the press, and as a consequence, he was not ashamed to acknowledge that the overall direction of CIA operations had become stalwartly controlled and predisposed to the United States Congress.

John was interested to comprehend what factors determine loyalty and motivate communist intelligence officers and how committed they could be to the communist doctrine and their motherland. His viewpoint that there should have been growing resentment among the intelligence officers and diplomats towards the superfluous communist ideology and towards the primitive ways of life throughout Eastern Europe was quite plausible and accurate. However, my own experience and observations intrigued the spymaster and he ornately highlighted some of my testimonials. Shifting to the *Solidarity* movement in Poland, Stain stipulated that the traditionally Catholic religious convictions of the Polish people and the enormous moral support from the Vatican and Pope John Paul II would inevitably weaken the foundations of the Polish communism.

Although John Stain had spelled out his limited time, specific interests quickly prevailed. Discussing the Pope's assassination attempt by Mehmet Ali Agca, on *St. Peters'* Square, he delineated Director Casey's and his own convictions that there existed a *"Bulgarian connection"* to the sinister crime.

The CIA analysts and DCI Casey had delicate reasons to believe that Clair Sterling's facts in her book *The Terror Network* had been a trustworthy synopsis of legitimate intelligence and comprehensive journalistic investigation. It was in reality a well-written book, based however, entirely on circumstantial evidences, and greatly exploiting beliefs and fears of a communist conspiracy to destroy the western democratic society. Convincingly Sterling had emphasized the Soviet support and training of *"terrorists"*, while it was short on explaining that the developing nations had been in need of security, military and management training. Based on this initially gained credibility, Sterling's writings in the late 1981 issues of *"Reader's Digest"* on Pope John Paul II assassination attempt had made western political and intelligence professionals embrace and consider her circumstantial findings and analytical assessments.

I vividly remembered the outstanding journalistic work by the American *TV* prime time *ABC* and independently by the *Washington Post's* Michel Doubts—irrefutably *"capo-de-cape"* American journalist in Italy, all diligently conducted just a few months earlier. The intellectual bash of political and intelligence maneuverings had attempted to accentuate on the presumably strong *"Bulgarian connection"*; especially through the swaying journalism of Clair Sterling and her "right wing" connections within the Italian media, government institutions and political analyst Michel Leadeen. The western media had masterfully manipulated specific facts in order to finger point at the KGB and State Security. Implicated into cunningly building up and supporting the radical, Turkish pro-fascist movement *"Gray wolves"*, and into facilitating terrorism and narcotics trafficking, the communists in reality had nothing to do with the planning and perpetration of the "crime of the century".

Deeply planted seeds of anti-communism and revulsion of the draconian Soviet security system made me a silent admirer of the unrelenting criticisms of the East European society. However, I was realistic and professional in my judgments, incapable of capitalizing on sentiments or contraptions.

John Stain became incessant in his pursuit of my proofs, discrediting Sterling's conclusions, somehow elucidating a preset milieu. Director Casey perhaps had been facing some in-house incongruity on the matter, hence calculatedly had arranged the meeting. I related facts-finding details to the DDO, frankly assessing the Bulgarian and KGB operations. My specific Information from reliable sources at the Communist party, KGB, FCD-foreign intelligence and

SCD-counterintelligence directorates clearly delineated a sharp contrast with Sterling's creative implications. A year earlier, in a highly professional and covert pursuit behind the Iron Curtain, I gathered conclusive evidence that the *"crime of the century"* was not State Security and KGB operation. Unmistakably, the facts pointed towards the fanatic Islamic movements and factions in Libya and Iran, and the radical and leftist global terrorist organizations, with strong connections to the PLO. An ample psychological profiling of Mehmet Agca, masterfully conducted by the mighty FCD and KGB residencies in Turkey and Lebanon, had identified him as a noticeable megalomaniac, disinclined to associate with the shambles of his wretched upbringing, unwilling to live in concealment since his daring prison escape. Agca had become psychotically possessed by an ill-fated requisite to be renowned and acclaimed center of attention. His near success of self-aggrandizement was perpetrated with the help of extensive Turkish and Iranian network of criminals and religious fanatics.

My highly structured facts and analytical standing made Stain's eyebrows hawkish in many instances, as his sharp eyes virtually attempted to bisect my mind. Astonishingly, I received the impression that my words about the Pope's attempted assassination did not reach a willful listener. Stain's standing and convictions on the matter were somehow predetermined as a result of DCI Casey's earliest assumptions, irrefutably and perhaps strongly influenced by persuasive biased journalism.

A phone chime among the four or five units on Stain's desk suitably dispersed the sudden chill overtaking our initially kind and forthcoming dialogue. It was DCI Casey, personally calling from his DC office at the Old Executive building. After a short conversation, Stain activated the speakerphone and Casey's difficult to understand mumbling voice greeted us. He was apologetic for the delay and kindly expressed his gratitude for my exceptional work and assistance for the United States government. After few more or less trivial words, he candidly acknowledged my highly esteemed findings and assessments on the Pope John Paul II assassination attempt. Still difficult to understand, he stated that my work had eventually helped him to modify his judgment on the matter. There was a short: "I have to go! So-long gentlemen!" and the DCI's line went silent.

John Stain looked at me and Ron McCarty with a conspiratorial grin and more or less disingenuously remarked: ". . . If your work had swayed Director Casey, perhaps I should accept your bona fide findings and professional intelligence as well . . ."

I left Stain's statement without comment, although the pervasive chill he had set off somehow persisted. Afterwards I learned that John Stain had without a doubt changed his professional standing on the matter and eventually had even fairly redirected the overall course of Agca's investigation in Italy. Following an extended exchange of thoughts about the increasing ingenuity of the KGB and the East European fraternal communist intelligence organizations in illegally obtaining restricted and embargoed technology from the West, my first meeting with John Stain was over. As a professional courtesy, John walked us to the Director's elevator and soon we disembarked into the main lobby, immediately becoming a focal point of curiosity from the crowded main lobby.

It was 4:35 PM, and many employees were leaving work for the day. We had spent almost two and a half hours with the chief of the most secretive directorate of the Central Intelligence Agency.

* * *

On November 17, 1983, I had the honor of meeting Director Bill Casey in person. The meeting was organized by the Agency's Directorate of Operations, and was aimed at familiarizing Casey with my personality on the eve of my forthcoming invitation to the White House, by President Ronald Reagan.

William Casey struck me as a somewhat informal and friendly personality, although a notably academic luster and intellectual supremacy vividly transpired from his words and expressions. Our dialogue quickly evolved around the East European totalitarianism and the volatile economy of the Soviet Union and the Council for Economic Cooperation (SIV) members. Casey uttered openly and rather surprisingly emphasized his disappointment that the United States' intelligence was not amply proficient in developing precise estimates on the Soviet economy and even obtaining reliable demographic data. My frank implication that even within the utmost communist leadership of the Soviet Union and the Warsaw Pact nations this kind of specific information has been sluggish and most often incorrect, made Casey grin behind his large spectacles, devilishly yet rhetorically rebuffing his own earlier critique.

The enormous KGB active measures (disinformation) operations and the Soviet Union's propaganda by a broad array of specialized communist institutions had been in reality creating perplexingly misleading assessments of the state of the economy and the achievements of developed socialism. I assured Casey of the complexity of the task, which had never existed as a final document in the Soviet Union or any of the satellite East European countries. The totalitarian communist leadership was apprehensive to disclose the real economic results even to the senior communist apparatchiks. Thus the totalitarian society's state of the economy was closely guarded secret not only to the West, but also to the senior members of the Soviet and East European communist parties. Conversely the results of some agricultural, metallurgical, energy generation and machine building enterprises had been intentionally inflated by the leading communist ideologists and consistently used to mislead the West, however, perhaps most importantly to proliferate and encourage the leftist movements around the globe.

These self-lies not only worked to catalyze the growing bubble of communism, but also would in time cause internal realization, pinpricks of reality that would soon shatter the Iron Curtain.

Credible facts on the Soviet achievements through prompt utilization of stolen western technology; know-how and advanced research evidently disturbed Director Casey, for he swiftly made annotations in a bulky leather bounded work agenda. Details about the close cooperation of Robert Maxwell with the KGB and State Security in transshipping embargoed technology to Eastern Europe opened the director's eyes very wide. Details on the Bulgarian military industrial complexes and the skyrocketing sales throughout the developing world irrefutably convinced the DCI to add few more words.

The American economy in the early 1980s was in severe stagnation and DCI Casey demonstrated remarkable knowledge about market trends and wise money management dexterity. Referring to the enormous wealth of the leading industrial giants of the United States, such as, but not limited to the monopoly-stained AT&T, Casey spoke like a father, offering me in reality the first professional advice on stock market operations. He went further, advising me to contact his personal broker Dan Wages (a former CIA officer and former station chief in Belgrade, Yugoslavia) at the Dupont Circle's downtown Washington D.C. office of E.F. Hutton. Soon thereafter Dan Wages became my personal investment banker, greatly contributing to my wisdom and wealth. Although it was rather difficult for me to understand Casey's words due to his lips strangely making him mumble, he astutely comprehended my testimonials, even to smallest nuances. I met Bill Casey two more times and still keep a sincere appreciation for his humble, human and professional attitude.

At the Agency, I quickly discovered that a rather egalitarian group of experienced senior operational officers had inherited the glamour and the challenges of the post OSS era of operations and had been guiding, managing, directing and controlling the destiny of many newcomers with impeccable professionalism and intelligence credibility. Bright and clever professionals, graduates from the Ivy League schools, such as Princeton, Harvard, Yale, Columbia, Dartmouth, and more, had emerged as an "*Old Boys Club*" of secretive members. They openly despised the lack of education, cross-cultural awareness, integrity, and intellectual and intelligence givens of some of the early 1980s new recruits.

Coming from the rather sophisticated environment of recruiting, managing and controlling the brightest academicians of the Soviet fraternity, I crossed the threshold into a new intelligence reality. With persistence we succeeded to utilize my acquired knowledge and consequently we enhanced the CIA's viable operations throughout Eastern Europe. Clearly defining KGB practices, clandestine methodology, communications, psychological profiling, industrial espionage, nonetheless subversive activities, helped the CIA to become an imminent force, capable of further eroding Soviet totalitarianism. Surprisingly, most of the KGB intelligence craft categories intermingled well with our slightly different American intelligence environment, despite the growing political impediments.

The macabre consequences of James Jesus Angleton's incompetent investigation of probable Soviet penetration of the CIA had irreversibly damaged the overall foreign intelligence process. Along with Church & Pike Senate Committee superfluous investigations, the Agency's Clandestine Services' morale and operations had further eroded and virtually shattered. National and strategic intelligence collection and analysis should had been sustained and developed further into an ultimate driving force of primary strategic superiority of the United States government. Instead; radical and almost destructive political wrangling had emerged on the Capitol Hill, especially instigated by the White House during the Democratic presidency of Bill Clinton.

BABE IN THE WOODS

At the age of fifteen, though one of the leaders of my high school's Young Communist Organization—"Komsomol", I had already become utterly disgruntled by the socialist confines. My father's unrelenting and intricately wise insights should be credit to my nonconforming wisdom. I read many of his "secret" documents with curiosity and in silent skepticism, and often listened to political dialogues with his colleagues and friends. Early on I learned essential facts about the power polarization between the capitalist West and the communist East, and came to live with a frightening awareness that we would be annihilated during the imminent nuclear war.

My maverick grandfather astutely guided me to ascertain that in reality our human fears and social uncertainty had been craftily manipulated by communist propaganda. This unyielding alienation from the socialist paradigm, bit by bit altered my conformist facade. I should today bestow tribute not only to my prudent grandfather, but also to my inspirational mother, for her consistent wisdom in teaching me the essentials of socio-economics that opened my mind. My mother Zvetana, nick-named Frieda after the renowned Mexican artist Frieda Kahlo*, was the vivacious daughter of an affluent and prominent landlord and entrepreneur. She had lived an aristocratic, privileged life until her prosperous realms had been brutally shattered by the destructive waves of the Soviet communist expansion throughout Eastern Europe. Family properties, agricultural machines, animals, grain silos and money had been callously confiscated and appropriated by the murderous new socialist radicals. My mother's elaborate stories about the entrepreneurial marvels of my grandfather Dimitrius and the wonderful wealthy life her family had enjoyed throughout the previous monarchist government were barefaced reminders of what I should be cherishing, admiring and perhaps pursuing.

I nostalgically remember the colorful stories of grandfather Zolo Dimitrius, about his outings throughout Europe: from Istanbul to Jerusalem, from Vienna to Budapest. I often sat on his lap as a child, mesmerized by his inspirational voice. He was not a gaudy aristocrat, shallow bourgeois or just another anti-socialist

---

*   Frieda Kahlo, Mexican abstractionist and leftist—wife of Diego Rivera.

reactionary. An exceptional intellectual and credible visionary, he consistently predicted the inevitable dissolution of the Soviet *"peasant"* socialism, grossly criticizing the thoughtless, shortsighted communal governing of the economy and the society.

Grandfather Dimitrius had never supported the monarch-fascist government of Saxe Coburg-Ghota; however, because he was a wealthy farmer and leader of the regional Agrarian party, the communists automatically had professed him as an enemy of the state.

During early 1947 my father was assigned by the Sofia County party bureau to conduct the communal appropriation of the wealth, land, machinery and livestock of farmers for the new socialist agricultural cooperatives. He was only 28 years old, with remarkable anti-fascist experience. By the virtue of knowing the region, he was assigned to be leader of an armed group of communist thugs and former partisans.

In next to no time my father's nationalizations group had appropriated for the new socialist state the region's largest farmhouses, opulent ranches and even most of my grandfather's vast estates. Almost unthinkably, in the gruesome process of repossession, the perpetrator paradoxically fell in love with an aristocrat's daughter. Fragile and frightened, deeply in love, my mother sheepishly would escape grandfather Dimitrius' strict control and strength of character moving to Sofia. In the glamour of the burgeoning capital she eventually got married to the fatherless young revolutionary.

*   *   *

My father's family heritage differs from the closely knitted descent of the Balkan's Slavic people. His father Ivan-Alexander was born in the post San Stefano, Austro-Hungarian Empire, and had grown up in a strict and affluent family. He had studied at the Vienna furniture design institute and Bucharest school of wood processing. Nick named *"Glockner"* he was inherent to the historic traditions of the region and the pan—Europeanism of his Austrian heritage and studies along the Danube River. In Bucharest and Vienna he was fascinated by the European culture and music, the philosophy of Marx, Engels and the Russian anarchists, the Bolsheviks and the exiled by the Romanovs democratic centralists.

Grandfather Ivan-Alexander had eventually embraced not only his new studies and knowledge in developing successful furniture design and manufacturing, but had also consciously and insistently disapproved of the Balkan War and soon thereafter the First World War. In few instances he had written letters to the Austro-Hungarian Court and personally to Ferdinand Hapsburg, expressing strong concerns about the war's devastating effect throughout Europe and the region. He was forcefully drafted in the army and sent to the Hungarian—Croatian battlefields. During an offensive near the town of Pecks, he was wounded and almost lost his life in a self-sacrificial, gut-wrenching hand grenade attack on an enemy ammunition depot. Even with a bullet lodged in his lungs, he survived, saved by his loyal comrades who drove him to an Austrian hospital.

After the First World War my father Panko was born. He grew in an environment of liberal thinking, pro-democratic trends and post war economic recovery. During the first European anti-fascist uprising in the fall of 1923, my grandfather, war veteran Ivan-Alexander, was arrested by the fascist police and was for days mercilessly interrogated. Confined to an old rusty cage in desolate isolation, he soon died from his broken ribs and collapsed lungs. My grandfather's revolutionary and free enterprising mind then led to tragedy. The comfortable childhood of my father and his family refuge had been tarnished. Public humiliation and social repression, persecutions and hard labor on the agricultural fields charted a new family destiny. The daily agro-labor was not only a common denominator, but also my grandmother's only hope to feed her three children.

After many missed meals and a plethora of deprivation and disease, my father nevertheless finished school and with the hope of a better life moved to the Bulgarian capital—Sofia. He enrolled in a military academy for tank commanders and after graduation was assigned to the Balkan's first motorized tank division.

The Austro-German Regent Tsar Boris III, Saxe-Coburg Gotha, had in the early 1940s aligned Bulgaria with Adolph Hitler's Third Reich. The Balkan tank brigade had emerged as a primary motorized military unit of Nazi Germany's regional interests and as a deadly tool for fascist repression. Unknown to the German General von Fritz and the intelligence residents in Sofia, Colonel Wilhelm Gellen and Dr. Dellius, within the tank brigade a strong clandestine communist group was working.

My father, as the son of murdered anti-fascist, was soon accepted as member of the underground communist party. As such he was assigned one of the greatest humanitarian missions, secretly thwarting the forced resettlement of Jews by the Bulgarian Gestapo's chieftain—Teodor Dannecor. From Moscow George Dimitrov had called on all democratic and anti-fascist groups in Bulgaria to avert the human malice. Daily tank tests conducted by the mechanized brigade of my father Panko Peshev and Stoian Luckov smuggled endangered Jewish families to safety through the fascist blockade of the only way to safety at the Arabakonak pass, near Sofia. Concurrently, my father's uncle Dimitar Peshev, a prominent Member of the Parliament (MP), had compassionately organized protests in Plovdiv against the anti-Jewish standings of Tsar Boris III and his monarchist government. Thousands of southern and central Balkan Jewish families were therein saved from inevitable extermination at Treblinka and

Auschwitz concentration camps. A year later, Tsar Boris III failed to endorse the German orders for forceful repatriation of all Bulgarian Jews. Nonetheless, Bulgarian military fascists and secret German commandos apprehended more than 10,000 innocent Jews from the new Bulgarian territories of Macedonia and Vardar Trace and sent them to certain death at Treblinka.

Thus the clandestine work of my father has began, later on to evolve into providing stolen fascist ammunition, food, weapons and explosives to the partisan brigade "*Chavdar*", a group whose political command was in the hands of Todor Zhivkov, the future General Secretary of the Communist Party.

When the Soviet Red Army advanced through the Balkans in September of 1944, George Dimitrov with the blessings of Joseph Stalin countered the Tsar Boris' fascist alliance with the German Third Reich, announcing the creation of a self-governing Peoples Republic of Bulgaria. The new country was immediately distanced from its monarchic and fascist past, joining the Red Army in the heroic struggle against Nazi Germany.

As a member of the communist party, my father was promoted to tank brigade commander and was ordered to sustain the Soviet offensives throughout Yugoslavia and Hungary. Near Maribor and Kriva Palanca, the tank brigade successfully had intercepted and heroically defeated retracting German forces from Greece. After the unconditional surrender of Germany in May of 1945, the Second World War was over. My father returned home as a war hero, marching his tank through the center of Sofia during the peace parade. Soviet and Bulgarian military and government officials awarded him seven medals for bravery and exemplary duty during the war. Under the red flags and the iron fists of the Soviet communism, a new stage in the history of Bulgaria was ordained, as new horizons promisingly had enlightened our family life.

Growing in the family of a State Security official, Fighter against fascism, a member of the communist party, and strict, demanding bourgeoisie-educated teacher was not an easy or flawless task for me. I was required by my father to be more than a role model of the socialist society, while my mother constantly disparaged the ways of the ruthless and ideologically stalled communism. I was taught and required to maintain a strict line of behavior, refined manners and to lead in mathematics, science and literature. Years later, this more or less Spartan upbringing soundly manifested my character, by helping me to maintain a proper state of mind in difficult and destructive environments, and by guiding me to a proper social, professional and family life.

*   *   *

At the Bulgarian State Security Border Guards Museum "*Kalotino*" in Sofia there lies information on a mysterious sixteen-year-old "*spy-defector*". Apparently an anomaly under the indoctrinatory orthodoxy of the Soviet might, such examples were often brewing in the minds of the people; very few had the means and the guts to perform on these hunches, however.

Despite my mother's discontent under my father's strict guidance and assertion, I progressed as a Komsomol activist and as secretary of my high school's young communist's organization.

Covetous high-ranking communist apparatchiks rebutted my father's appointment to a senior foreign intelligence assignment in Switzerland in 1963. He was maliciously accused of party revisionism and concealment of my mother's anti-communist sentiments and bourgeoisie upbringing. As our family's social standing more or less hastily deteriorated, tensions at home loomed. My father started showing signs of his degraded and crumbling morals by getting drunk and easily outraged. We were repeatedly punished and physically abused far beyond any human imagination and justification. Dark blue impressions of my father's belt buckle inadvertently showed on my body. My vivid and happy childhood was abruptly distorted into incessant physical and mental soreness and gruesome emotional agony.

In this dreadful atmosphere of my father's wretched misanthropy and disgruntlement with the prevailing socialism, I attempted to travel illegally to the West. It was not my teenage mind's misjudged temporary escapade, neither was my decision a spontaneous infatuation with decadent dreams fashioned by western propaganda. It was a miscalculated, genuinely immature revolt against the totalitarianism ubiquitously prevalent around me. My attempt to discredit the merciless socialist principles and restrictive human practices, terror and subjugation was the only workable solution to my struggles that I could carry out at that time.

This internal revolt all began with mounting bitterness and jagged repugnance of the socialist realities. However, slowly but surely, it evolved over the years into dyed-in-the-wool, perilous personal warfare. Years later, as Soviet communism disintegrated into the futile dust of modern history, I became especially proud of my sensible individual solution. Ironically, back in the 1960s my grandfather had already vibrantly foreseen the inevitable socio-political termination of his tormentors' dogmatic ideology and had came to a similar inner determination and resolve.

My father's connections, combined with loopholes inside the State Security system, worked to conceal my unorthodox escapade. For more than 30 years, these strokes of luck closely guarded my first rebellion against the communism, as the true identity of the mysterious sixteen-year-old known as Zorro, was never known to the public until now. Ironically, getting caught once due to imperfect planning and implementation proved an experience that I would never allow to occur again.

After graduation from high school, a State Security commission eventually positively assessed my personality, scholastic achievements and social standing and I was accepted as a member of a select State Security sports military unit. We tirelessly trained, incessantly practiced and fearlessly primed to protect the high-ranking members of the Political Bureau of the Central Committee of the Communist Party in case of war or sudden public unrest.

In the following four years, in addition to my complex duties, I four times became the national Judo champion. I won many international competitions and earned a plethora of awards, eventually receiving the national title of Master of Sports by the Bulgarian Committee for Physical Culture and Sports in 1971. Amongst many of my memorable international sports and educational events, one relates to modern times and illustrates how interconnected the KGB was with State Security: In 1970 our group spent 45 days with the Soviet Union's KGB team "*Dynamo*" at advanced Judo training camps in Moscow and Leningrad. We followed rigorous training practices and socialized with our enduring Russian hosts and renowned champions. Among our Russian counterparts were future brilliant KGB intelligence and counterintelligence officers. One of these judo players, Vladimir Putin, would during the 1980s become a KGB officer in East Germany and thereafter in the late 1990s rose as the most charismatic, democratically elected President of the Russian Federation.

The blond and petite Vladimir was a remarkably flexible and strong willed Judo player. Although I remember him as somewhat of a shy person and introvert, he was intelligent and quick in implementing and utilizing a broad spectrum of complicated ancient Japanese martial art techniques into his performance and competitiveness. His cool poker face and unreadable eyes were almost misleading with their lack of expression and sports zeal, and remarkably even his face did not get flushed under the strain of sport. He was a master of the *"Tai-sabaki"* (turning doors) and *"Uchi-mata"* techniques and wisely applied them to complicated situations. On one particular occasion, Putin had randoury (competition) with the Bulgarian champion—Zekeria Osmanov, and steadily the competition became fairly forceful as a result of both players' endurance and determination. After receiving a surprising *"vazaari"*, Vladimir almost surrendering smiled, a look of calm overcoming him. Then, with a sudden misleading twist to the left, he turned his body in the air to the right and achieved an impressive victory with an *"ippon"*. Vladimir perfectly executed the remarkably quick and unpredictable technique with flair. Filled with admiration at that moment, I realized that Vladimir Putin possessed stupendous willpower. Combining the sophisticated mind of an endearing warrior with the speed of lightning stratagems, the stoic Russian aimed at achieving his goals with finesse and striking efficiency. In Leningrad, Vladimir was often our guide through the wonderful city and the nearby Winter palace of Peter—the Great.

To the best of my recollection, the last time I saw Vladimir Putin was in 1972 during the international judo competition of East European and Cuban fraternal security teams in Kishinev, Moldova. The following year, in 1973, the State Security administration, in conjunction with the KGB, published my first book, co-authored by the renowned international martial arts judge Colonel Gencho Zarev. It was the first fraternal communist security organization's book on Judo and Karate techniques specially designed for use by operational officers. A copy of this book has been handy on the shelves of Mr. Putin's personal library since 1973. *

*   *   *

We lived in a house in the prestigious suburb of *"Lozenetz"*, near my Russian high school. Most of my friends came from elite communist and government families. We fittingly established a semi-secret fraternity, a private *"Boy's"* club. Playing cards, chess, and discussing different subjects at our home, we often skipped lessons and played hooky during the day, smoking cigarettes and even drinking alcohol at nights. Once Vovata Zhivkov brought a secret document from the General Secretary's office on the new communism of Joseph Broz Tito. It was very critical of Tito's policy against Stalin's Soviet Union and Khrushchev's Kremlin. With two of my best friends I jokingly suggested that we should bring the document to Tito in Yugoslavia. To my dismay, the spontaneous underhanded proposal was immediately accepted, and as I took sneakily possession of the document, we began to make plans.

In the meantime, I provocatively asked my father and his friends Boris Petkov and Stoian Luckov why the Yugoslavian communist party was expelled from the Cominform in 1948. As a member of national security group, my father had visited Moscow in the beginning of 1948. He had there met an old partisan friend from Tito's Yugoslav Liberation army with whom he had fought the Nazis north of Drava River. In tandem with General Hristo Boev, the future foreign intelligence chief, my father further befriended General Milovan Djilas** in Moscow, developing strong camaraderie through mutual understanding and fraternal conspiracy.

Boev was a more or less legendary communist intelligence officer, who had worked with Jan Carlovich Berzin*** in Moscow for many years, successfully

---

*   A Duma journalist's Moscow interview with Vladimir Putin, 2000.

**   In 1979 my father helped the senior staff of State Security to meet Milovan Djilas in Sofia, Bulgaria.

***   Berzin, a renowned senior Soviet intelligence officer and deputy chief of the NKVD (future KGB).

fulfilling Soviet intelligence tasks from Europe to Turkey, from China to Great Britain. For years thereafter he would maintain a stealthy relationship with Djilas, even offering him support while in prison.

At the 1948 Moscow meeting, Stalin eventually had sharply criticized George Dimitrov and Joseph Tito (represented by Djilas) about the planned but unapproved by Moscow creation of a Balkan Federation. The mighty Georgian had furthermore blasted both countries clandestine military support of the communist insurgence in Greece*. Stalin had evidently expressed to the leadership of both countries that any relations between the new socialist republics were not permissible if they were not in the interest of and had not been approved or coordinated with the leadership of the Soviet Union. Blatantly obvious to my father during this meeting was Stalin's unswerving announcement of the development of Eastern Europe into satellites; it was clearly aimed solely at securing, supporting and strengthening Moscow's global interests and domination.

As a faithful Stalin marionette, though potent Cominform leader, George Dimitrov had thereafter sightlessly carried out all of Stalin's Soviet directives. Quite on the contrary, Joseph Tito single-mindedly had elected to keep Yugoslavia sovereign, contravening the stern devotion and unquestionable obedience demanded by Stalin. Deeply suspicious of Djilas' role in these staggering international intrigues, Tito had mercilessly persecuted and in numerous instances imprisoned his most trusted general since early 1950.

A few years later, the new General Secretary of the Communist Party of the Soviet Union, Nikita Khrushchev, ominously assaulted Stalin's personality cult, his unforgiving communist purges and his imprudent economic legacy. Joseph Tito daringly stepping away from the Soviet ascendancy emerged as a glorified leader of the none-alliance global movement, greatly upheld by the Soviet discourse with communist China during the 1960s.

*   *   *

Meanwhile the Secret service (UBO) had contacted my father with an order to secure the vicinities of our home. He was visibly disturbed by the fact that we had been discussing issues deemed reactionary and anti-Communist. Almost immediately I distanced myself from Vlado Zhivkov, Krasi Bebov, Raichin Prumov and some other buddies directly related to these leaders, perceiving them as would-be *"turncoats"* of our fraternity.

---

*   Bulgarian and Yugoslav officials had provided secretly weapons and logistics to the leftist insurgence in Greece.

Based on our *"west bound"* plan, my group decided to take a train trip to the Yugoslavian border at *Kalotino*. We were inexperienced enough to think that the border was like a movie theater, that we could penetrate it without tickets by outsmarting and misleading the controllers.

During our trip, we puzzled a local peasant with our city cloths and attitude. Listening to our chat he advised us to get off the train in the next city and return home: ". . . You will be detained by the border guards boys, they check the documents of all people traveling to the border. You kids look too strange, although you are clearly not hooligans ready to escape to the west . . ."

He was a cynical, dirty nailed worker. His story about the local *otriadniks** collaboration with the border patrols in apprehending Bulgarian and East European nationals attempting to escape to Yugoslavia was a shivering warning. At the station Dragoman, we disembarked the train, visibly shaken not only from the evening chill, and quite ready to return to our homes' safety.

*　　*　　*

Unnoticed on the eve of the 47th October Bolshevik Revolution, I without fingerprint traces left two school windows unlocked from inside. These windows on the ground floor assured my stealthy access to the school that evening. Casually chatting with friends on the street, I later in the evening observed the maintenance manager turn off the lights and lock the school main gate. In the shadow of a large oak tree in the courtyard, soon I nonchalantly blended in with the darkness. I easily entered the building through one of the unlatched windows. Using a surreptitiously acquired key, I entered the Yang communists (Komsomol) room and locked it from inside. With a pounding heart, I waited to adjust to the dark settings, and then carefully traced the display case cables and twisted them together with two of the patriotic red flags. I opened the windows slightly, assuring an open flow of oxygen, and then stood still for few extra minutes. It was quiet and spooky, though I was unwaveringly in control.

A small burning candle carefully placed under the twisted electrical cables started to melt them, as the thick flags veiled the light. The flame steadily moved upward while I locked the door and nonchalantly vanished into the night.

Once at home, I joined the family dinner. Distant sirens however soon distorted the evening milieu. The startling noise of emergency and police vehicles approached our neighborhood and we curiously walked out onto the street with many of the neighbors. Black, thick smock and intense licks of fire treacherously crawled out of the school's Komsomol windows. Outside, the largest ornate banner

---

*   Voluntary member of the militia.

in the form of a waving Soviet flag soon caught ablaze, engulfing the vehement Russian slogan:

"*S Octomvriiskoi Revolutzii Vperiod k Nashem Budushti,*" or in English, "*With the October Revolution towards Our Future . . .*"

The setting was astonishing, as more fire-trucks and militia cars vociferously arrived. The extinguished fire transformed the once beautiful white main façade into a dreadful looking, ugly and intensely blackened horror.

The fire at the most prestigious Russian high school on the eve of the October Revolution celebration was something to remember. Not surprisingly, the censured national press and television did not report or mention the incident. Only on the following morning did the daylight reveal the astonishing consequences.

Dark residue on the outside walls made the damage from the fire look immense. The Bolshevik revolution had "inadvertently" gained a black eye, as the fire had destroyed the vast collection of Soviet and communist flags, banners and socialist revolutionary art and memorabilia on display.

Despite the substantial cleaning and face lifting of the school, that week of festivities contained some of the grimmest October Revolution celebrations I had ever attended. The material damage was limited; however the political and moral impact was overwhelming. Everyone at school, from the students to the janitors, deep inside them knew that it was not an accidental fire. As the Komsomol leader, I was one of the first students to be interrogated by militia and State Security (including KGB) officials immediately after the holiday. The lack of conclusive evidence of intentional or unlawful activity allowed me to firmly assure them of the accidental nature of the fire. An ironically unambiguous "perfect crime" was therein effectively perpetrated against the grossly detested Soviet Union.

*　　*　　*

During the final preparations of my adventurous attempt to journey to Tito's Yugoslavia, I discovered that a village near the border was named Osicovo. This fact helped me to formulate a legend in case of failure or apprehension. I came up with a simplistic justification for traveling in the region if questioned by the border guards. Osicovo was named similarly to my mother's births place Osicovitza, which was in reality located a hundred kilometers in the opposite direction.

At 4:45PM on the first Friday of November 1965, I boarded the train to Kalotino, carrying only a small bag with food and fruits. The steamer steadily moved through agricultural fields on both sides of the railway. After the harvest, the land looked desolate and unsightly. Black birds glided freely through the cloudy sky, once in a while graciously diving for the rare prize of a rodent or a forgotten stem of wheat. At the city of Dragoman, a few border officers and customs officials boarded the train. The guards were somewhat uneasy with my trip to Osicovo and oddly asked for my uncle's name.

Exiting the train car at the Kalotino station, I was intercepted by an officer and two border guards. Evidently the patrolman had given them my uncle's name, for the officer called me to stop.

". . . I don't know your uncle . . ." the officer mumbled, and, taking my bag, asked me to follow him. Quickly analyzing all of my vulnerabilities, I realized that I would be in serious trouble for the possession my father's gun. Instinctively, I pulled the German Mauser out of my pocket, and, using the darkness of the night and my body to screen my actions, prepared to drop it into the bushes. Suddenly a flashlight from behind filled me in an aura of light. Chilling metal sounds came from the Kalashnikov's safeties being released as I was ordered to freeze. An excruciating pain from a hit in my kidneys slammed me to the ground and a heavy boot viciously pressed my neck to the pavement. As a seeming proletariat punk, I deserved no respect. What occurred thereafter was a blur of brutality. They literally dragged me to the nearby office, where I was repeatedly kicked and punched. After a few minutes of deliberation, the guards stripped off my cloths and shockingly discovered a secret stack of documents. Unpacking them, the senior officer raised his hands to his brow. Suddenly the room was quiet with only few whispers of confusion. Reviewing the content of the documents, the Major had noticed that they were strictly for the eyes of members of the Political Bureau of the Communist Party. A teenager possessing top-secret State Security documents, a loaded handgun and a detailed operational map was an unprecedented event in the dreary and monotone daily practices of the border guards.

The Major instructed me to dress and ordered the guards to keep me under "shoot to kill" control. Apparently handcuffs were unavailable, for he hastily tied my hands with his belt behind my back.

A little past midnight I heard the screeching of car brakes. Spookily hollow steps mixed with whispering dialogue echoed down the hallway. The door swiftly opened and a burst of adrenaline chilled my body. The guards saluted the mustached Colonel, a figure disgustingly emanating alcohol and cheap tobacco. He heavily sat down and rested on a chair, then looked at me, visibly disappointed at my young age. Glimpsing through the secret documents, he checked my wallet, the handgun, counted the cartridges, unfolded the map and watchfully reviewed my student book. Finding my father's telephone number, he lifted his eyebrows, exclaiming to the Major that the number was of the Committee for State Security.

With a surprising thoroughness the Colonel reviewed the special papers of my detainment. As he completed the document, he signed and handed it to the Major. I had to repeat everything; I was calm and cooperating, even when the

Colonel came from behind the desk, sadistically grabbing my neck and spitting hysterically into my face.

"Stop lying to us small scum . . ." he yelled, "Otherwise we will shoot you right here . . . Where did you steal the secret documents? When? Who helped you? Who paid you? Why do you have a gun? Who is waiting for you in Yugoslavia . . ." Question after question, he became more agitated and sinister, practically choking me. He ordered the guards to remove all of my clothes again. The atmosphere began to gain sickening undertones as the face of the Colonel grew with rage. As it started to turn into a brutal affair, I began fighting and screaming for help. My resistance and cries for help eventually worked, as I was calmed. I then insisted for the Colonel to call my father. Gaining momentum and courage, I fervently threatened them with reprisal and punishment for my torture. Finally the Colonel picked up the secure telephone. After the verification of his name and position, the Colonel left his number with a duty officer and insisted for my father to call without delay.

Minutes later, a civilian entered the room and without formalities approached the table. Following interrogation protocol, he said nothing. However, knowing that the Colonel was waiting a call from the Committee of State Security, he curiously looked through the secret documents.

A telephone blaringly interrupted the sudden stillness. After a brief dialogue, the sheepish Colonel handed the receiver to the plain-clothed civilian. Introducing himself to my father, by rank as a State Security Captain, he stated his affiliations and responsibilities. Recounting to my father that I had been apprehended while attempting to escape to Yugoslavia armed and in possession of "top-secret" State Security documents hidden in my underwear, the Captain showed some attitude. Then my father spoke to me, and from his voice I noticed that he was quite shocked and disturbed by the development. With a naive and childish voice I explained that I had left a note at home and was going to spend my weekend with Uncle Basil in the countryside.

After a few more words were exchanged between my father and the Captain, I suddenly became a friend. The men all offered me apologies for the misunderstanding and gave me a military food ration with a warm cup of tea. The Major promptly retrieved his belt, which had turned my hands bluish. The State Security officer left the room, taking all my personal possessions and the interrogation papers. He unmistakably showed that State Security was in control of the situation.

Early the next morning, my father and a friend, Colonel Petko Lalov, Deputy Director of the Sofia State Security Administration, arrived in a distinct black *Volga* limousine, synonymous with the power elite of the Communist Party and the Committee for State Security. I was not involved in the meeting. About half an hour later, a junior officer instructed me to board the waiting car.

On the way to Sofia my father was quiet, noticeably embarrassed by the thoughtless event, and perhaps deeply remorseful for some of the physical excesses he had perpetrated upon me within last 18 months. Colonel Lalov was a tactful mediator, explaining to me that the border Commander had submitted the report on my apprehension to General Again, Director of Sofia State Security. Lalov suggested that my father promptly meet with him in order to close the case. Visibly humiliated, my father turned towards me and with a calm, unhappy face and asked,

"How should I explain everything to the General?"

I credibly repeated my story, especially in order to persuade Colonel Lalov of any doubts. With sincere guilt, I acknowledged that I had the gun to protect the top-secret documents, while everything else was just a coincidental mistake and the border guards' intentional misinterpretation.

The friendly manners of General Again, who received us at his office facing the Mausoleum of George Dimitrov and the King's Palace, were unanticipated. Years later I found that he was regarded as one of the most tactful, professional and intelligent military security officers in the East.

My explanation was calm and regrettable, as General Again did not challenge my recollection. The story of an attempted escape to the West virtually empty-handed was an odd and impossible invention of the border guards. Expressing sympathies for the cruelty I had undergone, he checked the interrogation protocol and glimpsed at the key "note" that I had thoughtfully left at home. This key evidence of my innocence, considerately emphasized by Colonel Lalov, helped the case to be immediately closed. General Again asked my father to acknowledge with a statement and signature on the file that I had been released to his custody and that he did not have any complaint. The Colonel firmly inscribed: "Case closed" on the folder and diligently dated and signed the file, asking Colonel Lalov to archive it.

My first somber act of dissent with the communist state, so sadly foiled at its inception, was soon covered up. Instead of my family name, I had given my mother's maiden name during the interrogations, thus predestining the files to disappear. The omission of key details from the interrogating officers irrefutably concealed my real identity and as a result I escaped the meticulous eyes and ears of State Security for many years to come. As a result of the strict internal requirements of the Ministry of Internal Affairs, a permanent record, #302/64, had eventually been created on my case. It was based on a border activities telex sent to the Committee for State Security:

"...*An armed Bulgarian citizen and suspected western spy: Zorro Ivanov— Tzolov was captured by watchful border guards. He was attempting to illegally cross the Bulgarian border at Kalotino KPP into Yugoslavia. Ivanov was in possession of top-secret State Security and Central Committee of the Communist Party documents deemed essential to the national security of Bulgaria and the Soviet Union . . ."*

Many family friends and relatives alleged that I had inherently exhibited the willful avant-garde character of my grandfathers. However, I truly attribute my pioneering to my father's revisionist wisdom and especially to my mother's astute bourgeoisie rearing. Stealthily asserting that communalism would vanish from the earth's milieu as abruptly as it had emerged was my grandfather's life inspiration and our family's hope.

THE STATE SECURITY ACADEMY

A fter a farewell *"night to be remembered"* with friends in mid September 1968, I reported to a top-secret air force unit in southeastern Bulgaria for my mandatory military duty. I was soon elected deputy secretary of the Komsomol, overseeing 82 solders and sergeants.

At the designated weekend day for our oath of allegiance, I was pleasantly surprised to see my parents and some relatives. It was a crisp, sunny day, once that brewed freedom and optimistic human identity. As I walked outside the garrison gates, I saw the hills and the sky in different colors; the hope that never comes for most came effortlessly to me. Three days later, unexpectedly interrupting our ongoing training exercise, the Captain-adjutant summoned me to the division commander's office. Colonel Draganov was forthcoming, and told me at once that he had received from the Minister of Defense Dobry Dzhurov an order for my relocation to a specialized unit in Sofia. He briskly handed me a pouch with transfer documents, and I was dismissed.

*   *   *

A few days later, I arrived at the well-guarded gate of the State Security Academy near Sofia. My name was on a special ledger, allowing me unrestricted access to the Academy. The guards respectfully welcomed me to the *"Sanctuary"* and after issuing me a photo pass directed me to the command center. I surprised Major Grigorov with my strict military manners and he soon firmly advised me to eschew such military protocol. Our elite group was relatively small; all of us were outstanding sportsmen from reliable communist families, and all had spotless personal backgrounds. Our assignment was to protect members of the Political Bureau of the Communist Party in case of war or social instability.

In early September of 1970, I informed the State Security Administration and the Ministry of Internal Affairs (MVR) of my acceptance at Sofia State University. On September 8th, at a special ceremony, I received the military officer rank of junior-lieutenant and was relieved of duty.

The university program was intense and demanding, but it did not prevent me from continuing my active judo and karate training with the sport team *"Levski-Spartak"* of the Ministry of Internal Affairs. As the result of my willpower, consistency in training and strong competitiveness during 1969, 70, 71 and 72, I won four highly acclaimed National Judo Championship titles and numerous international awards.

One day I received a phone call from an old family friend, Colonel Spas Petrov, to arrange a get together. He was a personable foreign intelligence officer, gifted and soft-spoken; his demeanor convincingly suggested the position of a university professor. At the designated day of our meeting, Comrade Petrov greeted me pleasantly and locked the door of the office of one of my professors in political sciences. Assessing my ample State Security experience, he explained that a West African student called Mr. Prince represented special interest to his office. He needed reliable information and data on Prince's personality, family background, friends and integrity. With my help Colonel Petrov soon recruited Prince's roommate as an agent, eventually providing detailed information and observations on the man. At the time a trendy pop star, years later Mr. Prince became the affluent Minister of Foreign Affairs of a West African country.

Similar examples from my student years abound, making me an integral part of the intelligence and counter-intelligence operations of the KGB and State Security. Intricate assignments allowed me to comprehend the operational and covert interests of the KGB controlled system. During these years my father gave me some of the most valuable lessons of conspiracy, analysis, clandestine observation, surveillance and astute comprehension of the political intrigues and the basics of ideological subversion and misinformation.

*   *   *

At the age of twenty-one, after a thorough background security check and lengthy psychological and medical evaluations, a special government commission appointed me as a State Security operational officer. After intensive specialized training at the State Security Academy in Simeonovo, I graduated with distinction and was assigned to the Second Independent Department (SID), the most secretive State Security Directorate. We specialized in clandestinely monitoring, controlling and analyzing the intelligence gathering and espionage operations of western embassies, diplomats and suspected western assets.

The vast and clandestine network assuring undetectable, virtually total control over any activities of western embassies, their diplomats, foreigners and domestic contacts was perplexing. These demanding and tedious around the clock responsibilities, consisting of never-ending invisible surveillance, disguised pursuits and followings, covert filming, photographing, conversations monitoring and identifying of any activities and contacts was indeed a craftily carried out course of action. Many advanced technical, bio-chemical, radioactive isotope, video and electronic methods were utilized in order to assure completely undetectable control of suspected western spies. A substantial fleet of modern and traditional cars with enhanced engines were used to tail targets, diplomats and their families all over the country. Surveillance methods included such tactics as the intimidating "Japanese" tailgating and blind spotting. Specially trained dogs with professional masters were readily available to nonchalantly stroll through streets, parks or mountain trails in order to pin down dead-drop sites or identify atypical objects manipulated by the targets.

After 18 months I completed the advanced KGB designed operational training. We traced and analyzed the activities of a broad spectrum of targets, ranging from genuine to dummy western spies and agents, to investigating terrorists, dissidents and even potential defectors to the West.

One of our most memorable and challenging spy-mastering exercises, consuming more than one third of our total rigorous training, was that of intense pedestrian and vehicular surveillance. Most intelligence officers came back to Moscow or Sofia for their annual reassessments and mandatory enhancement of their training. We joined them, as we had to follow our instructors, and then they followed us; complicated settings were created in elaborate pseudo spy games. Instructors and intelligence officers changed techniques constantly and at random. We loaded and unloaded dead drops, placed confirmation and execution marks, took pre-planned routes. With thrilling surprise I discovered that in intelligence and counter-espionage operations split-second decisions, perfectly executed procedures and great psychological strength separate the thin line between success and failure.

An operational officer under surveillance who is stationed abroad is normally not allowed to carry on specific intelligence tasks. During training however, we mastered an array of invisible or undetectable exchanges. These training procedures allowed us to prepare mentally and emotionally for thrilling and dangerous contacts with secret assets, momentous exchanges of information and nonetheless taught us proper surveillance and operations detection techniques.

Navigating through the crowded streets of Sofia, Moscow or Leningrad was a challenging endeavor. For the invisible followers' surveillance, the most importantly was the actual human stalking of the target; on foot, the greatest success was an unflappable escape from surveillance coverage.

For our training graduation, I designed with my KGB counterpart Evgeny Samoilov an intricate exchange of valuable information while both of us were under total surveillance. It was named *"Briz"*, after the calm Siberian winds, although, everyone called it *"Blitz"*: The brisk exchange of a cartridge with photo materials was scheduled to happen in the center of Moscow in one of the Arbat's under passes. We planned to utilize the human eyes' light adjustment, the transition from the brightly lighted street to the semi-darkness of an underpass, to assure the invisible exchange.

At the technical center I designed a photo cartridge with an anchor of two three pronged fishing hooks. The half of my clenched fist near my thumb would hold an umbrella, while the pinky side tightly gripped the cartridge. This photo cartridge tweak came to the common observer as a natural extension of my umbrella handle. As Evgeny walked by, his slightly flipped open raincoat would catch the photo container's hooks to its inner lining. We calculated by the second the distance and the timing, allowing for the exchange to occur at the bottom section of Evgeny's staircase, as to fully benefit from the sudden change in daylight to the meager underpass lighting.

Evgeny and I decided that as repayment to the rest of our comrades who had sadly failed the test, we must succeed and pay a little vengeance to the academy's egotistical instructors. However, executing one of the most complicated emergency exchange operations in the intelligence game was almost unthinkable, and required much care. A time of only two hours and 30 minutes was allocated for us to execute this most difficult task. From utilizing the public transportation and the metro to visiting the city's library and the main shopping center GUM, we established signal and verification sights and meticulously measured our steps through a few under passes. Nonetheless we replaced two of the linings of Evgeny's raincoat, assuring texture that would flawlessly catch the virtually invisible triple fishhooks extruding from of my outer fist.

In order to spawn confusion and unforeseen disorientation to the already comforted and perhaps fatigued surveillance teams, we determined to slightly change our appearances a few seconds before the set exchange. We were to use the wardrobe shift as a last confirmation to undergo the exchange or to calmly alter our course, due to uncertainty or imperfect tribulations. I had to lift up my coat lapels, which ingeniously changed to a light browned texture and nonchalantly put on a matching color hat, while Evgeny planned to do the same, momentarily disorienting the surveillance crews.

Most of our classmates failed miserably at their surveillance tests, and became the laughing stock of the instructors and colleagues. Thus our success had more than professional connotation, as it was our final opportunity to prove that we had learned well and were ready for the challenges of the intelligence or counterintelligence careers ahead of us. Knowing that the instructors had unsurprisingly secured the cooperation of the technical staff of the Academy, we fashioned three different demands for components and camouflages, in order to misinform and intentionally mislead the surveillance teams about our plans and intend. Furthermore, we shaped two misleading plans, which we submitted to our own instructors for verification and modification, knowing that they would "accidentally" reach the desks of the controlling instructors.

*   *   *

On the designated day, while nonchalantly holding a roll of the "Pravda" newspaper, I spent seven minutes watching the main entrance of the city library from a nearby kiosk. At exactly 2:30PM I entered the library and calmly ordered a reference book to be available at 4:00PM. I noticed that the surveillance team had dispatched a youthful lady to the foyer, for she made a stealthy move, covertly taking my photo as I conversed with the librarian. Perhaps in the shrewd anticipation that I could enter the large facility on Lermontov Square, surveillance had ingeniously covered the facility in advance. Since its inception, our game promised to be a dramatic cat-and-mouse performance.

As the minutes ticked by, Evgeny and I established remote visual confirmation marks of each other at a GUM appliances store. I was on the third floor and he was at a jewelry kiosk on the ground floor. We were able to confirm to each other the availability of surveillance coverage and to nonetheless observe some of the counterpart's surveillance officers in action. Personally, I was surprised to discover how many officers had suddenly filled up the crowded, narrow and in a way dilapidating space of the Central Shopping Mall (GUM). Although it was a landmark building, it was far from a modern commercial center. We each had to calmly divert our surveillance team's attention without them knowing we had identified them. Then, with a sudden tactical change, we were to execute the *"Briz"* and thereafter continue calmly through our planned walkway until 4:15PM. We then planned to simulate slight anxiety and to within 3 minutes of each other visit the linguistic section of *Tchehov* bookstore.

At the time of the exchange, I casually waited at a city bus stop until I noticed Evgeny across the street preparing to enter the underpass. He casually adjusted his French beret and as he positioned it on his head I imitated frustration towards the bus's delay. I entered the busy passage, indifferently mixing in with a group of students. In the initial darkness, I quickly put on my hat while my left hand easily affixed a large grayish mustache to my face. With a raised coat collar, I was suddenly transformed into an aged man. It took a few seconds until my surveillance team recognized me in the darkly lit tunnel; however, by that time I was too far ahead to allow them to scrutinize any of my movements. As I had experimented and found twice within the last 75 minutes, my surveillance had kept a generous distance while going through the street underpasses with me. There was no reason at all for them to change the established pattern, perhaps the most dangerous and misleading intelligence routine.

I spotted Evgeny as he gradually approached the lighted bottom section of the stairs, and as he casually sneezed, his right coat section easily flipped open and my outer right fist slid through it until I felt the pulling grip of the hook. We achieved the virtually unthinkable just a few steps from the well-lighted exit stairs. Not far behind Evgeny, I saw mixed into the crowd a youthful man with an unusual western looking briefcase that was in disharmony with his common clothing. Obviously the crowd had obscured the cameraman's view and he was too far and too late to catch any symptomatic motions from either one of us. At the same time, I was perplexed to see a face that I had identified earlier, a man from my surveillance team, casually walking towards me in an apparently well-managed up-front control of my whereabouts in the underpass. With my hat and thick mustache, he did not recognize me and anxiously passed, pursuing my lost phrenology.

Notwithstanding the enormous psychological pressure from the tight surveillance, we maintained cool demeanors and casually prepared for the final, although highly misleading operation. Entering the *Tchehov's* bookstore on Vasilevskii prospect, I strolled through the linguistic section and was astonished not to find a tail. While taking notes from a Chinese grammar book, I casually removed my mustache and with my bubble gum affixed a 10-kopek coin under the metal corner of the bookshelf. At the same time I left one of my used trolley tickets between the pages of the book I had been working on. With the tip of a casual looking multi-colored pen, I affixed a microdot on page 38, which was the reverse number of the final digits on the tram ticket. At 4:40PM I left the bookstore and from the adjacent pirogues coffee shop, while casually reading my notes and sipping a cup of tea, observed Evgeny enter the bookstore. In the course of the underpass crossing my surveillance team had lost track of me, while Evgeny's remained tightly present. After a few minutes, I emerged from my refuge and strolled to the front of the bookstore, patiently waiting the seconds' hand of my watch to pass the 4:50 mark. It was the end of the intricate exercise and in a few minutes I entered the designated safe house in order to write my report.

Unknown to me and Evgeny, on this crisp autumn afternoon of 1976 we had achieved the unthinkable; we had flawlessly executed the most efficient intelligence exchange operation in the most recent history of the Academy, without being detected by the watchful eyes of the vast surveillance layout.

The next morning, Vitaly Serov, our instructor, was more than jubilant as we greeted each other. He promised to show us a remarkable movie of our actions. The class had already heard the rumor of our success; nonetheless, no one knew the real truth. Colonel Gromov (all of our names, as well as these of our instructors, are assumed), the leader of the surveillance-training program, was a colorful and erudite former intelligence officer with many years of experience working throughout the world. He had the unique ability to quickly and invisibly master camouflage and facial disguises, and became suitably worthy of his nickname *"Babushka"*, or the Old lady. Perhaps I should credit his knowledge and expertise in teaching me the immense power of the proper disguise and of human psychology. Gromov had also been one of the best students of the legendary Colonel Mangasarov, the KGB's former resident in the Middle East.

The analytical assessment of our performance was left for after the end of the surveillance team's audio and video materials. With much surprise, I discovered that video and audio coverage had been craftily performed on my first contact with the librarian. Thus, I learned a timely lesson; perhaps the young woman's unorthodox emphasis on taking my photo had in reality distracted me from the main surveillance operation, taking place just behind my back.

A variety of video segments were selected to recount our proper or incorrect activities. They overlapped, setting an almost unfair comparison between my demeanor with the sly and devilish conduct of Evgeny. In a few instances, the cameras had even caught his eyes intensely searching for surveillance. My slightest touch of the handrail in the first underpass was clearly caught on video, as was the entire run-through of the second; however the overcrowded environment of the third had created blurry and distorted two-way video coverage. It turned out that the staircases had been greatly miscalculated by the video technicians, for in all instances the different elevation had distorted the coverage. Furthermore: the transition from the bright light to the dark underpasses had consistently distorted not only the officers' vision but also the sensitive video electronics.

My unanticipated and sleek disguise upon entering the *"Arbatskii"* underpass had effectively deceived the surveillance to the extent that they had lost not only video but also the tails' control on me. The "face catcher" (front surveillance officer) had failed to recognize me among the students. Perhaps the most intriguing recognition came later, as an event at the bookstore. A distantly positioned officer had successfully caught on tape my elaborate "get rid of the gum" motion, while utterly failing to identify my bookwork and the microdot positioning. Continuing video surveillance had scrutinized Evgeny as he got the book from the section, purchased it, and departed, all the while not collecting my old gum. This all added to the overall confusion and fretfulness of the surveillance.

Going through the written reports of the surveillance teams and thereafter through our own (separate) assessments numerous times triggered instructors' comments and laughter. It was perplexing to see the faces of some of the instructors and the surveillance officers as they learned from our two independent reports about the multifaceted operation that we had carried out under their noses. Perhaps it was one of the proudest moments in my professional career when the *"Babushka"* shook my hand, expressing his appreciation for indisputably taking aback the best of the best of KGB surveillance.

This disclosure should plainly elucidate that Soviet and the East European fraternal State Security officers were developed not only as enormously potent tools, but also as almost supernatural wizards. We were capable of utilizing complex and surreptitious means to monitor, control and manipulate human destiny and to fulfill any intelligence undertakings.

KGB MASTERS

V iktoria, the strict secretary of General Neshev, urgently summoned me to his executive office on a foggy day in early May of 1973. The General greeted me with a friendly smile as he stood up from behind his desk, and after a firm handshake, he invited me to the comfort of his brown leather sofa. Following some brief small talk about daily operations, the General almost incontestably stated: ". . . I have selected you for an important enterprise. Based on your integrity, I have confidence in your ability to adeptly fulfill this very important assignment . . ."

Sitting on the edge of the sofa, I expected additional instructions; however, General Neshev merely silently measured me with his intense eyes and then started reading a document. Seconds later the secretary announced the arrival of a visitor. The KGB chief in Bulgaria, General Ivan Savchenko, a charming, heavyset, graying official, entered with a smile. For more than an hour we conducted another routine dialogue about the country, the government and KGB and State Security. Evidently the two generals were cunningly evaluating my knowledge and credibility in order to approve or veto my selection. To my surprise, and proving his on-the-spot decisiveness, the KGB general in the end invited me for a tennis match the following day at the *"Levski—Spartak"* courts in Liberty Park.

The meeting was exceptionally important to the generals, as it assured my astute political and professional character. A senior member of the KGB brass was soon scheduled to arrive from Moscow on an official visit and vacation in Bulgaria. General Savchenko sketched out some specific details of the pending visit and suggested basic arrangements for proper security, anonymity, and nonetheless a joyful vacation for the VIP Soviet guests. Masterfully melting the initial ice, he craftily transformed the meeting into a show of camaraderie. Ivan Savchenko perceptively proved to be a great manipulator, a perfidious given that put me on alert right away. In any case, the delegated responsibility was a stupendous honor and opportunity.

*   *   *

General-lieutenant Alexey Alexeevich Bureniok, Chairman of the KGB training academy *"the Barn,"* and his wife Tamara had never been to Bulgaria. The new Bulgarian Minister of Internal Affairs, General-Colonel Dimitar Stoianov, had officially invited the KGB General, and their first impression was to be in my hands.

Prudently, General Neshev avowed: ". . . Perhaps you will chart your future far beyond any imaginings . . ." For some time his implication remained firmly lodged into my mind, but without setting off any leading predilections. I was at the time conceivably too youthfully innocent and bluntly straightforward to grasp the pending opportunities. Following his directives, I put aside all my duties and developed a comprehensive guest's schedule. Coordinating details directly with the Regional directors of State Security throughout the country made me an instant insider. Further, I was to be the family's escort and would join in all events during three weeks of vacationing at the Black Sea resort of Nesebar.

My assignment was complex; from official translator and driver, I was also to be a security guard and photographer. Most importantly, I was supposed to be an intelligent and friendly guide and companion of the Burenioks. Besides the trivial undertaking of assuring a comfortable and relaxing vacation, there were strong political implications as well, which both generals delicately mentioned: General Bureniok's visit would inevitably bring a comprehensive first hand assessment about State Security to the KGB Chairman Yuri Andropov.

During the first official visit of Todor Zhivkov to the USA two years before, he had received the gift of a bright yellow convertible Cadillac El Dorado from President Richard Nixon. This state-of-art western *"decadent symbol of prosperity"**, seldom seen outside the secure facility of SID, was assigned to be General Bureniok's car. I was ecstatic; out of the blue I became responsible for one of the most valuable cars in Bulgaria and perhaps for the well being of one of its most important KGB guests. Also, in addition to professional photographic training, I was taught by an expert from the BTV (Bulgarian National Television) how to operate a modern movie camera **.

Upon the arrival of the international train from Moscow, many people, including former minister Angel Solakov, deputy ministers, high-ranking officials, and KGB General Ivan Savchenko and his assistants greeted General Bureniok

---

*   Todor Zhivkov's testimonial to General Ilia Kashev,during a Rila Mountain hunting trip in 1977.

**   My films about General Bureniok's visit became part of the historical archives of State Security.

and his personable wife Tamara Ivanovna. After prolonged warmth and friendly greetings, we swiftly departed to the hotel *Balkan*, currently *ITT Sheraton*, escorted by a police car. The same evening, we had a delicious dinner at the hotel's main restaurant with plenty of vodka and countless toasts to communism and security, friendship and cooperation. I realized that the new assignment was a more than promising endeavor, for most Bulgarian officials were surprisingly limited in their knowledge and even understanding of Russian. The necessity of becoming a permanent translator and most importantly of building up liaisons for Bureniok with senior State Security and KGB officials was a thrilling and rewarding task. With huge control over words and what each side understood, I steadily came to manage and even stage all parts of the event.

Our first countryside trip was to the Danube port city of Vidin, organized by General George Mladenov, an SCD deputy, as a meeting with the Secretary of the Regional Communist Party Marin Atanasov. We received splendid accommodations at the *Old Palace*, Ludmila Zhivkova's Ministry of Culture residence, where I selected for myself her own personal and comfortable flat. Seven years later, in an ironic turn of events, I once again actually returned to the same lodgings, but was then accompanied by Ludmila.

Visits to the famous *Belogradchik* rocks and caves permitted us to take pleasure in viewing nature's mesmerizing beauty, where over the course of centuries wind and water had carved spectacular rock formations. The millions of years old crystalline stalactites and stalagmites at *Ledenika* cave were perhaps some of the most illustrious in the world. A special cave section, ingeniously developed into a modern Champaign processing winery, even allowed us to taste a few sparkling elixirs.

By that time, General Bureniok had awkwardly suggested that his oldest daughter Larissa was soon to be married in Moscow. Thus, he needed special gifts from Bulgaria. The General then obtrusively asserted himself and used the famed Bulgarian hospitality as a scapegoat, delegating to us the task of obtaining these presents.

The General took my professional demeanor and quickly progressed into closely scrutinizing and manipulating my camaraderie to his advantage. Although I remained solemn, reserved and considerate, Alexey Bureniok repeatedly persisted on informal and casual association. Soon I realized that the Burenioks were cleverly pursuing an ulterior rationale; the beautiful country and the hospitable people were mesmerizing them, evidently instilling visions of retirement years in the vicinity as frequent joyful escapes from grim Soviet realities.

General Dimitar Stoilov, Plovdiv's Regional State Security director, organized various other lavish and enchanting festivities. At the *Bachkovo* monastery we had the rare opportunity to visit the treasure vault and touch priceless antiquities and national treasures that were meticulously maintained and preserved from generation to generation by devoted monks. Paradoxically, our esteemed orthodox host, Deacon Ignatii, was a secret agent of the notorious Sixth directorate. A trip south of Plovdiv allowed us to enjoy the beautiful, breathtaking ranges of the Rodopa Mountains. Through the magnificent fortress of Bulgarian Tsar Asen, we entered the narrow and treacherous gorge of the only mountain pass to the Aegean Sea. For centuries it had diligently guarded and protected the territories of Byzantine, Greek, Roman and Bulgarian tsars and emperors. An extraordinary "stargazing" dinner with folklore dancers at a Pamporovo resort meadow then offered us deliciously roasted lambs and baby piglets that were well complemented by local Thracian wines.

A day spent with the Burenioks at the ancient capital of Veliko Turnovo, one of the oldest strongholds of the East Orthodox church, revived our admiration of the rich cultural and historic heritage of the region. Walking through the masterfully restored castle/fortress *Tzarevetz* confirmed the greatness of the Bulgarian and Byzantine tsars who had successfully ruled over the Greeks and the Romans for centuries. The fortress and the surrounding enclaves were unique, for they had been the last fortifications left after the Sultan Mahmud's clever conquest of the Byzantine jewel of Constantinople during the 14th century, which would stall the Seljuk and Ottoman Turks' advance on Europe.

A few days later we arrived at General Nikola Cherkezov's Regional directorate and received a warm welcome from the local State Security administration at the exclusive Black Sea resort.

As I had prearranged, General Bureniok received a multitude of gifts during these trips: opulent crystal candelabras, leather winter coats, dining sets, silver artwork, original oil paintings and few cases of special Champaign and red wine partially completed the carte blanche shopping list of the KGB General. The insatiable greed of Bureniok was beyond belief. A notion crossed my mind that the General could have easily been developed into a western asset based on his wickedness and insatiability. My own moral and psychological tenets silently detested the Russians and their palpable primitivism.

General Bureniok willingly made assessments of the leaders of State Security. From chronic drunkards to morally decayed sex buffs, he did not save vibrant words in describing the intimidating incompetence of some of his friendly and *"God-obvious imbeciles"*. Bureniok has been a master spy and senior military officer prior to becoming Chairman of the KGB Academy. He had spent almost 25 years on KGB foreign assignments. Well trained in military strategy, psychology, foreign intelligence, surveillance and counter-espionage, he was a resourceful and intelligent mentor and storyteller. Clever and provocatively menacing while in action, he was a calm and charismatic personality while with friends and family. His bright blue eyes were extremely intense and even frightfully hypnotizing at times. Alexey's slightly corpulent and always smiling wife Tamara habitually joked that he resembled a snake, as she was never able to recognize when he was ready to "strike".

*   *   *

For at that time unknown reasons, General Bureniok involved me in unexpected narratives about the KGB's domestic and international operations. Initially, I thought that the General was craftily attempting to impress me with his knowledge. Then I came to think that it was more or less his growing pre-retirement syndrome, revisiting the past. Soon, however, I came to discover that it was in fact part of Bureniok's sagacious personal agenda.

The fact that he was teaching and writing on variety KGB operational and training matters was in my mind. I was regrettably unable to distinguish where the astute realities started to intermingle with imaginations or contraptions. The General was highly structured, loaded with information and not surprisingly; I accepted his testimonials as the uncontaminated truth. Besides, Bureniok was persuasively manipulative and thoughtfully skilled in extrapolating information. Within days of his arrival, he had craftily cross-referenced my upbringing and family genealogy. An almost super-natural power facilitated his rational, deductive memory, allowing him to reincarnate facts or statements with appalling accuracy.

Bureniok's most astonishing disclosure was that the KGB had penetrated the inner sanctum of the political, economic and military structures of the developed west. This was achieved not only through the recruitment of highly placed western agents, but also with well-situated sleeper cells of illegal officers. The General became energized as he described how the KGB had developed deadly subversive forces inside the United States, Great Britain, France and West Germany. He was fond of declaring that within a day, the entire Western world could not only be immobilized, but could also be virtually annihilated by functional and highly trained KGB professionals (illegals), mortally disrupting the main transportation networks, energy generating plants, nuclear silos and most strategic military facilities. My prudent interest about the KGB illegal operations somehow made him cautious, though he eventually became fond of my desire to one day perhaps become a part of the challenging process.

Tamara Sergeevna was a wonderful and down-to-earth woman. She had spent many years abroad; however, she was untouched by western sophistication or superficiality. Discussing the beautiful countryside one day, she casually asked me if I could invite their youngest daughter Kathy for a visit to Bulgaria. In order to further cultivate Bureniok's comradeship, I invited Kathy to be our family guest during the 1974 Christmas and New Year holidays.

We accepted Kathy as openly and considerately as possible and she easily indulged in our joyous holidays. The Burenioks fervently anticipated her likely Bulgarian marriage. On New Year's Day 1974, my parents left to the countryside, visiting relatives and delivering our traditional gifts and blessings. Kathy woke up early in the afternoon and as soon as she understood that we were alone cheerfully opened a bottle of vodka. Nude under her robe, she soon seductively and pleasantly approached me. With the rhythm of the music, her untamed body motions were thrilling. The day evolved into a wonderful moment in the life of two youngsters.

After Kathy's return to Moscow, intense correspondence took place and we planned to spend Christmas of '75 together. However, due to the distance, or my being swayed by my mother's uneasy acceptance of the Russian bold attitude, our friendship gradually faded away. In June of 1975 we entertained Burenioks for two days at our family countryside ranch. It was more than perplexing to me how well Bureniok and my father bonded as potential in-laws. During my training at the Academy in 1977, I was surprised to find out that General Bureniok had become retired and was working as a deputy director of the KGB sports club *"Dynamo"*. My wonderful friends invited me to a lavish dinner at their Moscow apartment, near *Luzhniki*, acquainting me with what became a steady and relentless family heartbreak. In 1980, I was saddened to learn that the Burenioks had not succeeded to turn away Kathy from her ceaseless alcoholism. Sternly rejected by her family and by privileged society, she was sent by the communist authorities to a "recreational Siberian camp."[*]

---

[*] Growing number of disillusioned children and family members of the privileged KGB and the Central Committee of the Soviet Communist Party have been sent to a "Gulag" type recreational camps near Khabarovsk and Sochi.

KIM PHILBY'S DECEPTIONS

General Bureniok informed me that at Nesebar the legendary British mole, Harold Russell, well known as Kim Philby, would vacation with us. After few chilled Stolichnaya shots, Alexey conspiratorially lowered his voice and with almost academic certainty stated: "... You will have the opportunity to personally meet Kim Philby and learn a lot from him ... here are some basics ..."

"*Kim*" *Philby,* aka Harold Adrian Russell, was an outstanding student of aristocratic ancestry, a graduate of Trinity and Cambridge College in England. By 1934, the young socialist had grown frustrated and disappointed by the global recession and the dilapidating stagnation under the imperialistic British Crown. He had also become outraged by the surprising downfall of the promising British Labor Party. On the other hand, he had grown terrified by the emerging National Socialism and Fascism in Europe. Philby's extensive knowledge of the German language had then helped him to obtain a *Goethe* Institute scholarship in Austria. There, he had closely followed the German trial in Leipzig against the Comintern leader George Dimitrov, solidifying his secret communist inspirations.

Socialist and communist ideology grew to become Kim's enthrallment and future infatuation. He eventually concluded that he could dedicate his life to becoming a full-fledged communist and even a secret Soviet emissary. Recruited as a secret agent by the Soviet intelligence in 1933, initially he was used as a Moscow's secret courier with the Austrian communist party. However, by 1936 Philby had emerged as a credible journalist and a social scholar. Hastily marrying a licentious, divorced, underground communist Jewish girl in Vienna had made him vulnerable to the growing Austrian pro-fascist reactionaries. On Soviet advice, Philby timely returned to London with his wife, escaping an imminent arrest by the Austrian secret police. Working for *The Times* of London, in 1937 Kim Philby had reached prominence by covering the exceedingly contentious Spanish Civil War from Spain. After a remarkable stint in Seville and Burgos, where Philby had befriended and dully exploited an aristocratic senior *Abwehr* officer (German military intelligence), he eventually was ready for more serious Soviet assignments. Together with a few socialist-oriented British intellectuals (all Cambridge graduates) Kim Philby had been cleverly developed and indoctrinated by NKVD (Russian foreign intelligence—the future KGB) into an unyielding clandestine devotee to Soviet communism.

With convoluted and thorough Soviet support and guidance, Kim Philby eventually succeeded in attaining high-security jobs in the British SIS*, including a top security job for the British foreign intelligence.

Although factually unsupported, General Bureniok was categorical in stating that Philby had long been suspected by the NKVD and then by KGB management of being a double (MI6/Abwehr), and even a triple (MI6/OSS-CIA/Abwehr) agent for years. Some specific reporting omissions by Philby had been analytically linked to an incriminating pattern dating back from the Spanish Civil War, through the Second World War, and well into the early 1960s. After his exfiltration to Moscow, the "skipped fine points" mold had suddenly vanished, greatly reinforcing Soviet security concerns about Philby's credibility and perhaps stealthy deceptions. During the Second World War, Philby had then provided the Soviet Union with substantial information about the military strategies of Germany, England and the USA, including but not limited to gathering information and performing joint intelligence operations with Richard Sorge**. Unrelentingly, Philby had provided the Soviet Union with invaluable intelligence for many years after the Second World War. Quickly ascending to a senior British SIS-MI6 foreign intelligence and counter-intelligence officer had further perplexed the Soviets. The NKVD leadership had never accepted Philby as a bona-fide asset. Perhaps the most stunning of Bureniok's revelations about Philby was the fact that he had been targeted for assassination by Beria's*** henchman. NKVD leadership and Lavrentii Beria had personally reached to the conclusion that Philby was untrustworthy and hence should be assassinated, setting a vivid example to other assets of the consequences of double or unfaithful collaboration. A senior member of the French resistance and of the communist party had apparently written a letter to Stalin, expressing concerns of Philby's activities and associations during the Spanish Civil War, grossly incriminating him of being German asset, and resolutely rejecting to work with him during Second World War.

Joseph Stalin himself had blocked Kim Philby's assassination, astutely fearing that the purging of Philby could trigger objectionable alienation and

---

*   British Secret Intelligence Service

**   Kim Philby and Richard Sorge apparently never knew of each other or worked together. This was an apparent disinformation by Bureniok or simply incorrect knowledge of the real facts.

***   Lavrentti Beria had replaced Yezhov as head of the Soviet NKVD-OGPU, the future KGB. He is credited with emptying Lublianka's KGB offices by systematic executions of officers during the 1937—1939 purge.

fear among future assets willing to perform espionage on behalf of the Soviet Union and the global communist fraternity. This had happened in 1941-42, around the time that Stalin had realized that major damage had been inflicted by Beria's relentless philosophy of duplicity, deception and mistrust. It was the time of Stalin's megalomaniac attainment of a close thoughtfulness with Churchill.

Bureniok explicated that he was perhaps the only KGB official ever to review and study all of the Philby files* dating back to the early 1930s. He acknowledged that the NKVD had hideously suspect Kim Philby, for he was the only western Soviet asset ever to work for free. Bureniok had also just completed a top-secret FCD analytical study** on Kim Philby's secret relationship with the Soviet Union; describing how purely ideological convictions had made him one of the most brilliant communist spies ever. Nonetheless, Bureniok clearly outlayed Philby's credits for developing and training some of the best KGB—FCD foreign intelligence officers, such as Victor Cherkashin, Oleg Kalugin, Rem Krassilnikov and Leonid Shebarshin.

Philby's name had been intentionally surrounded by riddle and heroic mysticism by the KGB and the Academy. After the Second World War and especially after his near betrayal by the inner NKVD/KGB leadership, most of his clandestine operations became closely guarded secrets. Bureniok's thorough knowledge of Philby's operational files was overwhelming. The General's candor and credibility warranted all information, not to emphasize that he has started perceiving me as his certain soon-to-be son-in-law.

Philby's covert work on behalf of the Comintern, Cominform and the Soviet Union, can perhaps be better understand today not only through my personal observations, Gerneral Bureniok's assessments, but also and especially by Philby's own personal accounts and those of few independent writers. The alluring communal philosophy of Marx, Engels and Lenin had been the Philby's main rationale in generating fondness and association with the British socialists, consequently leading to his inevitable communist deceitfulness and hideous infidelity to the British Crown. The same utopian idealistic devotion and ideological "veneer" had made the formation of clandestine networks of Soviet supporters possible in Great Britain, the Americas and all over Europe.

---

* KGB's, FCD—counterintelligence directorate has been maintaining Philby's file active (none was in the KGB archive in 1973) it was an overwhelming record kept in three main safes at Yasenevo.

** *"Philby's agenda"* KGB, 1973, Leutenant-General A.A. Bureniok #128-373PS

*　　*　　*

The trans-Bulgarian sightseeing trip was enormously satisfying to the guests. They soon realized how ancient, rich and controversial the Balkan Peninsula had been over the centuries. Bureniok discovered firsthand the reasons why the Russian Tsar Alexander Romanov had disregarded the expansion of Russia to the East and instead had decided to pursue greater Russian influence (*Russophile*) and hegemony throughout the Balkans. It had been a wise geo-political balancing act of the Russian Tsar, strongly influenced by the strategic positioning of the British Crown within the region. Not surprisingly, Josef Stalin had pursued a similar agenda during the Second World War, countering Hitler's Third Reich regional politics and inclinations.

Kim Philby had achieved his first successful work in Bulgaria years earlier. As luck would had it, he had received his NKVD nickname "*The Lucky Kim*" during a secret British SIS* regional operation. This had come from a unique assignment he was entrusted with, replacing his boss in the last moment. He was supposed to debrief, cross-examine and recruit a Soviet GRU would-be defector in Istanbul, Turkey. However, this intelligence officer had turned out to possess first-hand knowledge of Philby's secret misdeeds with the Soviets. Instead, with Philby's stealthy related information accompanied by some amazing luck, the NKVD and GRU had perpetrated a cunning deception and were able to withhold the man from divulging the information to the SIS.

The Ministry of Internal Affairs resort at Nesebar was our next stop. It was like an opulent oasis dropped in the middle of the unmatched tranquility and beauty of the desert sand dunes. It had been developed over the years into a luxurious resort for selected members, guests and senior officers of the East European security institutions. A private road led to the guarded compound and a parking lot, while a well stocked bar and an open-air discotheque offered exceptional time for relaxation and entertainment. The exceptional abundance of amenities conveniently eliminated activities outside the two resort buildings.

The resort's manager, Major Tomov, was well prepared for the arrival of the "big boss," and we promptly received wonderful accommodations. A discrete VIP section at the restaurant veiled us from any curiosity, while special servers waited on us at all times of the day. It was the epitomized "lazy vacation". However, every morning after Burenioks had comfortably settled at the beach, I had to drive

---

*　　Kim Philby was assigned as a SIS (MI6) Chief of Station in Istanbul during 1946-1949. During 1945 Philby had betrayed to the Soviets would-be defector Voronin, a member of the GRU station in Istanbul, a credible source of Philby's double crossings. Voronin was apprehended and executed as a traitor by the NKVD.

to the Sunny Beach Regional State Security directorate to collect mail, office messages, papers and magazines.

On the second day of this deed, while driving back to the resort, I noticed a girl walking in my direction, near the Sunny Beach Park. She had long dark hair, wore a bright summer dress, and hid her eyes behind designer sunglasses. She casually held a beach bag over her shoulder. Instinctively I diminished speed, but untouched by the car's elegance, the girl unflappably continued. Quite shocked, I became slightly boorish, and shifted into reverse. As we aligned, I finally attained her attention.

It turned out that the girl was walking towards the nearby bus stop for a ride to Nesebar. Solemnly pointing out the irregularity of the local transportation, I invitingly opened the door. The somehow shy and reluctant girl looked in both directions of the deserted road and with a brief snippet of gratitude accepted the temptation.

Exiting the woods I pressed the accelerator as the road accommodatingly stretched parallel to the sandy beach. I kept cool and silent, as the girl tactfully matched the moment. It was an almost picturesque moment on the background of an eternally blue sea. In tandem with my jovial companion, I was taken in by the speed, the music and the semi-decadent comfort of a newly discovered world. Wordlessly, soon we arrived at the Nesebar's harbor and I stopped at the main parking lot.

Admiring a nearby medieval windmill, the girl turned in my direction and before I was able to react, quickly kissed my cheek.

"... This trip gave me so much joy; it was terrific. Thank you!" She stepped out, gallantly closed the door and walked away, vanishing in the crowd of the Old city gate.

No name, no address, no phone, just a remote trace of lipstick on my cheek and a light perfume fragrance, both which quickly disappeared with the salty wind. My supposed "cool" attitude had perhaps inadvertently chilled a potentially promising social contact. I had to return to the Burenioks in two hours for our lunch. Covering the automatic roof of the convertible, I spotted my passenger's Chinese umbrella on the floor of the car and hurriedly decided to find her in the Old city.

The early walk through the narrow streets lined with Mediterranean style homes and Greco-Roman ruins was pleasant. I logically came to the conclusion that perhaps I was under surveillance by either State Security or the KGB. The remote pick-up place of the girl and the strange circumstantial developments perhaps justified a foreign intelligence undertaking, aimed at Bureniok or even Kim Philby. How had the "nymph" arrived at that remote spot of Sunny Beach forest and how was she so prudent as to predict my approach? I was flabbergasted at thinking that my beautiful passenger was perhaps a professional plant.

I stopped in front of an old facade and "read" its moldy bronze plaque, and casually probed and examine the umbrella. While my fully-fledged professional "paranoia" swiftly prevailed, the search turned clueless. Calming down, I walked back through the streets, setting off some surveillance swiping aimed at losing tails. A few blocks of intricate "evasion and detection" techniques assured me that I was clean. Through the Roman gate, far below, I soon noticed my car surrounded by few inquisitive buffs. A lady on a bench nearby, with a straw hat and colorful dress, suddenly shifted my attention. Intricately watching a group of fisherman repairing nets, my companion peripherally observed my approach.

I greeted her kindly. "... What a wonderful surprise to find you here!" "I looked for you all over!"

The girl lifted her head, looked at me over her sunglasses, and provocatively smiled. Touching the hat's edge, she graciously explained, "... In the meantime, I found a wonderful replacement for my old Chinese treasure ..."

Extending her hand to take the umbrella, she revealed the pale skin of a beach newcomer.

"Thank you for your honesty." She stood, tall as me on her modern sandals, compellingly gorgeous.

"My name is Zorro". I introduced myself with my pseudonym.

"Hello, Zorro, my name is Sashka." She responded and in attempting to sit back on the bench, found that one of the fishermen had nonchalantly taken half of it, carrying a plethora of fish, seaweeds and cheap tobacco scents with him.

"... I saw you yesterday with your parents on the beach. Is your mother Russian? Yesterday you were walking on the beach in front of our resort and I heard you speaking Russian," She asked with a minor southern accent.

"I am on an assignment with government guests from the Soviet Union." I cautiously mumbled.

"Your car is awesome and must be very expensive."

"It is an official diplomatic car for VIP guests, and I am fortunate to have this nice car for my guests."

"Are you a driver?" She asked disrespectfully.

"No! I am translator and a trip coordinator at the Ministry of Foreign Affairs."

Glimpsing at my watch, I offered Sashka a ride to her resort and our dialogue continued surprisingly effortlessly and friendly. I learned that she was looking into learning to sail and that same morning had visited the students' sailing center "Academic", a walking distance from the place I had picked her up.

In front of her resort, Sashka swiftly got off the car, just as a heavyset lady rushed through the front doors towards us, loud-mouthedly reproving Sashka, who barely succeeded to wave goodbye.

TACKLING THE FISH CALLED PHILBY

In early June 1973, at the Black Sea resort of Nesebar, I met for the first time the notorious British communist spy Kim Philby. Surprisingly tall, standing on top of a sand dune in front of our building, Philby was visibly captivated by the tranquility of the low tide and the rising reflections of the morning sun. He was also seemingly intrigued by my martial art sequences, for the grayish man in a long green with red stripes western robe walked towards me. He emanated the aura of a regimented, powerful and controlling man, but perhaps what I saw was simply well trained conduct, or facade.

For most vacationers, Kim Philby would have been just an unknown KGB VIP. However, for me he was a mysterious and worthy fable, a presumed "brilliant" Soviet master spy, a spook; he was one who for years had simultaneously worked with the three most powerful intelligence organizations of the world. In reality, he had been both sought after and enviously protected by all of them at the same time. Besides all of his KGB glories, Philby was a pathetic epitome of utopian communist imaginings gradually degraded by the Marxist-Leninist communal, economic and moral failures.

Philby accepted my greeting with a reserved smile. I took the initiative further and nonchalantly inquired if he enjoyed the beautiful morning. Kim was pleased by my attention and in surprisingly limited Russian stuttered acknowledgement of the beautiful morning.

"Perhaps I should speak English, sir?" I cordially introduced myself, disclosing that I was a State Security officer. Expressing my great honor of meeting him in person, I felt that the initial distance shortened with our warmth handshake.

"... I greatly admire your immensely successful work for the KGB. Your memoirs are the most fascinating intelligence writing I had ever read!*". My expressions were frank, but not flattering.

---

*   Kim Philby, "My silent war"; The soviet master spy's own story. Grove 1968 (KGB censored account)

Philby more or less conspiratorially looked around, and while guardedly raised a finger in front of his lips, slightly bowed, expressing gratitude.

To thwart Philby's suspicion or misinterpretations that potentially could implicate me in a blatant transgression, I made it clear that I was a State Security escorting officer of General Alexey Bureniok and that we had arrived at the resort the previous day.

I mentioned our floor and apartment number, which caused Philby to look back at the complex. With surprisingly clear English he asserted fast that we were just a flock of stairs apart. Then, wishing him a wonderful day, I left him to complete his morning walk, triumphant of my newly established liaison.

A few minutes later, Kim Philby approached the beach showers at the end of the serpentine walkway and while washing his sandy slippers cautiously gazed around. Oddly slapping his wet slippers, he walked towards the building and waved politely as soon as spotted me on the balcony.

At the breakfast table around 8.15AM, someone softly tapped my shoulder. I noticed the devilish shock on Alexey Bureniok's face and spun around. However, this surprise came from my innocent professional mistake in not divulging to Bureniok the fact that I had met the British man of whom we had so often conversed. In refined and unperturbed Russian, Kim introduced his wife Rufina Puhovich and himself as Andrey Feodorovich, and without any signs of stuttering, pointed towards his chubby Russian escort Lavrenty or Lev. Appropriately, I introduced General Bureniok and his wife Tamara. Bureniok's brusque greeting with the Philbys came somewhat disingenuously, perhaps deviously preset. Rufina exchanged a few friendly words with the look-alike Tamara and smilingly shook my hand a second time. Moscow was obviously concerned with Philby's contacts and security, for I noticed Lev's more or less constant control of his whereabouts.

Todor Boiadzhiev, an FCD-foreign intelligence officer, soon joined Philby's table and cordially shook my hand, anxious to introduce him to General Bureniok. Apparently he was assigned to assist Philbys, for their breakfast continued in English. A year earlier Boiadzhiev had returned from a lengthy stint in New York as a Science and Technology intelligence officer. His wife Radka was a German translator at the Fourth department. During 1976 and 1977, I would work with Boiadzhiev in the field of science and technology intelligence, when he functioned as a deputy of Lubcho Michailov. Towards the end of 1977 Todor was assigned as chief of station in New York, under the cover of representative to the UN. Upon his return in early 1983, he was assigned as chief of the Sixth department, the analytical and information arm of FCD. It was considered one of the most mundane and demoralizing jobs available in State Security. However, Todor Boiadzhiev had quickly climbed the ladder of success as a result of nepotism and of his family's communist and resistance background. However, neither

Kim Philby, nor my future boss, Ognian Doinov, would prevent Boiadzhiev's derailment into a long-justified dead end FCD fate.

I was taken aback by Kim Philby's approach, but soon grasped that the KGB had all along kept him aside, not only from the reach and hold of western intelligence, but from the Soviet society as well. Throughout our association I repeatedly observed Philby's palpable wisdom. Kim's acquaintance with Lev and the superficial Boiadzhiev gradually became a transparent repugnance with the reality. Lev was not only his bodyguard, but more or less an official censor, supposed to not only monitor, but also to control Philby's activities and contacts. Boiadzhiev, on the other hand, appeared to be ashamed of his duties as a guide, and narcissistically attempted to be Philby's professional acquaintance rather than his convenient services provider.

During the following two weeks, I mastered many meetings with Kim Philby, most of them without Lev or Todor. Several of the "incidental" get-togethers took place as I walked on the beach early in the morning or evenings and Kim unexpectedly showed up with a book or newspaper in hand. Perhaps Philby used the reading materials as a justifiable excuse to be left alone on the beach, or the KGB and General Bureniok deviously guided him to study and perhaps develop me further. The coincidences made me slightly uneasy, for I kept in mind Bureniok's opinion that the Cambridge group had been homosexual by nature.

Our dialogues about the socialist system and western pluralism gradually became trivial. Soon we explored the demanding role of communist intelligence agencies and officers. Perhaps eager for attention after years of oblivion and mistreatment by the Soviet bureaucracy, Kim Philby became more than a mentor; shortly put, he started to treat me as a sibling. He perceptibly played politics by affirming the superior standing of State Security. For yet unknown reasons, he made palpable parallels with the strength and the capabilities of the Israeli's Mossad and the British MI6. Openly and some times very perilously Philby critiqued the KGB staffs' inferiority and their semi-peasant or apparatchik demeanors. Nonetheless, he was not short of criticism of the CIA's domination of the western and global intelligence since the Second World War. Elaborately justifying his assessments and in-depth knowledge, Philby often mentioned that he had been the official British MI6 liaison with the CIA in Washington, D.C. for many years. Thus, he was more than "on the ball" with the development of the nuclear equilibrium. His frank confession that this was his first trip outside the Soviet Union, since his mysterious Lebanon* disappearance was puzzling to me.

---

* Ten years earlier, as an Estonian seaman, Philby had escaped to Moscow on a Soviet commercial ship from Lebanon.

After a decade of growing frustration and deepening disillusionment with Soviet communism and the developed socialist society, the new KGB* management had eventually started treating Philby in a different way. Most of Philby's Cambridge comrades had lost their human identity through the Moscow labyrinths, succumbing to alcoholism, mental disorders and dilapidating health. Praising the visionary style of the KGB chairman Yuri Andropov, Philby was evidently not flattering his master; he was just hopeful of an improved and perhaps more considerate KGB.

Philby elaborately linked the ongoing KGB changes with the colossal problems that Soviet foreign intelligence had suffered two years earlier by the defection in London of Oleg Lyalin. Although the case was a closely guarded secret within the KGB and State Security, I had some limited knowledge from the top-secret bulletins assessing the global press.

Lyalin's disclosures to the British intelligence and thereafter to the British press about the multifaceted KGB operations against the United Kingdom in case of war, including but not limited to the plans for assassination of the British leaders and conducting subversive activities against the London subway systems, power generation and nuclear stations and the main water supply systems had sent chills and waves of shock around the western world.

Covert Soviet operations in England had received a mortal blow: more than 100 KGB officers had been expelled and a restricted diplomatic status was imposed on the Soviet's London mission.

Philby was clearly living with a heavy moral burden, perhaps as a result of mounting remorse from his duplicity and his ever-lasting love for England. He had irrefutably recognized the utopian nature of the communalism and that it had not been worthy to hurl to certain death more than 100 spies and to viciously destroying so many would get unstoppable in his criticism of Soviet society, even in front of General Bureniok. During some of these binges Kim made the most accurate assessments of his esteemed Cambridge University communist fraternity. His elaborate story on Anthony Blunt resembled a eulogy of the social philosophy and his own disdain of the British society during the Depression of 1930s, and to him somehow mitigated his socialist transgressions.

Growing up in a rich and affluent family, Blunt had fallen in love with the Soviet communism and its influence while at Cambridge. He had started questioning the Crown's superficial luxuries and decadence, while squalor and poverty had been widely spreading throughout the kingdom and the colonies. A brilliant scholar and historian, Anthony Blunt's noble ancestry was a sufficient guaranty for his acceptance to Windsor and his appointment by Queen Elizabeth

---

* Confirmed by Gordievsky in New York, 1999 and Kalugin in Washington, DC, 2000.

as a Royal art curator, successfully shielding his leftist orientations and communist spy activities. Having been a former intelligence officer of the Crown during the Second World War and advisor to MI5 and MI6 after the war, he had virtually unlimited access to Allied and British secrets thereafter. In his ambivalent capacity as a Royal confidant and a member of the secretive Cambridge communist clique, Blunt had learned in the early 1950s from Philby (assigned by MI6 to Washington D.C.) about the ongoing investigation and imminent arrest of Guy Burgess and Donald MacLean. Stealthily warning his London KGB contact, Blunt was able to prevent their apprehension. To the great embarrassment and humiliation of the British government, the KGB agents successfully arranged their exfiltration to Moscow.

Kim Philby's defection to Moscow in 1963 had finally exposed the Cambridge spooks, corroborating their grave misdeeds. Blunt lost his knighthood in disgrace; however, stone faced and aristocratically composed, he had managed to secretly confess to MI6 about his KGB activities. He had masterfully double-crossed the KGB, working until the late 1970s for the British Crown.

Reminiscent and nostalgic like Philby, Guy Burgess became disillusioned with the socialist realities and willingly, or perhaps with a devious help, had succumbed to a slow-imposed alcohol-related death by 1969.

Catching on to Philby's references about the Israeli Mossad's efficiency, and in order to further expand his trust, I told him about a great State Security and KGB fiasco during the 1960s.

MOSSAD'S MAGIC TOUCH

It was a warm summer night in the middle of the 1960s. A highly trained by the KGB, State Security technical team had stealthily entered the Israeli Embassy in Sofia, Bulgaria. The officers had started the elaborate installation of electronic bugs and microphones in order to thoroughly monitor the controversial Zionist establishment. It was the result of a long, intricate chain of events, consisting of surveillance, analysis and now successful infiltration by an attractive State Security agent (a former prostitute), posing as the girlfriend and lover of one of the lustful Jewish embassy guards. Every detail had been carefully evaluated and approved by the KGB and the Moscow instigated operation was set off.

The seductive "girlfriend", lusciously embracing the gullible lover, called her mother to inform her that she would be late for dinner. The monitored call meant that the embassy was empty and she was engaging the guard in a passionate session and sedating him with a laced bottle of Champaign.

However, every deception can be deceived. Unknown to KGB and State Security, a renegade, patriotic Jewish operational officer had acquired knowledge of the pending bugging operation of the Israeli Embassy. As a translator of the Israeli communications intercepted by State Security and KGB, he had worked covertly for the Israeli Mossad. As a result of his information, and undetected by the State Security and KGB, a team of Israeli commandos had entered the Embassy one by one as visitors. The Israeli Mossad craftily envisioned gaining a more than valuable bargaining chip to then silently demand and impose stern political action on the part of the Communists. They would thereby curtail the growing Soviet support of fundamentalist Arabs and Palestinian causes and their escalating persecution of Jewish intellectuals across Eastern Europe.

The technical team, assured by surveillance that the embassy's premises were clear and that the guard was drugged, entered the compound through a side door. Promptly entering the Ambassador's office, they covered the windows with thick curtains and without delay started invisibly hiding remotely activated sensors and microphones that were capable of eavesdropping on any word or phone conversation made in the Ambassador's office.

The summer temperature inside the south-oriented room was well above normal. Most of the officers removed their jackets, setting aside even their personal guns.

A sudden bang blistered opened the two wide-paneled doors. Masked commandos with short Uzi machine guns swiftly stormed the ambassador's office, thwarting any resistance or communication. Three technicians from the Fourth department and two counter-intelligence officers from SCD were caught "red handed". Summarily gagged, hooded and cuff linked, the perplexed State Security officers were quietly spirited to the underground bomb shelter for interrogation. Personal weapons, security ID cards, instruments, technical components and documents were collected. The communications equipment was hastily stripped off of the officers' bodies and therefore prevented any warnings to the outside security details. Deep underground, the gagged and stripped necked culprits were soon securely tied to chairs.

Israeli diplomats surprisingly popped up in three different locations on the nearby streets, taking clandestine photos of the surveillance teams and the technical communications car. This cunning Israeli operation, conducted in the heart of the communist fraternity, was deemed on of the worst blows ever to the integrity and the professionalism of the KGB and State Security. It had exposed and made extremely vulnerable both the Soviet and the Bulgarian governments for not pursuing and employing the consistent and unbiased policies assured by the constitution of the country.

After a few months of looming bilateral discontent, the affair had been quietly settled, but not before the Bulgarian government had changed its international policy towards Egypt, Syria, Iraq, Lebanon, Libya and the Palestinians. The stealthy victory achieved by Israel, however, would become irrelevant soon, for Bulgaria dramatically changed its policies. As a consequence of the Arab-Israeli war of the 1964-67, Bulgaria unilaterally closed the Israeli Embassy in Sofia, expelling the Israeli Ambassador.

The Soviet/Bulgarian intelligence fiasco at the Israeli Embassy in Sofia and the newly imposed government policies towards the Jewish state orchestrated by the Soviet Union's leadership resulted in the blunt expulsion of thousands of Jewish officers from State Security, the Ministry of Foreign Affairs and the Ministry of Defense, although most of them were longstanding and even ranking members of the communist party.

PLEASANT ENCOUNTERS

I gradually got into the habit of relaxing and reading books on my balcony after our sumptuous meals, and was often captivated by the tranquility of the sea and the mesmerizing beauty of the sunset. On Bureniok's instructions, I had begun to more or less permanently watch over Kim Philby, frequently joining him for walks. Now and then, we would sit on the dunes, practically in silence, while he stared far out over the sea, contemplating a few sentences. Sometimes walking with Philby for hours, I relentlessly extrapolated his knowledge, experiences and deeds. I had in reality an amazingly well versed and erudite mentor, perhaps a sincere comrade.

I was reading a Soviet documentary on Fidel Castro's Cuban revolution when an enchanting voice called my name from beneath.

On the alley was Sashka, barefoot with a hat in one hand and a pair of sandals in the other. Affectionately waving, I silently pointed to the entrance of the building. With a pounding heart I arranged the room and hurriedly rushed down the stairs.

"Hi Sashka! So nice to see you!" I friendly extended my hand.

"The pleasure is mine." She replied with a smile, kissing my chick.

Holding her hand I invited her to be my guest upstairs, taking the sandals. It was just before 7 PM and I had plenty of time for my guest.

"What a wonderful view!" She exclaimed as we entered my room.

"It is so nice to see you again."

Sashka did not resist my hug and I felt her trembling body tightly pressed against mine. Wonderful and exciting feelings were in the air between us. She allowed me to kiss her neck, as my hands tenderly held her enviable body. Sashka was quiet and astoundingly eager to go on with our passionate escapade.

The room was filled by the sun's golden radiance, and breathless and joyfully embraced, before long we rested on my bed. The hugs and kisses grew into a wonderfully sensual cuddle of two youthful and energized bodies. Rapidly, the sun descended behind the hilly western horizon, bringing chilly wind. Unperturbed in the comfort of a warm robe, Sashka apologized for the weird behavior of her over protective mother. Her last two years at the university had been the most wonderful and happy time in her life. Away from home and from her difficult mother, she had discovered a new world.

"Do you know that you are the first man with whom I am in bed?" She whispered as I kissed her velvet lips, unashamed of being a 20-year-old virgin. Surviving the challenges of her student life in Sofia and the unquestionable pursuits of her admirers was surprising.

Sashka came closer and playfully kissed and cuddled my body. Evidently she was mentally and physically geared up to be sexually active. Yet I could sense some willful resistance to a concluding encounter, for perhaps the unknown scared her. I grasped that I had to play an almost asinine game, giving her time to comprehend the inevitable situation. The last thing I wanted to become was an unwanted perpetrator.

Our bodies gradually immersed in the pleasing embraces, rousing contacts and sensual kisses. Before the night could cover the sea in darkness, our irresistible determination made Sashka a woman*.

$$* \quad * \quad *$$

The phone ringing made us jump out of the pleasurable cuddle. General Bureniok asked if we could leave earlier to take a tour of the Sunny Beach yacht club with the local State Security chieftain. Glancing at the time, I agreed to leave in about 15 minutes.

Within minutes Sashka was surprisingly blissful and ready to go.

". . . I'll see you at the beach tomorrow." Sashka lovingly kissed me and almost conspiratorially vanished into the falling night as I followed her waving silhouette through the dunes.

The Yacht club was a relatively small facility on the main Sunny Beach resort, with only few berths for motor and sailboats, most for rent to western tourists.

Our sister cities dinner was well organized from the wonderful and colorful folklore dancers to the traditional abundance of food and drinks. A well mannered gentleman from the Baku mayor's group cordially approached me and asked if he could have a word with General Bureniok, introducing himself as a KGB Colonel, Sergeevich Piotr, Chief of Baku's City KGB directorate. My Russian fluency made him assume that I was Bureniok's assistant. Piotr turned out to be a former student of the Academy and a fraternal bond soon prevailed as he joined our table. With a few vodkas our discussion progressed around the growing problems in Baku and the surrounding municipalities. The largely Muslim population strongly resented the cultural and ideological values of Soviet socialism. Evidently, the KGB had

---

*　As leader of the Dimitrov's Young Communist Organization—Komsomol, in the early 1980s, Sashka Shopova (A) became a secret lover of the General Secretary of the Bulgarian Communist Party, Todor Zhivkov.

been facing identical problems as experienced in Bulgaria with the pro-Turkish (Pomak)* movement and the strong revitalization of Islamism.

Sipping the traditional vodka, Colonel Sergeev corroborated that the Soviet Union had serious minority problems in most of its southern republics. Sharing some of the problems of the Bulgarian government with the Turkish and the Macedonian region cunningly catalyzed the subject, provoking more and more disclosures.

The KGB officials clearly reiterated that the brotherly State Security had been the KGB's primary provider of strategic intelligence on Turkey and Iran, and nonetheless played a pivotal role in the overall intelligence operations of the region. The role of the Bulgarian Muslims emigrating to Turkey, Iran, Iraq, Afghanistan, Pakistan and Lebanon and clandestinely working as KGB and State Security agents was delineated as one of the most successful cooperative efforts.

General Bureniok become somewhat agitated on the subject and sarcastically delineated the fact that the KGB had learned a scornful lesson in allowing Russian Jewish KGB agents to immigrate to Israel. Jewish immigrants would within days of arrival to their Holy land reveal sensitive KGB secrets to Shin Bet (Israel's State Security). It was the first time that I become consciously aware how much information can flow and be gathered in "the darkness" of a casual conversation with colleagues, especially over drinks.

The next day we enjoyed an early morning outing of deep-sea fishing and a thrilling mid-afternoon sailing. I discovered another joyful dimension of the privileged life of the reach and powerful. The "Bennetton 36", a fine-looking and modern luxury sailboat, was one of only three expensive rentals of the Bulgarian Tourist Agency *"Balkan Tourist"*. The challenging exposure to the sea and the wind steadily revitalized my hidden obsession with sailing, which in turn grew up to become my family hobby many years later in the United States.

*   *   *

I continued to artfully exploit Kim Philby's almost fatherly attention. A sneakily overheard telephone conversation he had with Bureniok unambiguously tipped me off about Philby's stealthy coordinates. At that time, I was perhaps too shallow to comprehend the mind-numbing process of diversity and the complexity of the KGB's plans and interests. I was much more concerned about the fact that for two days I had not seen Sashka, instead of attempting to unravel an ongoing KGB stratagem.

---

*   Bulgarian Muslim believers, mostly non-Turkish or Arabic speaking ethnic minority.

My poignant wishes led me to Sashka's resort. The outlandish attitude of Sashka's mom made me slightly tense when I knocked on their door.

"Hi Zorro!" Sashka opened the door with a pleasant smile and politely asked me to wait for a moment.

"I will be back after dinner . . ." She announced to her parents and cheerfully pulled me down the staircase. Stopping on the lower level she awarded me with a seductive kiss. It was a mesmerizing evening due to the purple sunset's reflections on the calmed sea. A long stroll on the beach, with sandals in hand, allowed us to joyfully chat about life and our interests. We stopped occasionally, passionately and warmly embracing each other.

At the resort we joined an ongoing Polynesian party and had a few drinks enhance our joy. Surpassing my judgment, reality was transforming our friendship into a love story in the making. Unsure of who made the first move, and driven by mutual passion, we escaped to my room. The rest of the evening we were passionate lovers, filled with fervor never experienced before. Hand in hand we walked back to her resort, to find in the main lobby her mother in the company of a distinguished looking grayish man.

"I am going to be in trouble!" Sashka comically bit her lips and after a fly-by kiss ran sheepishly inside.

I greatly desired to see Sashka before our departure, as a last minute change had been made to General Bureniok's schedule. The resort management and the local State Security directorate organized a wonderful farewell dinner. I expected to find Kim Philby among the guests; however, he was regrettably out of town.

The immensely enriching experience and the extraordinary contacts I had been fortunate to develop with General Alexey Bureniok, Kim Philby, Ivan Savchenko, the elite of KGB and State Security, became a solid step in my professional and personal development. I grasped tightly to the sheltered world of power, perks, luxury and benefits set forth for selected government and party officials and their families. So much was happening in our relatively modest social environment, whereas the national doctrine of equality and communality, through its persistent socio-ideological manipulations, in reality continued to greatly mislead the ordinary people.

*   *   *

Upon arrival in Sofia, I promptly reported to General Neshev on key details about the Bureniok's trip and vacation. He requested a written report and made clear that I was expected to make a prompt call to General Savchenko.

The KGB master invited me for a tennis game at 10:30 the next morning and clumsily suggested a lunch thereafter at the Ministry of Internal Affairs' club *"Slavianska Beseda"*.

General Savchenko arrived late for our morning tennis and jaggedly called me to the bench.

"... I will get your detailed report on General Bureniok from comrade Neshev, but before that I need some information: I have learned that you befriended comrade Feodorovich in Nesebar and apparently discussed professional matters with him!"

He was a bullish and somber, intimidating old man. The sparks in his eyes and his firm intonation revealed a man of dangerous intensity and attention to details. I calmly smiled and attempted to overpower the spymaster with my roundabout retort.

"Comrade General! Are you referring to the stuttering comrade Feodorovich who preferred to talk to me and Todor Boiadzhiev only in English?"

"Yes! Tell me everything you know and everything comrade Feodorovich had told you about the KGB or any other intelligence matters!"

I was facing a different Ivan Savchenko, not the mellow, friendly person I had known for almost three months, but a dangerously inquisitive and demanding superior, with owlishly eyebrows and icy cold blue eyes. I explained how comrade Feodorovich had approached me on the beach as one of the individuals eating at his reserved area of the resort. He funnily stuttered his Russian and because I had noticed him reading an English book I spoke English with him thereafter. Describing Feodorovich's fascination with the Bulgarian land, folklore traditions, literature and ancient culture, nonetheless I summarized his fondness of the Russian culture. Assessing that comrade Feodorovich had been exceedingly introvert, I mentioned the fact that his reluctance to discuss any details about his personal life and work drew me away.

Savchenko's intensity was gone, or perhaps his artistic talents had run out of steam, for he intriguingly smiled and invited me to attend the following Monday a special meeting with comrade Feodorovich at the State Security's executive conference room on the third floor of the Ministry of Internal Affairs.

"Do you realize that you had befriended one of our most important western intelligence assets ever?" Savchenko asked rhetorically.

"Well done partner, let's play, but before that, let me tell you that I received a controversial report from Moscow about your relentless meetings with Kim ..." He stopped short of spelling out Philby's name and smirked on the unintentional slip. We played until noon when I noticed his profuse perspiration and deep, choking breathing problems. Tennis games and his love of walking had become the only viable deterrents against his body's obesity and premature aging, but his lungs had been clearly irreversibly damaged by more than a half-century's abuse of tobacco and alcohol.

ITALIAN CONNECTION

L ater in the day, General Ivan Savchenko carried out one of the shrewdest psychological KGB drills I have ever been exposed to. He blatantly subjected me to a ferocious mental experiment, perhaps elaborately attempting to check my stability and determination. I sensed thereafter that I had been accepted not only as his tennis associate, but also more or less as a bona fide asset.

General Ciril Neshev and an unknown KGB Colonel Vasilii Serov waited for us at the executive's club-restaurant. Serov's introduction was brisk, delineating the official nature of the meeting. Promptly the conversation evolved around the fraternal security cooperation and General Neshev surprisingly asked me to translate to the Russians his testimonials. The KGB center in Sofia had been maintaining in strict secrecy an office; conducting special technical tasks, surveillance and training. Colonel Serov vaguely introduced details of a sensitive, top-secret assignment, linked to the impending trip to Sofia, of a KGB illegal officer deeply infiltrated in Italian political circles.

The KGB spook, a flamboyant and vivacious Russian named Alexandra Melnikova, had stealthily penetrated the highest socio-political strata of Barry. She had seduced and married an affluent Italian magistrate, while secretly maintaining a relationship with her Russian family, conveniently relocated to Sofia. The KGB intelligence planners had arranged for Melnikova to visit Bulgaria under the auspices of setting an export-import commercial business and simultaneously spending time with her two teenage daughters. She was also scheduled to undergo a KGB advanced operational and active measures training.

The KGB code-named Melnikova "*The Lioness*" and while in the country she was to be under our surveillance monitoring and control. We had to eliminate any potential exposures of Melnikova's rendezvous with the KGB. Colonel Serov was assigned as a controller of the program.

Alexandra Melnikova arrived in Sofia with a flashy turbo-coupe *Lanchia Stratos* with a Redgio Emilia, Italian registration. Sporting modern leather pants, ultra modern Italian designers' cloths, and sensual appeal, Alexandra soon overtook Sofia's main establishment with class, finesse, splendor and egotism. She displayed acumen for money and entrepreneurial talents. Her sporty and forceful driving manners become a major headache for the surveillance. Shrewd and intolerable, she had once even approached a surveillance car and rudely raised a middle finger at the officer, commanding him to get lost!

These incidents eventually became known to the KGB center and new surveillance techniques had to be utilized. Soon we found why *"the Lioness"* feared our presence; she had not only been a shadowy Soviet spy and a bullish businesswoman, but also a regularly licentious female. Surveillance in numerous instances documented her convoluted engagements in philandering activities with a business partner and a prominent Bulgarian politician. For me, *"the Lioness"* became another confirmation about the questionable qualities the KGB employed in pursuits of foreign intelligence. For my colleagues, it was an appealing intelligence subterfuge. I, however, considered it a blatant illustration of Kim Philby's KGB critiques.

A few years later, the CIA eventually tipped off the Italian magistrates on Melnikova's KGB and State Security operations during the investigation of the assassination attempt by Mehmet Ali Agca on the life of Pope John Paul II. As a result of the masterpiece Italian investigation, a major network of deeply rooted Soviet agents was methodically unraveled and a major political scandal shook the utmost democratic foundations of the Italian Republic. KGB and State Security intelligence operations throughout Italy and Western Europe received another mortal blow due to the loss of its Roman sources.

*   *   *

I was delighted by General Savchenko's invitation to attend the meeting with Kim Philby. However, I was too late to obtain the necessary official permit to enter the MIA's (Ministry of Internal Affairs) building. To sustain the absolute secrecy of SID (surveillance) department, the administration did not allow even us to overtly access the MIA. Our State Security red ID credentials had been issued without the necessary red stripe (one or two) in the upper right corner, which would otherwise allow complete access.

Late Saturday evening, I obtained my father's State Security ID credentials in order to assure the identical color and length of the red stripes. These little markings were so crucial in opening so many new doors of opportunity. After a few minutes, my forged ID card was ready, with no visible differences from my father's original.

Calmly approaching the main gate of the MIA on Monday morning, I kindly greeted the guard, who glimpsed at my "enhanced" ID card, saluted, and let me in without hesitation. My first wholly unlawful penetration of a high-security communist institution was triumphant. Because of this "enhancement," from this spring day of 1973, I did not need any special permits to freely visit the main archives of the MIA and State Security. As a result, I was able for the following three years (until I was transferred officially to the HQ of State Security) to conduct any research throughout the secret archives and to visit and develop many friends all over the system. Especially rewarding were my contacts at SCD-counterintelligence, the Ministry of Internal Affairs, the Central archive and the foreign passports office.

I had already developed lasting discontent with socialism and had started to intentionally collect intelligence on the totalitarian KGB and State Security system. As randomly, or as specifically as I could, I surreptitiously and stealthily gathered state, political, military and diplomatic secrets and documents. The critical defenselessness of the supreme communist security system, not from powerful external forces, but from stealthy turncoats within, was perplexing.

As Kim Philby eloquently wrote in the title of his first book, practically copying Hitler's "My Struggle", it was *"My silent war"*. However, Philby's war was not silent; it was, after all, a blindly fought war by an ideologically brainwashed *"Bolshevik soldier of utopian fortune"*. He became in the process a doomed to disgrace individual, one whom I had the chance to meet in person and intentionally befriended, solely to learn his misdeeds and expose his moral downfalls. In my case however, the underhanded KGB did not miss the opportunity to use Kim Philby as my leading personality assessor and my indoctrinator, facts that were accurately confirmed by General Ivan Savchenko and his deputy Colonel Ferov*. Yet again, however, the great master turned out to be blind to reality.

---

*   Anticipating my marriage to his daughter Kathy, General Bureniok had greatly utilized his nepotism, not only to develop me as a furtive KGB asset, but also to closely ally me with Kim Philby in the process.

THE GLORIES OF A MOLE

The meeting with Kim Philby was conducted in English, with Todor Boiadzhiev and Dimo Stankov serving as translators. Philby's spiral notebook from Nesebar had the questions that had been submitted earlier as well as his elaborate penned answers. After expressing gratitude to the Minister of Internal Affairs, General-Colonel Dimitar Stoianov, for the wonderfully arranged vacation, Philby made a brief parallel between his visit to Bulgaria this time and what had happened exactly 40 years earlier in the Viennese park *"Belvedere"*.

Philby's studies in Austria had been instrumental not only in his mastery of the language of Goethe and Hegel, but also most importantly in his stealthy connection with the NKVD. Soviets had carried out Kim's recruitment and trained the Cambridge student to become a Soviet spy. The agent *"Sohnen"* (the Son) was developed in the lush Viennese park by the NKVD Colonel Otto Lang. In Vienna Philby was introduced to the global Comintern movement as the only viable antifascist alternative and had been made to believe that his clandestine work would help in the inevitable destruction of National Socialism and Fascism in Europe. The persuasive context for Philby's unyielding recruitment had been the fascists' trial in Leipzig against the Chairman of the Comintern, George Dimitrov, charged of the torched fire of the German Reichstag. However, Philby stopped short of acknowledging that there had been conclusive evidence of pertinent NKVD complicity to the Reichstag's affair.

For more than two hours Philby described subjects such as:

> *CIA and MI6 cooperation.*
> *Operational structure of MI6 and the British counterintelligence.*
> *Government and diplomatic covers for operational officers of MI6 and*
> *   military operations abroad.*
> *British operations on the Balkans and in Bulgaria.*
> *Goals and methodology of achieving results.*

I was the only youthful operational officer present besides Todor Boiadzhiev. There were about 20 senior State Security officers and five or six KGB representatives in the conference room.

One of Philby's most striking statements was in reference to the Secret Intelligence Service's process of personnel selection. Without hesitation Kim Philby disclosed that the superior quality of intelligence work by Great Britain and the United States of America had unquestionably been based on their proper selection of professionals with aristocratic background and Ivy League education. The working class was not recognized in any capacity, nor did party affiliation bear any criteria during the selection process. The palpable parallel he made with the Soviet and the Bulgarian realities, where the selection of communist party apparatchiks and leading representatives of the working class were the dominant method, was a brilliant subtle criticism. In an analytical manner Philby presented specifics about overall MI6 and CIA operations and cooperation. During his work in the USA he had discovered that the Americans possess great and vastly growing resources to pursue global dominance and to set standards of intelligence gathering. He foolishly complained that the Americans demanded all information gathered by British agencies without any reciprocity. Philby cunningly recommended the State Security and KGB officials to work on identifying and manipulating specific cases of mutual interest for MI6 and CIA:

". . . Because of the lack of cooperation and exchange of intelligence, MI6 and the CIA very often approach identical targets of political, economic and military interests around the world, "de facto" compromising each other, instead of coordinating and consolidating efforts for mutual interests and benefits . . . *"

Philby revealed his believe that the CIA distrusted the MI6, as well as most western agencies. The failures of some of the most famous cases of the century, such as "the Atomic spies" had developed the CIA into a group of *"disinclined paranoids"*.

As a balancing act, the CIA's failure to professionally handle the GRU spy Colonel Oleg Pencovsky was outlined as one of the never ending interagency *faux pas:* Philby admired the KGB's crafty surveillance and apprehension of Pencovsky, which had exposed not only his latest CIA contact Jacobs, code named *"Librarian"*, but had also blatantly compromised the SIS (MI6) resident in Moscow-Chisholm, code named *"Connoisseur"*, especially his wife Jinee and the go between businessman Wynne. Some nuances behind Philby's testimonial intricately delineated Kim Philby's connivance in Colonel Penkovsky's downfall.

In an inimitable moment after the meeting, everyone shook Philby's hand. Minister Dimitar Stoianov was self-righteous, for he had the audacity of inviting Philby to visit Bulgaria. I stood silently away until Philby openly waved me over. Embracing the old spook, we surprised some of the officers with our vivid

---

*   Kim Philby's exact quotation, June 1973, Sofia, Bulgaria

friendship. Kim Philby's lack of clever perception and visionary nimbleness to recognize the blind alley of the communist doctrine was bewildering; however our acquaintance at the time was more than an eloquent professional commendation for me.

I wrote an October Revolution day greetings card to the Philbys in Moscow just prior to New Year 1974, and received a surprisingly wonderful and warm response. Kim Philby had hand written his letter in English and Rufa wrote a kind New Year greetings card. General Savchenko personally delivered the letter to me, and a few days later, using the same channel I responded thankfully to the Philbys.

*　　*　　*

My relationship with the KGB spy and conniving mole in the British MI6 and the American CIA, the notorious traitor of the British Crown, the aristocrat who had elected the misanthropy of the communism, the man known as Kim Philby, received surprising new developments in the summer of 1974.

Once again at the Black Sea resort of Nesebar, I organized the second vacation of General Alexey Bureniok and his wife Tamara, where again I was amiably astounded to encounter Kim Philby and Rufina Puchovich. This time the KGB had sent Philbys without an escort. Although I had written to Kim Philby twice since Christmas 1973, I had received only one letter in response, with early spring good wishes. Philby's assessments of their comfortable family life in a newly remodeled Moscow apartment were somehow superficial and dry. Perhaps Kim was cautiously accentuating on his rather mundane and still restricted life.

This time we drove in a simple, common Soviet made *"Lada"*, *as* Todor Boiadzhiev, who was Philby's conventional companion once again, drove in a light blue *"Vauxhall"* station wagon, perhaps intentionally selected to revitalize Kim's old sentiments. Peculiarly, Boiadzhiev displayed a disgustingly superficial and narcissistic attitude, greatly reinforcing the common dislike between the intelligence and counterintelligence officers.

General Bureniok silently was directing once again most of our daily meetings with Philby, often guiding us through the never-ending labyrinths of the intelligence crafts and deceits. Endlessly we discussed professional topics such as cultural heritage, active measures, methods and strategies in recruitment of westerners and especially Americans, western society subversion by distribution of drugs and influencing the development of the youngest generations, and the sponsoring of right and religious extremists and terrorists.

Philby had visibly aged; his puffy face and eye pockets bared the trademark of alcohol abuse and the imminence of ailment. He was a pleasant, semi-phlegmatic intellectual and connoisseur; however, deeply into his light eyes an attentive observer would notice overwhelming discontent. A deep repentance and perhaps a growing sense of guilt for his tremendous past transgressions somehow manifested themselves in his demeanor. He almost calculatedly emphasized on some of the most secret and successful KGB illegal operations. With a penchant for methodology, he told me stunning details about one of the KGB's very successful illegal officers in Great Britain, Gordon Lonsdale, a man who had been closely connected and even controlled by the Bulgarian intelligence. At that time I did not realize that General Bureniok and KGB management had perhaps deliberately selected the subject matter.

The KGB successfully had stolen the identity of a deceased Canadian named Gordon Lonsdale. After a few years in Canada, Konon Molodoy a.k.a. Lonesdail spent some time in Australia polishing and accentuating his English. Thereafter the KGB sent him to London with solid credentials, including a diploma from the London School of Economics. With readily available cash and entrepreneurial passion, Lonsdale developed a successful commercial enterprise. He astutely penetrated the British biological warfare centers, obtaining samples of the most advanced bacteriological agents and weapons ever developed. For years, until the early 1960s, Gordon Lonsdale worked unnoticed by the British secret services, directing and controlling a vast network of Soviet agents. However, a Polish defector eventually gave the CIA sufficient circumstantial evidence to direct the British authorities to Lonsdale and most of his contacts. Arrested, the illegal KGB Colonel, Konon Moladoy, "Gordon Lonsdale," was convicted and sentenced by the British court to the longest imposed solitary confinement ever of 30 years. Within few years, however, he was exchanged at the East Berlin point *"Charley"* for G. Wynne, the convicted British spy in the Soviet Union and Colonel Penkovsky's liaison with SIS.

Philby was elaborate and proud of the intelligence work consummated by Lonsdale and his extensive network. He knowledgeably revealed that in numerous instances the Bulgarian resident in London, Dimo Stankov*, had directed and assisted Lonsdale during his challenging British endeavors.

During these particular discussions, I noticed for the first time Philby's carefully formulated questions, that he often asked out of the blue hypothetically, tackling my operational opinion and psychological assessments. Until that moment I have not realized the elaborate KGB pitch in the making.

A memorable moment for me came with Philby's cleverly extrapolated confession that he was in fact not recruited by the Soviets, as had been blatantly exaggerated by the British media and rumored by the KGB. Philby himself had

---

*   Former Resident in Paris and Active Measures chief, Colonel Stankov was Philbys guide in Sofia during 1973.

approached representatives of the Socialist International in London, inquiring about information for a study conducted in Cambridge on Soviet socio-economics. Once in Europe, Philby had contacted the Soviet Embassies in Switzerland and Austria, palpably offering his services to the Commintern.

"... I was a young socialist, captivated by the Marxist-Leninist communalism and democratic centralism. Offering my services to the Commintern, I expected to be summoned to Moscow for academic studies as promised by the Soviet Consul General in Bern ..." Philby smiled:

"... Instead, I became a clandestine, underground courier between the Austrian communists and the Kremlin ... and years later ... a Soviet citizen ..." Kim Philby was actually reciting essentials from his unorthodox resume, dictating how his clairvoyant dreams, deceitful life and double-crossings had led him to short-lived KGB and Soviet communist "stardom".

*   *   *

While Kim Philby presumably did well for the communism, his father Sir Saint John Russell had devoted himself to the fanaticism of Islam. Evidently, they fit the mold of *"like father, like son;"* both had wittily displayed a heretic family pedigree, wholly deplorable by the commonality of modern humanity.

One day General Bureniok wittingly directed me to organize a dinner with the Philbys. As a go between of the two KGB masters, I set the dinner at the renowned *"Neptune"* restaurant at the Sunny Beach resort.

General Bureniok laughably ordered Philby to be flanked at the head of the table by Rufa and Tamara. To my surprise, Bureniok and Philby that evening demonstrated their close comradeship.

Philby's Russian language limitations, even after more than a decade spent behind the iron curtain, soon become evident. He gladly transitioned to English, and I started translating into Russian.

Accentuating the beauty of the seaside and the Black Sea resorts, Kim became rather philosophical about the strategic significance of the country and especially of the *Bosphorus* and the *Dardanelle's* straits. Conveying his special knowledge about the Turkish, British and the American interests in the region, Kim Philby revealed to us something of historic significance:

"... Perhaps, Bulgaria's key positioning on the Black Sea, the Balkans, and the straits, and the relevant strategic interests of Nazi Germany and the Soviet Union should be attributed to the development and the destructive commencement of the Hitler's plan *"Barbarosa"**. Philby's seemingly

---

*   "Barbarosa"—the code name of Hitler's plan for Nazi Germany to attack the Soviet Union.

unsubstantiated admission was also surprising to General Bureniok. However, Philby went on at length to describe how the British SIS-secret intelligence services had not only successfully intercepted and deciphered the Bulgarian government's communications with Hitler's Germany, but had also closely followed the vital negotiations of Stalin and Molotov with Hitler and Ribbentrop. The British Crown and Winston Churchill had personally perceived Stalin's failed shuttle diplomacy with Tsar Boris III, Saxe Coburg-Gotha of Bulgaria and Nazi Germany as the foremost catalyst of Hitler's growing war inclinations.

The British assessment concluded that the German Third Reich and especially Hitler had lost trust in Stalin's non-expansion communist geo-political goals. Therefore, Molotov's official 1941 visit to Germany was abruptly cut short, especially after Hitler's blunt criticism and condemnation of intended Soviet positioning of military divisions in Bulgaria. This prevented the imposition of Soviet communist control over the Danube channels of navigation in Western Europe and over the strategic maritime *Bosphorus* and the *Dardanelle* straits. Conspiratorially lowering his voice, the assertive Philby compellingly concluded:

"... Hitler's exasperation and ultimate mistrust with Stalin's communist nationalistic and international policies should be considered the foremost reason for the development of the plan *"Barbarosa"*, and thus for the beginning of the Second World War ..."

The strategic interests of the Soviet Union in the Balkans and especially in Bulgaria catalyzed and prompted the Nazi Germany to initiate the Second World War, which Philby categorized as a "National-Socialist war against the growing spread of the Soviet communism". Philby's disclosure was a rather staggering and perplexing rationalization of the most atrocious event of the 20th century, the beginning of the Second World War. Under different circumstances, his implications would be an uncontestable warrant for a one-way trip to the Siberian *"Gulag"*. However, we were listening to his bigheaded unilateral assessments with undeniable glamorization. Kim Philby knew details that only a few had been privileged to know.

Translating the specifics, I attempted to diminish the idiosyncrasy of Philby's chronicle. However, the hawkish eyes of General Bureniok were already indicative of his deep repugnance and disagreement with the testimonial. Perhaps the General's English was far better than I had anticipated, and he more or less comprehended Philby's fine historic points and authentic British intelligence that was long suppressed by the KGB. Alexey Bureniok was a highly decorated Belorussian partisan and the Second World War hero, and he clearly foresaw western deception, instead historic accuracy, in Philby's testimonial.

*   *   *

Working on my Ph.D. thesis in 1979-1980, I gained access to the secret communist party archives. I was astounded to find a file with designation "G. Dimitrov museum," consisting a stack of unpublished George Dimitrov letters to Vasil Kolarov. One, dated August 13, 1939, was a plain forewarning to the Bulgarian leader of potential German-Nazi occupation of the Balkans as a result of Hitler's strategic interests in the region. Compounding on Philby's Second World War assessments, I had found a trustworthy testament that corroborated his statements.

In 1977 and 1978 I spent time at the KGB academy and twice visited the Philbys at their flat in Moscow. General Bureniok was instrumental for my first visit to the retired spy. A replica of an old Ottoman flintlock handgun, a gift from "me" it became Philby's possession instead of Bureniok's, a clear indicator of the "son" that Bureniok considered me. Alexey Bureniok had also granted Kim Philby the status of lecturer at the KGB Academy during the late 1970s. With the General's retirement, however, Philby was slowly but surely cut off to his Moscow apartment and was even often been under intimidating KGB surveillance. Was this a result of Philby's growing resilience to the misleading Soviet enigma, or perhaps a result of his growing alienation from something too different from his roots of upbringing?

Although I profoundly detested Philby's betrayal of the western democratic universe, I never despised the noble and gentle man whom I befriended. Deep in my cunning mind, I regretted that I did not possess a viable option to deliver Kim Philby to the British or the American authorities. Option, that we explored carefully with the CIA during 1979 and 1980, however without result, for during this time Philby visited Sozopol resort in order to meet his grown daughter and his first grad child, a "get together" operation that was conducted under rather surprising security precautions. Philby's devilish and devastating treason somehow mobilized my own personal commitments to achieve just the opposite. Inevitably our relationship catalyzed my willingness to fight, harm and discredit the totalitarian communism, a system in which Kim Philby had so naively believed and to which he had inescapably dedicated his misanthropic life.

Kim Philby was discarded as an ideologically handicapped, prematurely aged and emotionally down in the dumps alcoholic. To his last hours, he was a victim of an immature student dream of utopian socialism, Marxist-Leninist human equality and communality. Philby eventually became an insufficient consequence of the Stalin's ill-fated global communist expansion. More or less, Philby became a "hero" of Soviet wickedness, similar to a plenitude of communist "heroes" already forgotten by history.

Perhaps it would be worthy to close the chapter on Kim Philby with a small tribute to his reasonable judgment on global Islam: As a vivid expert on Turkey and the Middle East, Kim Philby had greatly enhanced his theoretical wisdom by sharing the exclusive knowledge spawned by his eccentric father:

In the mid 1950s Sir Saint John Russell had become a leading expert on Islam, eventually converting to be a Muslim. Mesmerized by the pan-Islamic Arab culture, ethnicity and ethnography, nonetheless the abundant religious heritage of the Middle East, he had developed exclusive relationships with King Feysal of Saudi Arabia and countless Arab religious and tribal leaders, such as but not limited to Abu Griad and Bin Saud. He became one of the last thorough mentors of Kim Philby in Beirut, Lebanon on the subject of Islam and the Muslim righteousness. Despite Kim's deeply rooted fondness for socialism, he was eventually diligent enough to listen and embrace his father's academic knowledge on the subject matter. Thus gradually emerged one of the strongest opponents of rising Islamic fundamentalism, contrary to, as many would speculate, the idea that Kim had become just another critique of Sir Saint John's adventurism.

Kim Philby was clearly never thoroughly listened to by the KGB, nor were his intelligence assessments considered. Philby's information on the first secret "*Turan pan Islamic*" meeting, (attended in absolute secrecy by Philby's father—Sir Saint John a.k.a. Mahmud Bey Oglu) stealthily conducted in Al Islamia, Egypt in 1956, should have become a serious point of concern for the new Soviet leadership and the KGB. Nikita Khrushchev encountered the first Muslim ethnic troubles in the southern Soviet republics immediately after Al Islamia's resolution reached the believers. It would take the *Turan Islamite** 45 years to hit in the heart of New York.

During my meetings with Kim Philby in Nesebar and Sofia, among the many intricate subjects about global politics we discussed, he was the first person to evidently express unyielding fears about the growing Islamic fundamentalism and the fanatic multiplication of their sacred *Turan zeal* throughout the Balkans and the world.

Philby was genuinely concerned about the consequences of the rising religious malaise, although he never envisioned the critical impact it could have on the Balkan and Middle East's regional stability. During 1976, I shared Kim Philby and his father's astute points on Islam with the chief of the Sixth directorate, General Petar Stoianov** and the KGB expert Colonel Levan Galustov.

---

*   Turanian movement, the latest pan Islamism, an early 19 century Osmanic (Turkey, Iran, Saudi Arabia, Iraq, Syria and Edypt), religious doctrine, based on global dominance of the Islamic fundamentalism.

**   General Anton Musakov, deputy director of Sixth directorate, quoted Philby's assessments on the rising danger of the Islam on a State Security conference, September 08, 1978 at the Ministry of Internal Affairs.

COMMUNIST UTOPIA

SOCIALISM AND ECONOMIC PROSPERITY

High-level political consultations in mid 1976 Moscow, between the Warsaw Pact leadership and the COMECON-Committee for Economic Cooperation charted a follow-up meeting in Sofia between the KGB and State Security. The secret gathering started at the State Security Academy in Simeonovo and surprisingly expanded to the government residency *"Boiana"* with the General Secretary Todor Zhivkov's participation on the second day. Main focus was development of a joint operational strategy for essential advancement of key industrial sectors. Through timely utilization of high technologies and industrial know-how stolen from the West, Soviet and East European socialism was going to attempt to survive and even thrive in the high paced world of tomorrow.

Parallel to the main functions of FCD—Science and Technology foreign intelligence, a foreign academic exchange group was established at Sixth directorate of State Security. After a formal interview with General Peter Stoianov, Chief of Sixth directorate and General-Colonel Mircho Spasov at the Central Committee of the Communist Party, I was assigned as leader of the new specialized task force and transferred to the Ministry of Internal Affair's main HQ.

Until mid 1983, I for eight years managed the international academic and scientific exchange programs of Bulgaria and numerous Soviet institutions. It was a complex intelligence-gathering machine, fine-tuned to aggressively pursue industrial R&D, scientific and technological secrets by dispatching to the West the communist nations' brilliant minds. In a well-centralized manner, I coordinated these cumbersome activities with the intelligence, military, counterintelligence, industrial, educational and academic institutions of Bulgaria, the Soviet Union and East Germany.

During all these years, we worked closely with some key government leaders and the intellectual and academic elite of Eastern Europe. My group (detachment) audaciously and persuasively recruited, trained, directed and controlled the best academicians and intellectuals of our time as communist agents and collaborators. The adherent KGB/State Security goal was to diligently study all western scientific and academic institutions and foundations. With detailed strategies we penetrated them and boldly tried to steal new research

87

and developmental projects, modern high technologies, and obtain samples of embargoed products and systems that greatly promoted the communist society and in essence persistently profited the shallowly "developed" socialist economy. It was a rather vital developmental task, and hence was consistently coordinated with the KGB, the foreign intelligence directorate (Sciences and Technology department—seventh) and the Central Committees of the fraternal Communist Parties.

By mid 1970s, the developed West imposed a strict COCOM embargo on key exports to Eastern Europe and many Third World (Developing) countries in order to prevent the proliferation of Western technologies intellectual pirating, computerized and automation systems copy-cat, and biochemical and pharmaceuticals use for competitive advantages. Many intellectual properties, such as but not limited to computer software, hard discs and drives, memory components and etc. became imperative to the development of the Soviet economy and the Warsaw Pact military and space industrial complex. The virtual isolation of the Warsaw Pact members from the rest of the developed world was silently professed as the main reason for the sluggishness of the economic and industrial growth of the socialism. During this time few powerful government sponsored *"bootleggers"* of communist origin silently emerged on the world stage, becoming experts in smuggling intellectual properties, stealing advanced computerized and automation systems, pirating software products and blatantly engaging in economic and industrial espionage.

East European leadership blindly embraced the top-secret Soviet directives. Highly skilled forces of science and technology operatives were directed to shrewdly perpetrate some of the greatest modern era economic, industrial and intellectual property crimes against the developed West. Since 1975, the Science and Technology Department of FCD-foreign intelligence and KGB developed and managed the modern and vital *"Center of Applied Information"* and the *"Central Institute for Scientific and Technical Information"*. The centers processed information gathered by Science and Technology intelligence abroad and by our network of valuable spies returning or working in the West. They evaluated, analyzed, utilized and implemented all information gathered.

Some of our assets, after returning from the West, continued to further develop their scientific projects and sophisticated technical research, achieving splendid results and academic recognition. The Centers coordinated an elaborate planning and cooperation process with all leading institutions and ministries, in order to identify key components, ingredients, chemicals, automation and computerized systems, instruments or machines that had to be obtained from the West through clandestine intelligence and commercial methods. In order to properly pursue specific projects, based on economic necessities and feasibility, S&T intelligence officers were assigned under cover as scientific coordinators and technology consultants to the leading ministries.

The Science and Technology foreign intelligence department of Colonel George Manchev and his deputies Lieutenant-Colonel Luben Mihailov and Major Todor Boiadzhiev, and my international academic exchange detachment, worked since early 1977 with about 780 professors and academicians, and more than 3250 scientists, scholars and specialists.

My appointment to the Academic foreign exchange, managed by the State Security's Sixth directorate, overlapped with the creation of a powerful working group, specialized in the coordination and implementation of the scientific and technological progress in the Central Committee of the Communist Party. One of the newest and rather controversial members of the Central Committee of the Communist Party, Ognian Doinov, became leader of the new group. Doinov was known for his bullish careerism and lack of professional experience. He was a State Security's Science and Technology foreign intelligence agent in Japan for almost 5 years. Major Alex Ivanov was Doinov's control officer and Major Vladimir Moscow, the future foreign intelligence resident in Tokyo and Singapore, was his supervising intelligence manager. My first cousin Ivan Dimitrov (inadvertently) further developed Ognian Doinov's relationship with numerous Japanese government institutions and officials *.

Towards the end of 1977, Ognian Doinov was appointed by the Council of Ministers to oversee and control the Science and Technology foreign intelligence and our international academicians' and scientists' exchange operations. Doinov's silky and lustrous business acumen, proletarian adventurism and reputed party reliability, contributed to the transformation of the Bulgarian and the Soviet national identity and credibility into an allegedly well-organized semi-criminal enterprise of international thugs, smugglers and intellectual property crooks. From his predecessor at the Central Committee of the Communist Party, Professor Ivan Popov—Chairman of the Committee for Science and Technological Progress, Doinov inherited a team of highly professional intelligence officers and specialists in industrial espionage and illegal transfer of high technologies, whom he greatly continued exploiting.

After for years successfully conducting high scale science and technology thievery in Vienna, Austria, as a Chief of station, Colonel Stoian Evtimov in 1977 became one of Doinov's personal advisor. As a stealthy balancing component,

---

* Dimitrov's father-in-law Dimo Dimov was Counselor (FCD cover) at the Tokyo Embassy during Doinov's Japanese stint.

another officer closely linked with Doinov's "partner in crime" Andrey Lucanov soon joined the group. Colonel Petur Hristozov had maintained secretive intelligence connections with Lucanov in the 1960s, while the latter was working as trade representative in Switzerland. Our secretive fraternity directed individuals or professionals to literally steal any western intellectual and technological achievements they could. Paradoxically, the aim was an ill-destined attempt to build up a prosperous utopian socialist society at the expense of western democratic attainments and clever ingenuity.

After more than decade of intricate totalitarian scams and the illicit creation of various industrial, military, chemical and electronics conglomerates, Ognian Doinov was boldly and mercilessly removed from his leadership position in the communist party and with the collapse of communism was publicly indicted as a common criminal, a scapegoat for the large scale economic failures.

The State Security and KGB leadership insisted for us to aggressively penetrate Western scientific, research and developmental centers and multinational corporations. In the United States of America we broke into many Ivy League universities and top tier educational institutions, such as Princeton, MIT, Harvard, Yale, Columbia, UCLA, USC, Cornel, the Fulbright and Mellon Foundations, IREX and the National Science Foundation. In Western Europe, we targeted institutions such as: The Max Plank Institute, DAAD, Carl Duisberg, Alexander von Humboldt, the Goethe Institute in Germany, the Sorbonne and SIAL in France, Cambridge, Trinity and Oxford in England, and Trondhaim and Gothenburg Universities in Sweden.

The most advanced R&D programs of these institutions were subsidized and directly linked to major Western multinational corporations and their long-term business planning and economic interests, so Doinov's aim was for us to greatly abused this liaison and cooperation. Blunt industrial espionage, unauthorized gathering of technical and bio-chemical know-how, smuggling of systems, prototypes, components and illegal copies of proprietary and secret R&D data was conducted, taking advantage of the openness of the western pluralistic and democratic society.

In essence, this stealthy process made possible the survival of the Soviet and socialist economies and even miraculously sustained their growth.

ZINTI (Central Institute for Science and Technical Information) was reorganized in 1976 and relocated to a new building in Sofia. It was equipped with the most advanced computerized systems obtained illegally from the USA through bogus sales to the University of Limassol in Cyprus, despite the strict western embargo. A leading Greek politician and affluent businessman boldly perpetrated the technology transfer with the help of the East German foreign intelligence HVD (Stasi*) and the professional efforts of the future chief of the Bulgarian foreign intelligence—Brigadir (Brigo) Asparuhov.

Working with the academic elite of the nation was a demanding and intellectually challenging process, often influenced and complicated by the subjective opinion of top-level communist party officials and government bureaucrats. Notwithstanding being a master communist recruiter, controller and intellectual's ideological manipulator, I secretly and unmistakably embraced democratic western values. Perhaps I unwittingly was helped by the best independent and unbiased sources available—my intelligent assets. I found myself increasingly upholding the values and the merits of western society, its free market economy and its freedom of belief, and pursuits of happiness.

*   *   *

Since its inception until its abolishment in early 1990, the main function of the powerful and sinister institution known as State Security was to uphold the never-ending fight against the socio-economic and political enemies of the socialist state and the communist party. Any individual, any institution or sovereign government proclaiming anti-Communist sentiments or acting that way was officially declared an "Enemy of the Communist State," thus becoming the target of KGB and State Security. Around the mid 1970s, the Sixth directorate of State Security emerged as a powerful, virtually uncontrollable, *"State inside the State Security State"*. Identically as the Fifth KGB directorate, it evolved secretly into an absolute omnipotent powerhouse, above and beyond any governing laws, party control, and even the country's sovereign constitution.

The operational staff of the Directorate had some unique characteristics: Most officers were members of the Communist Party and had undergone substantial and excellent State Security and KGB training.

All possessed a minimum of one university degree and all had previous experience at local, regional or national communist institutions or the giants of the socialist industries. Most operational managers were former antifascist fighters, partisans and communist party apparatchiks. The fairy-tale of the longest standing Minister of Interior and Chairman of the State Security, General-Colonel Dimitar Stoianov was similar. The General Secretary of the Communist Party, Todor

---

*   The German BND unmasked the Greek businessman in 2000. Utilizing covert connections with the former Bulgarian State Security he purchased one of the largest Bulgarian telecom companies in 2001 with questionable communist funds.

Zhivkov, in early 1973 appointed him directly from his post as a Veliko Turnovo regional communist party secretary.

Many of my colleagues and especially most of my professional "friends" had graduated from the leading universities and possessed exceptional education, erudition and intellect. However, they were profoundly stage-managed by the communist party. Incapable of perceiving the reality behind Marx's dialectical materialism, these apparatchiks did not possess the decency or courage to confront the utopian dreams of Lenin's proletarians, nonetheless to critique the crumbling socio-economic paradigm of the pseudo developed socialism.

"How could you be such a blatant disgraces to humankind? How could you be such narrow-minded misanthropes, concerned only about your privileged life and your fat pay check, viciously enjoying limitless power, while deliberately smothering society and countless decent human destinies?"

These are my simple metaphorical questions to all of these ideologically and intellectually handicapped individuals blindfolded by communist doctrine, power hungry and unscrupulously malevolent toward humanity.

The KGB and State Security were intended and destined to preserve the integrity of the communist party and the socialist states. In reality they grew to become powerful oppressive apparatus, evolving into secret institutions, functioning without any oversight control and legal guiding principles. Bribing and recruiting foreign nationals, intellectuals and journalists, the State Security and KGB aggressively influenced the democratic processes in the western world by supporting and manipulating leftist, communist, socialist and terrorist organizations. The communist leadership paradoxically envisioned monstrous western forces engaged in complex subversive activities against the basic foundations of the communist states. Almost ridiculously all means of western media coverage, from radio, press, TV, theater, art, as well as all channels of international exchange of scholars, athletes, tourists, intellectuals and businesspeople, were intentionally declared as capitalism's organized form of influencing, destabilizing and discrediting the socialism.

A joint KGB-State Security analysis conducted in 1976 identified more than 100 western centers actively involved in anti-Communist activities. A group of "Enemy Radio Stations"—such as but not limited to: "Radio Free Europe", "Voice of America", BBC, "Vatican Libere", "Douche Welle", "Turkey News", "Thessalonica Greece Radio", "Radio Tirana", "China Daily", "Iberian Radio Liberty" and limited number of private radio hosts were declared anti-Socialist as well.

Most Bulgarian emigrants to the West were actively investigated and monitored. The Bulgarian National Committee and the Bulgarian National Front in New York published the periodicals: *"Free and Independent Bulgaria"* and "*Fight*" and became the most aggressively investigated organizations in the USA by FCD—foreign intelligence and Sixth directorate. Anastasia Mozzer*, one of the leaders of the Bulgarian emigration in the USA, together with Dimitar Kravarov, Ivan Dochev, Dinko Statev and others, became targets of investigation, malicious disinformation and agents infiltration. Agrarian National Council of Tzenko Barev and Jordan Georgiev and the Bulgarian Liberty Movement of Blago Slavenov and Dimitar Mollov in Paris, France, together with the Bulgarian Social Democratic Party of Stefan Tabakov in Vienna, Austria, and the Bulgarian League for Human Rights in Amsterdam and Rome, became another aggressively investigated "enemy" emigrant organizations.

In Munich, Germany, Radoslav Kosovski led the powerful Bulgarian Democratic Alliance in coordinated efforts with Enrico Del Belo's Rome based Bulgarian Help and Assistance Committee.

The KGB and State Security developed an "ad hoc" approach towards these organizations. They established a peculiar and imaginary role of the western intelligence services of intentionally guiding, supporting and financially backing these ordinary forms of opposition to communism in Eastern Europe. Short sighted in comprehending democratic pluralism, the Soviet communist leadership justified enormous spending for illegitimate operations with questionable results.

Some State Security and KGB activities aimed at assassinating or kidnapping people in the West were well speculated and publicized. In order to neutralize some of the most active exile leaders, State Security devised elaborate programs. Luring unsuspected individuals to neutral European countries for legitimate reasons and thereafter kidnapping, drugging and bringing them in for highly publicized trails in Bulgaria became reality.

"If a knife or sharp object is used, penetrations should be inflicted fast and repeatedly in the area of the heart and the chest, until the target is surely dead. If a hard object is used, the first strong blow should be aimed at the head. The most efficient method to prevent and eliminate eventual noise and screaming is to inflict additional mortal wounds, instead of suffocation of the mouth. If introducing poison to the target, strictly follow the relevant instructions in order to eliminate suspicions and early warnings and to disallow the target to call eventually for help . . ."

This very disturbing paragraph is part of an official State Security document: Secret operational file *"Terrorist"*, #9867/1973 of SCD counterintelligence. It

---

*   After 1990 Anastasia Mozzer, daughter of the liquidated by the communists M.P. G.M. Dimitrov, become Member of the Bulgarian Parliament and leader of the Agrarian Party.

outlines the specific actions and instructions given to an agent who had been directed to assassinate Bulgarian emigrant Boris Arsov in Denmark. Moreover, this file should exemplify clear evidence to the actual methodology and cruelty of the East European secret services in fulfilling the most sinister orders from Moscow.

Before escaping to the West, Boris Arsov was one of the thousands of citizens subjected to repression, persecution and imprisonment by the communist government for his affiliation with the previous regime. He was jailed and incarcerated numerous times for anti-government activities and criticism of the Soviet Union's "occupation" of Bulgaria. In 1970, avoiding a forced deportation to one of the rugged regions of the country, at age 55 Arsov escaped Bulgaria. Initially in West Germany and thereafter in Denmark, he worked a variety of mundane jobs, supporting new Bulgarian emigrants morally and financially. His popularity and past persecutions by the communist government were well respected and he was elected as a Board Member of the Bulgarian Human Rights League. In 1973 he became a managing member of the Bulgarian National Front in New York, where he established the Bulgarian Revolutionary Committee with HQ in Denmark. Boris Arsov's monthly magazine "Levski" was the strongest and the most prolific critique of the Bulgarian and Soviet communist party's lies, lawlessness and human oppressions.

As a result of his activities and eventually as a consequence of uncorroborated State Security agent insinuations, General-Colonel Grigor Shopov, Chairman of the State Security, declared Arsov *the most dangerous enemy* of the state. Thereafter General Shopov approved a complex and elaborate operational plan for the neutralization (murder) and/or bringing to justice (kidnap), of the leader of the Bulgarian Revolutionary Committee, Boris Arsov. FCD—foreign intelligence, SCD—counterintelligence and Sixth directorate—internal intelligence received a *"carte blanche"* for masterminding a most outrageous intelligence operation on the territory of a foreign sovereign nation.

General-Colonel Grigor Shopov was one of the founders and long standing leaders of State Security, a member of the Central Committee of the Bulgarian Communist Party, and a close personal and professional adviser to the General Secretary of the Bulgarian Communist Party, Todor Zhivkov. Thus, it is undeniable today that the Bulgarian totalitarian leader Zhivkov personally granted the final approvals for any kidnappings or assassinations abroad. The oldest son of General Shopov, Lubomir, was assigned by the Ministry of Foreign Affairs as an under cover senior diplomat to Switzerland, in charge of managing and controlling in essence the secret funds of the Communist Party and the personal finances of Zhivkov's family.

Four years after the kidnapping of Boris Arsov in Denmark, the 1978 murder of the Bulgarian dissident and writer George Markov in London shook the world, especially after investigators conclusively and unequivocally ruled assassination. Witnesses thereafter would successfully describe the evident assassination and even the brainy murder weapon: an umbrella-disguised gun that silently propelled at high-speeds a miniature hollow pellet loaded with the lethal poison *Ricin*.

A week before Markov's murder, an attempted assassination on Vladimir Kostov, the Bulgarian State Security defector to France, failed to materialize. It was attempted with a matching weapon, and the poisonous pellet had even penetrated Kostov's body. However, it had eventually become lodged in a thick fat deposit, preventing the prompt release and absorption of the *Ricin*. The British investigation into the subject of Markov's murder triggered a major French examination, reconfirming to the stunned world the unofficial standing of the notorious State Security and KGB on communist defectors, affluent dissidents and "enemy" emigrations.

Although as a professional precaution State Security had succeeded in eliminating any official documentation of these cases in Bulgarian secret archives, it would be years later, in 1994, when the stunned world learned the truth directly from the KGB General Oleg Kalugin, former Chief of the KGB's counterintelligence foreign operations. Kalugin knowledgeably implicated the KGB and State Security in many closely coordinated operations, but especially in the planning and the perpetration of George Markov's murder.

SILENCING THE "ENEMY"

For two hunting weekends in 1977, the guest of our group was Colonel Angel Topkarov, director of the Pazardzhik high security prison. Behind the colonel's ice-cold eyes was hiding a devilishly sadistic mind. A former partisan against fascism, he was a long-standing communist and a loyal State Security officer.

While we were warming up and relaxing around the fire after lunch, a confused young boar ventured through the nearby grazing land. Topkarov, without any remarks, swiftly grabbed his rifle, and before anyone had taken any notice, the boar was motionless. We lightheartedly encouraged the Colonel's mastery, and someone even behind his back sarcastically implied the necessity of him being a good marksman, in order to prevent any prisoners from escaping. The same evening, some alcohol inadvertently improved the quality of our *tête-à-tête* and proliferated the plentitude of shaggy dog stories. I instigated Topkarov to sit next to me and elaborated upon, about the work of Sixth directorate officers monitoring his prison. Manipulating fine points, stealthily assembled from Captain Emil Milanov (Sixth directorate, Fifth department—"*Enemy Emigration*") about Boris Arsov's case, I put forward a challenge:

"*. . . Comrade Colonel, you have done an excellent job with Mr. Arsov . . .*"

Topkarov's eyebrow lifted in a devilish frown, and glimpsing at me, his answer was not far off from an orthodox priest's confession:

"*. . . It was the only way to take care of the old plague . . .*"

Captain Milanov's old testimonial that the NTU, in conjunction with the Military Medical Academy, used prisoners as "Guinea pigs" for different toxin and psychotropic drug experiments, proved to be a perplexing and disturbing admittance of callous totalitarian transgressions.

In essence, the complex operations of bringing Boris Arsov to stand trial in Bulgaria had specific and sinister political reasons. The Communist Party's leadership wanted to clearly accentuate on the growing efficiency and immense capabilities of State Security, and to send a strong message to any emigrant and enemy organizations, that they were vulnerable even abroad or in exile.

After successfully abducting Arsov, State Security attempted ineffectively to convince him to become a public "*propagandator*" of a critical and erosive anti-emigration campaign. As an effective tool of demoralization of the emigrant's organizations and communities' abroad, Boris Arsov was supposed to commence a series of pro-socialist reports through the radio, national TV and press. However, his unyielding rejection to cooperate with the communist authorities became an astounding government disappointment.

Arsov then boldly escaped from a securely guarded State Security villa in the Pancharevo resort, which triggered an aggressive manhunt. Apprehended overnight, Boris Arsov was indicted and a fabricated trail for treason and subversive activities convicted him to 15 years of solitary confinement. Condemned to the Pazardzhik high security prison, Boris died within a week. Under doubtful circumstances, the conscious voice of an avid anti-Communist and an upright fighter for democratic values, freedom and national sovereignty was viciously silenced.

*   *   *

The 1977 Conference of the Secretaries of the Communist Parties of the Warsaw Pact countries in Sofia delineated some serious Moscow anxieties. Leonid Brezhnev, the General Secretary of the Communist Party of the Soviet Union harshly, addressed the communist leadership of Eastern Europe on the necessity:

"... *of radical security measures against the activities of dissidents and enemy emigration organizations in destabilizing the Developed socialist society and the moral values of the proletariat* ..."

Brezhnev's razor-sharp requirements received immediate attention and set in motion coordinated meetings and planning sessions of the KGB leadership in Sofia with the State Security Collegiums*. All foreign operational functions of SCD-counterintelligence were transferred to FCD-foreign intelligence, Sixth directorate-ideological subversion and enemy emigration.

---

*   Ministry of Internal Affairs governing body.

BULGARIAN UMBRELLA

George Markov was a prolific Bulgarian writer affiliated with the ruling communist elite and personally with the General Secretary of the Communist Party, Todor Zhivkov and his daughter Ludmila. Sixth directorate's Colonel Ciril Kulumov cunningly had recruited Markov as a secret agent of State Security in order to monitor and report on the activities and the dissent among members of the writer's guild of leading communists and intellectuals. For his loyalty to State Security, the mighty institution deviously built up Markov's reputation.

With the indispensable help of Colonel Kulumov, Markov developed the scenario for a TV show about communist intelligence, "*On Every Kilometer*". Markov's writings extended further, covering subjects such as the "Success of the Socialist Revolution", and numerous other flattering articles about the daily life of the communist leadership and the working class proletariat. As a result of George Markov's secret affiliation with State Security, he was clandestinely prepared and directed to London, the opulent center of West European anti-Communism.

George Markov successfully hid his secret affiliations with the KGB and State Security from the British authorities. Well trained by his communist spymasters, and greatly assisted by Petar Uvaliev a.k.a. Pier Roof and his intellectual verses, Markov soon received the opportunity to work in some of the utmost propaganda centers, such as BBC's "Radio Free Europe", "The Voice of America" and others. Markov married a British socialite, Annabelle, and within a year they had a daughter, although as a result of a childhood illness he was sterile. The liberties, creativity and prosperity of the democratic western world gradually eroded Markov's duties as a communist secret agent. His gifted and creative mind inevitably recognized the misleading nature of the socialist utopia, especially in direct comparison with the enormous values and achievements of the developed West. His knowledge of significant facts about the life of the communist elite and the growing problems of the socialist fraternity inadvertently magnified his gradual rebellion from communist ideology and the totalitarian security institutions.

From a deeply rooted secret agent within London's emigration and a cunning communist mole in the British high society, Markov would embark on a new mission of palpably discrediting and tarnishing the realities behind the "*Iron Curtain*". Out of his comprehension and his writers dazzling resourcefulness, stunning critiques of the Bulgarian and Soviet fraternity gradually emerged. Revelations about the staggering incompetence of the Bulgarian and Soviet communist leadership *"with limited peasant's minds"*, comically shocked the globe. George Markov entitled his works *"Extramural Reports on Bulgaria,"* and the leading western radio and TV stations published the reports not only in English, but also in Bulgarian and Russian, all over the world.

Markov's controllers grew dumbfounded and disturbed. He started shunning prearranged clandestine meetings and rebuffing even official contacts with embassy officials. Before the London residency and FCD could truthfully assess George Markov's dissent, the General Secretary of the Communist Party Todor Zhivkov was flabbergasted by an unusual call. Directly from his Moscow's office, Andrey Gromiko, Minister of Foreign Affairs and senior member of the Political Bureau of the Central Committee of the Communist Party of the Soviet Union, contacted him with very critical remarks on Markov's anti-Communist innuendoes. This triggered Zhivkov's rage* and belief that his image had been irreversibly tarnished.

A year later, during the 1977 conference of the East European communist leaders in Sofia, Leonid Brezhnev, General Secretary of the Communist Party of the Soviet Union, harshly addressed the audience on the dissident movement and the ideological subversion against Developed Soviet socialism. Not surprisingly, soon thereafter on request from the General Secretary Todor Zhivkov, a senior State Security official** approached the KGB Chairman, Vladimir Kruchkov through General Ivan Savchenko***, asking for help and assistance with the physical elimination of the communist renegade George Markov****. Markov's highly critical writings and disparaging publications had become sternly nerve-racking not only to the Zhivkov's long communist reign, but also to the fundamentals of the Soviet elite.

A team of ruthless assassins, members of an exceptionally stealthy group *"Zvezda"* (Star)***** was dispatched to Moscow. Trained by KGB experts to

---

*   Luben Bozhev's disclosure to my father 1977, Vidrare.

**   General Stoian Savov, Deputy Minister of Internal Affairs, responsible for foreign intelligence operations. Instead of facing trial for the assassination of George Markov, he committed suicide in mid 1990s.

***   General Savchenko tipped me on Markov's recruitment by Colonel Kulumov during a tennis practice in 1977.

**** In 1994, KGB General Oleg Kalugin at last confirmed the KGB complicity surrounding the 1978 assassination of George Markov in London.

***** The group of General Slavcho Trunski, carried on various top-secret assignments for the Communist party.

murder without traces, they were soon ready for the gruesome job. The team was not amateur to the "*wet affairs*" business: The old communists had perpetrated bold and senseless murders as members of underground communist resistance cells during the fight against fascism in Bulgaria and the Soviet Union.

FCD would craftily involve an intelligence asset of Italian origin, a bearer of a Danish passport who was recruited in the early 1970s through a customs scam in Bulgaria. He was to divert any possible attention from the main perpetrators, while assuring the actual assassination with a second shot.

*   *   *

Two weeks before Markov's assassination in London, the controlled hand of an assassin pulled the trigger of an inconspicuous looking umbrella-weapon in Paris. Major Vladimir Kostov, a State Security defector, was calculatedly shot with a miniature bullet that carried a lethal doze of *Ricin*. Even while critically sickening Kostov, the Paris assassination failed; an unforeseen deposit of body fat inexorably had prevented the poison's proper disbursal.

The suspicious death of George Markov in London prompted the French forensic experts to reopen Kostov's case in Paris. They stunningly unraveled indisputable corroboration of complicity. As the baffling death of the renowned Bulgarian dissident writer and BBC columnist perplexed the Londoners, news from Paris reverberated throughout Europe, conveying a shivering communist plot.

Vladimir Kostov was the director of the Bulgarian National Television and Telegraph Agency in Paris, and Vice-president of the Bulgarian journalists association. Under deep cover, he was a foreign intelligence officer. With his wife, a talented writer and translator, they gradually became discontented with communist realities. Vociferously defecting to France, they initiated an aggressive media campaign against totalitarianism. Renouncing his communist membership, State Security and KGB affiliation and his nationality, Kostov disclosed to the French security and the media vast quantities of information about KGB and State Security intelligence operations in France and throughout Western Europe. Kostov was eventually triumphant, winning one of the greatest journalistic awards in France, *"Journalist of the Year,"* for his human decency, consciousness and courageous journalistic mind and plausible anti-Communist publications.

Concurrent to Kostov's fond appreciation of their new way of life, a secret military tribunal in Sofia expeditiously had condemned the Major to "Death by firing squad" (in absentia) for his defection to the West and for high national treason. The execution (assassination) was carried unsuccessful in France.

While recovering from an apparently severe food poisoning the day of Markov's death, Kostov called to mind a momentous sting inflicted ten days earlier at a Paris bus stop. He then remembered an inconspicuously looking passenger or pedestrian at the stop casually brandishing an umbrella walking away. A promptly summoned French medical team immediately discovered an unusual inflammation on Kostov's thigh and was astonished to recover a miniature pellet, craftily designed to carry poison in its hollow cavities. Experts succeeded in retrieving residues from the fatty pouch, and unequivocally indicated the presence of the extremely lethal substance *Ricin*.

The French authorities circumstantially linked Kostov's case with the veiled in suspicion death of George Markov. This prompted the British authorities to immediately exhume Markov's body for an additional autopsy, which the French suggested corroborated and paralleled their suspicious crime.

British forensics discovered a pellet in the early stage decomposing Markov's body. A series of spectral analyses thereafter determined with reasonable certainty the matching origin of both poisonous pellets. These new evidences led to criminal investigations and the establishment of an eventual Bulgarian connection. Regrettably no indictments were filed due to the absence of substantiated evidences, witnesses and suspects. The case in France was dropped, while the case in England has lingering for decades and is still open. In July 2001, British Prime Minister Tony Blair, while congratulating the former Bulgarian King Simeon II Saxe Coburg—Gotha, on his election as Prime Minister of Bulgaria, tactfully emphasized his expectation for Markov's murderers to be brought to justice.

*   *   *

Vladimir Kostov was recruited as a secret agent by counter-intelligence in the mid 1960s inside the national radio, television and writers' circles. Besides being a cunningly productive secret informer, he was a promising and well-versed journalist. By intuition Kostov discovered early in his career that in order to achieve results and grow up in the competitive intellectual's stratum, he had to be affiliated with the communist party and most importantly with the notorious State Security and KGB institutions. Strong willed and persuasive, he was introverted and goal oriented: qualities that were positively evaluated by State Security foreign intelligence managers. During the late 1960s Kostov was assigned as a journalist covering Bulgarian government visits to France. His efforts were recognized by the foreign intelligence resident in Paris, Peter Stefanov, and thereafter by Colonel Raiko Nikolov.

As a journalist for the newspaper "*Pogled*" (View) in Beirut, Lebanon, Kostov befriended Colonel Bogdan Hristov, the foreign intelligence resident. Kostov's prominence glamorized Hristov and soon he was lured into proposing a plan for Vladimir Kostov's involvement as intelligence officer. After some bureaucratic wrangling, the highly motivated and restless Kostov eventually approached

General-Colonel Mircho Spasov and Luben Bozhev at the Central Committee of the Communist Party. By the means of his fame, eminence and substantial support from high-ranking members of the government, Kostov was appointed as a State Security intelligence officer.

For years Kostov used the code name *"Krustev"* under his reports, astutely maintaining his secret attachment with the intelligence institutions. Kostov's knowledge about FCD operations and intelligence officers should be deemed marginal, for he did not maintain an office at the foreign intelligence directorate. He was more or less a prominent figure in the Committee for Television and Radio, than a cunning intelligence spook.

As a foreign political-intelligence officer, Kostov became a well-versed collector and insightful analyst of foreign economic and socio-political information. His inability to recruiting foreign agents was his most crucial operational shortfall as an intelligence officer.

Under the watchful eyes of Colonel Dimo Stankov*, the Paris resident, Kostov was directed to befriend and develop western journalists including some Americans. At that time Kostov had already established a semi-clandestine relationship with an American correspondent. Paradoxically, Colonel Stankov was silently and methodically pitching for recruitment the same American, unaware of his stealthy liaisons with Kostov. Incapable of setting an inescapable net around the targeted American, Stankov repentantly discovered that in reality he had been providing the information most of the time, becoming in reality dependent on the leading strategies and unambiguous CIA's demands. The bigheaded Stankov, inherent to his runaway peasant upbringing, has become an inescapable casualty of his own entrapments.

Unknown to Kostov, one of the greatest KGB intelligence assets ever in France (managed by State Security) flew up through the French government hierarchy, attaining the portfolio of Minister of Interior. So important was this communist asset that Colonel Raicko Nikolov was assigned to the Paris residency with the sole purpose of maintaining a secure and secretive liaison with the French agent *"Marrat"*. In the late 1970s Nikolov replaced Stankov as Chief of station and resident of FCD's intelligence operations in France.

---

* Colonel Dimo Stankov, former Chief of "Active measures" department of FCD-foreign intelligence directorate, and a State Security acquaintance of the British communist spy Kim Philby.

FRENCH GRAPES

During the 1970s, the immodest KGB and State Security intelligence planners grossly miscalculated a potential target's fondness with the misleadingly promising communist ideology. As it had been with the communists' successful handling of *Marrat,* the leading French official and Minister of the Interior, their new target was an astute American, under whose prominent journalist's cover, unknown to the Soviets or the French, was functioning an exceptionally capable CIA operative.

As a stealthy *"go between"*, Vladimir Kostov provided consistent reports and analytical assessments of his relentless acquaintance with Donald Ratner (A). Perplexingly unforeseen by Kostov, however, his scrupulous work gradually entangled him in a pre-determined relationship. The KGB and State Security's foreign intelligence management soon made professional assessments and concluded that the CIA was slowly aiming towards Kostov's recruitment.

Surpassing resident Stankov, the FCD and KGB conducted comprehensive preparations and developed a new and "promising" endeavor of allowing Kostov to be recruited by the CIA. The KGB correctly envisioned potential conflicts of interests between Kostov's new task and the traditional intelligence operations of his Paris residency. Thus, Kostov was ordered to separate from the intelligence community and the ongoing operations, discontinuing his accountability to the growing apprehensive Dimo Stankov. A KGB experts group* was established at FCD, Sofia's center, to work in secrecy with Kostov, and manage the upcoming events.

The growing paranoid Vladimir Kostov, however, would envision behind the new operation an immense and sinister trap set fort to expose him. He truly believed that the complex intrigue was set forward to provide evidence to the KGB and State Security that in reality Kostov was an active CIA spy, an asset craftily recruited by Stankov's insightful and enigmatic American contact Donald Ratner.

Eventually a leading pitch from the Americans and specific information that Kostov had covertly conveyed to Ratner prompted him to suppose that he was

---

*   Details from FCD archive materials on Kostov's operations in France, 2001.

in effect under investigation by State Security and the KGB. In reality, Kostov had been unofficially providing information to an old CIA friend for more than three years. Silently paranoid by nature, he lived with an excruciating sense of danger that was craftily stage-managed by the CIA to assure Kostov's one-way ticket to the West. Lavish and chic dining, gifts and expensive trips to the castles on the Loire and Seine Valley, exploring the tranquility of Samoa River in the Ardennes, along with crafty American feedback on some of the most sophisticated NATO nuclear missile facilities, already made Kostov a pawn in the global stage of intelligence mastery and active deception.

Kostov befriended the people he was suppose to be most afraid off, and seemingly fell a victim of the advanced intelligence games of the CIA; however, it was also possible that everything was an inevitable outcome of Kostov's growing anti-Communist sentiments and intellectual rebellion against the totalitarian socialism.

Under similar circumstances, Kostov's gaudy and egotistical boss, Colonel Dimo Stankov, was not even able to detect how naturally he had been played into feeding back to the Americans the information they have been looking for. It was truly the astute art of espionage in the making: the recruiter has fallen victim of a greatly anticipated asset for recruitment. These were mundane but important trivial pursuits that were long overlooked and perhaps idealistically subjugated. The communist ideology was truly a utopian, peripatetic delusion!

The sinister intent of the KGB and State Security to turn Vladimir Kostov against centuries old western institutions, or perhaps in the anticipated process to verify and expose his stealthy association with the West had plummeted: Vladimir Kostov and his family elected with dignity and pride to duly pursue their human happiness, freedom and prosperity, away from the chokehold of the communist realities. Astutely defecting to France, they made public and exposed the ruthlessness of the communist society. Kostov should be credited for the discovery of the evidences in the attempt on his life and nonetheless, for the irrational murder of the writer George Markov in London.

*   *   *

The First and Sixth directorates aggressively recruited intellectuals for specific assignments to the West. To allow them quickly and legitimately integrate within western targets and emigration centers, often these agents were declared dissidents and had craftily fabricated legends.

The KGB and State Security sent the illustrious Bulgarian movie director and producer Hacho Boiadzhiev to France during the mid 1970s. Exploiting Boiadzhiev's connections with the French aristocracy, intellectuals and the large Turkish and Bulgarian emigration, Colonel Dimitar Vandov, the FCD resident in Paris, recruited some lasting assets for the KGB and State Security with his help and assistance. After years in oblivion, in the early 1980s Hacho Boiadzhiev returned to Bulgaria and for many of his "dissident" connections surprisingly received high government recognition and was assigned as a Managing Director of the Bulgarian National Palace of Culture (NPC), an ultimate communist reward for his loyal "treachery and deception" for the state. Furthermore, Boiadzhiev's NPC office became overnight a safe house for clandestine meetings with foreigners in Bulgaria, recruited as State Security agents by Vandov's son, Svilen, a Sixth directorate officer.

*   *   *

During a visit to Sofia in 1977, the IOC's (International Olympic Committee) President Juan Antonio Samaranch was deliberately introduced and thereafter masterfully seduced by Kamelia Hristova, a multi-lingual university student from Varna and a registered prostitute. Craftily directed by the Sixth directorate and KGB officers, Hristova embarked on closely monitoring Samaranch's activities, conversations and contacts directly from his bed. The technical team developed substantially compromising XXX-rated videos and photos of the IOC President for future blackmail operations. To the best of my knowledge, during 1979 and the early 1980s, the KGB stealthily representing the Soviet Union's Olympic and political interests, and cunningly manipulated Antonio Samaranch's critical decisions as leader of the IOC. Another western aristocrat and renowned international executive has fallen a victim in the hands of the merciless communist secret services. Sergey Avdeev, an IOC member and a stealthy KGB Colonel, can perhaps corroborate the Soviet glories carried throughout Samaranch's devious transgressions.

POLITICAL POLICE IN ACTION

The operational activities of Sixth directorate covered not only groups or individual representatives of different fractions or institutions, but most importantly covered the operational security of all institutions of the country. This demanding process in reality assured the State Security and KGB relative transparency of any business, personnel and management, and international or political activities. Under the guidelines of the KGB and the Central Committee of the Communist Party, a main emphasis was placed on the intelligentsia, the intellectuals, academicians, students and the sports organizations. Perhaps as strong was the operational control and monitoring activities of the leaders of the Communist Party, the Government and the pro—Turkish nationalist movement of the *Pomacs*.

The main duty of an operational officer was his ability (or inability—leading to his dismissal) to recruit agents. This ultimate ancient art required specific talent, knowledge and tact, sensitivity and intelligence, persuasion and conviction.

It would be socially deplorable today to delineate how many intellectuals, academicians, professors, ministers, priests, architects, Ph.D.'s, artists, poets, writers, actors, journalists, producers, researchers, scientists, musicians, conductors, singers, Olympic and World champions, and regular citizens were recruited as agents of the notorious State Security and the KGB. Sixth directorate's 220 to 260 operational officers managed and controlled during mid 1984 a permanent contingent of 3,500 to 4,000 agents. The KGB and State Security were constantly growing in all operational directorates, from late 1970 to the early 1980s. Most of the institutions they controlled were monitored and managed with an iron fist, and gradually became wholly dependent on the operational officers for any management, personnel, economic or even financial management decision. Although the process was in line with the totalitarian approach of the Communist party and the growing dependence of the state on policing any segment of the public and private life, it evolved into a dangerously unraveling thread, out of both party and the constitutional control.

Under the Communist Party's ideological and manipulative nurturing, the Soviet KGB and State Security developed an extremely powerful system of monitoring and investigating the activities of virtually everyone in the country.

Agents and secret collaborators, members of the communist party, and informers devilishly contributed to the conversion towards a virtually translucent society. State Security's Sixth directorate and the KGB's Fifth directorate became masters of penetrating and controlling not only the social and individual life of citizens, but also of any spheres and aspects of governing and political oversight. Operational officers were skilled to monitor with agents, technical and eavesdropping systems, and support personnel almost any event or development throughout the country. Reacting fast, bluntly and mercilessly in preventing any dissent, ideological subversion, nationalist propaganda or anticommunist activities of organizations or individuals made State Security a venerable force. In essence, the totalitarian leadership inadvertently created a Stalin type Political Police, which became so powerful that it functioned in absolute secrecy, out of any party and government control.

*   *   *

Not popularly known due to the implication that it could be one of the most powerful attempts ever made by political dissents in Bulgaria against the totalitarian rule of the General Secretary of the Communist Party, Todor Zhivkov, the "*coup d'etat*" of Generals Ivan Todorov-Gorunia, Tzviatko Anev and Dimitar Tzolov vehemently showed the internal chaos against the strict regime.

The leaders of the renegade old communists succeeded in the late 1960s to unite more than 120 senior State Security, army and navy officers in an attempt to remove Todor Zhivkov from the communist party leadership and impose a revised socialist system. Under strong pro-Stalinist, Maoist and Titoist influences, the conspirators prepared to steal the control of the Communist Party from the authoritarian command and dictatorial hold of Todor Zhivkov and his small cohort of brigade "*Chavdar*" partisans. They planned to revise the socialist model of the country, but without abolishing the communist society and the dialectical materialism of Marx-Lenin's ideology. The group intended to limit the Todor Zhivkov's power over the communist party, rather concentrating party control within the hands of a political bureau that was periodically elected by a party congress.

Colonel Boian Velinov, a Sixth directorate officer, deeply infiltrated the renegade's group and was positioned to peacefully change the course of intended actions. However, the highly disgruntled Zhivkov proved unyielding and more than implacable. Most of the dialogues between the "*coup d'etat*" leaders were effectively monitored by some of the most modern listening equipment provided by the KGB, including, but not limited to miniature American transmitters masterfully implanted into the military cards of the generals' hats. The Fourth department officers even monitored the generals Gorunia and Anev's most secretive dialogues with absolute precision; amazingly, these audios have been obtained while the suspects walked through the Park of Liberty. As soon as the renegades proceeded to mobilize and recruit new members, the Sixth directorate orchestrated a clever "active measures" operation:

An anonymous caller ingeniously tipped off General Gorunia that the Committee of State Security had discovered his plot and arrests were imminent. The strategy was aimed at identifying the few secret cells that were intelligently developed and placed under deep cover by General Anev. They were the only missing links in State Security's overall investigation of the first "*coup d'etat*" in Eastern Europe after Nagy in 1956 Hungary. In the final dramatic stage of the operation, a team of operational officers was dispatched in North East Bulgaria to apprehend General Gorunia. Few were aware of Todor Zhivkov's secret order for General Gorunia to be murdered, a decision made in order to eradicate any schismatic consequences within the communist party's leadership.

Two former partisans and operational officers, also elite members of the special group "Zvezda"* (Star) managed by General Slavcho Trunski, cunningly staged an apparent suicide as the cold-blooded method of General Gorunia's murder. After a week in hiding, General Anev was also apprehended, and was soon quietly sentenced to a lengthy prison term together with most of the members of the failed *coup*.

* * *

In 1970 a secretive group of General Gorunia's followers consolidated with the anti-Zhivkov's group of Doctorov/Naidenov and formed a new wing of the communist party—"*Blagoev/Dimitrov Communists*". Their goal was the separation of the Bulgarian communist movement from Soviet influence, to take control over the activities of the communist party, overthrow Zhivkov's "*cult of personality,*" and take down its tyrannical Stalinist pedestal. Riddled with Sixth directorate secret agents and technical monitoring, the renegade (dogmatic) pro-Maoist group was successfully eliminated at its inception.

The non-conforming members were sentenced to the harshest prisons and the lengthiest terms, unequivocally sending a serious message and warning to any future political dissidents about Zhivkov's blunt cruelty and intolerance.

---

*   "Zvezda" members assassinated in 1978 Bulgarian writer and anticommunist George Markov in London. They attempted to assassinate Vladimir Kostov in Paris and in 1988 were ready to murder the author in Antwerp, Belgium.

*   *   *

In the spring of 1978, a Bulgarian emigrant in the Netherlands, Anton Krustev, approached Amsterdam's "Human Rights Association". The young dissident was searching for assistance with an aggressive anticommunist propaganda campaign in Bulgaria.

Offering Krustev monetary assistance and logistics support for his altruistic mission behind the "Iron Curtain", the Dutch human rights organization gladly embraced his courage and dedication. Traveling on assumed identity papers, Krustev settled in Sofia and a nearby town, where together with his girlfriend Kati and a childhood friend he created an insightful human rights pamphlet entitled *"Declaration 78'"*. Printed in English and Bulgarian, the pamphlets were distributed to numerous international institutions and western embassies in Sofia, appealing for the support of the Bulgarian human rights movement.

During the activation of a semi-automatic gadget on the roof of the "Students Club", the illustrious Bulgarian wrestler Boian Radev and a group of State Security officers who were coincidentally walking out of the next-door bar-restaurant "Sofia" apprehended some members of the group. After a lengthy investigation and nasty interrogations, Anton Krustev and his accomplices were sentenced to 15 years imprisonment at the high security Pazardzhik prison.

Similar consciously provacative activities should be attributed to Dr. Nikola Popov and Nenko Nenov, former communist party members and creators of the *"Bulgarian Manifest"* and *"Charter 77"*. Their unswerving anti-socialist protests and critiques of Bulgaria human rights violations were instrumental in engaging western watch groups' attention. By constantly monitoring the telephone conversations of foreign Embassies in Sofia, the State Security's Fourth department successfully intercepted most of Popov and Nenov's conversations with western representatives and craftily controlled all of their covert initiatives. Thereafter a simple technical operation of redirecting upcoming calls to the American Embassy in Sofia to a control center of State Security exposed the dissidents' upcoming *"Charter"* initiative. English speaking "embassy receptionists" directed Popov and Nenov's calls to an apparent American press attaché and journalist who was in reality an English speaking State Security officer. The dissidents were apprehended through this sinister operation, believing to the last moment that they were in contact with legitimate western representatives. After eagerly disclosing their connections, operations, supporters and newly planned activities, the dissidents Popov and Nenov in reality sufficiently self-incriminated themselves, guaranteeing a guilty verdict and a lengthy Soviet type "Gulag" imprisonment.

*　　*　　*

The Sixth directorate during the 1970s infiltrated and arrested a large group of Bulgarian and White Russians connected with the Paris based *"People's Labor Council"*. A group of more than a hundred members led by Vladimir Macarov and Teodosi Beliakovskii, they were harshly persecuted for anti-socialist propaganda and anti-government and anti-Soviet activities. The French exchange scholar at the Bulgarian Academy of Sciences, Catherine Lvov, and the freelance French journalist, Andrea Savine, both members of the group, smuggled to the Soviet Union and Bulgaria thousands of forbidden publications by Saharov, Solzhenitzin, Svetlana Alilueva as well as anti-Soviet propaganda materials. The Central Committee of the Communist Party of the Soviet Union (CPSS) instructed the KGB center to assist State Security in summarily and severely punishing the perpetrators. Not surprisingly, Macarov, Beliakovskii and Lvov were sentenced to prison terms ranging from 3 to 5 years. Caterine Lvov, however, was transferred to the custody of the French authorities, alleviating the growing strains in the trilateral relations of Bulgaria and the Soviet Union with France. Skillfully disguised and concealed, Lvov was in the end inconspicuously spirited out of Sofia's French Embassy.

While supervising Sofia State University in 1976, Major George Krustev infiltrated the inner circle of one of the talented students at the History & Philosophy faculty. Nikolai Giakov had written an elaborately critical analysis of the moral and ethical failures of the socialist society in Bulgaria and Eastern Europe, decisively paralleling the malice with Soviet realities. With brilliant language and literary style, Giakov concluded that life under communism was absurd; it was a life without freedom, creativity and spirituality, a life destined to swampiest existence, human decay and inevitable moral degradation. Promptly expelled from the University, Nikolai Giakov was condemned to prison for anti-government and anti-Communist ideological subversion and propaganda.

During 1981, George Krustev and his underling: Dimitar Dimitrov and Pavel Terziev received the nicknames *"The Butchers of Sofia University"* for their senseless, sinister and brutal approach against students, academic and operational staff and professors. Their demonic motivation and mindless interpretations of bogus directives from the Communist Party were some of the most blatant forms of political policing of the most prestigious university in the Balkans. The modern new and democratic Bulgarian intellectual society should not forget the *"Butchers'"* merciless abuse, persecutions and malevolence.

The Bulgarian Communist Party's secretive and steady policy of ongoing fusion with the Communist Party of the Soviet Union and especially the growing autocratic totalitarian rule of the General Secretary Todor Zhivkov started receiving sharp disagreement from leading members within the party. Hristo Kumanov, the former powerful and well-respected Party Secretary of the Pleven region, led one of the most potent renegade communist groups during the 1977.

Seriously disturbed by evidence of dissent in the party, Todor Zhivkov personally demanded State Security's Sixth directorate to thoroughly monitor and investigate the anti-Communist activities of the communist renegades. Two surveillance operational units with more than 20 cars had been dispatched to the city of Pleven for one of the lengthiest investigations of communist officials. During this time the sinister State Security reached further into aggressively utilizing radioactive isotopes and potent spy dust for tracing and controlling movement of people and documents. Infiltrated by cleverly manipulated agents, the group was gradually destabilized and its leadership apprehended. Convicted behind Stalin era "closed door" court procedures, Kumanov and seven of his key followers were sentenced to harsh imprisonment.

*　　*　　*

In 1982 President Ronald Reagan initiated one of the most important moral and political campaigns against the worldwide presence of communism. In his June address to the British Parliament, Reagan announced the new American position on the totalitarian Warsaw Pact:

"... It is time to see Communism finally and forever discarded at the garbage dump of world history ..."

The program "Democracy", which was significantly subsidized by the United States, was developed in order to aggressively support opposition and anti-Communist movements around the world. Radios "Voice of America" and "Free Europe" became leading providers of reliable and credible information about western society's democratic values and prosperous life, as well as unbiased critiques of the socialist realities. They gradually evolved into credible vocal "Agents of Change" and moral consciousness among the anti-socialist opposition behind the "Iron Curtain".

The Polish "Solidarity" movement gradually grew from a confined labor movement of Gdansk shipyard workers into a powerful and irreversible human march in search of democratic freedom and independence from the Soviet Union's oppression and grave influence.

The consistently evil enlargement of totalitarian power and the ruthless suppression of the population by State Security's Sixth directorate reverberated into a powerful call for human rights and democratic pluralism. During 1982, Janko Jankov, a Ph.D. scientist at the Institute of State and Justice of the Bulgarian Academy of Sciences, initiated a lengthy complain against the lack of liberty, justice and human rights in Bulgaria. Forced out of the Academy, he was interned to the rugged Bulgarian North where he continued his anti-communist and anti-government activities. Jankov's book "An Epistolary Novel" was successfully distributed by western diplomats to some International institutions, and generated solemn foreign governmental complains as it officially incriminated Bulgaria of Helsinki Accord human rights violations. Arrested by ruthless Sixth directorate officers, Dr. Jankov was cruelly persecuted and sentenced to high security prison for 12 years.

Vladimir Nakov shared a similar destiny, as he was convicted for alleged "anti-government and anti-Communist propaganda". Nakov persistently criticized the Soviet Union and the Communist Party of the Soviet Union as a tireless warrior for freedom and human dignity. With numerous official letters and blunt black and white assessments to western leaders, he complained about the Bulgarian and the Soviet Union's violations of the Helsinki Accords and the brutal suppressions of the elementary human rights and liberties of the Bulgarian Muslims (Pomacs). Yet again, however, the Sixth directorate apprehended the "blasphemer." He was viciously persecuted and thrown into a high security prison. Once in the communist's "Gulag", however, Nakov's persistent anticommunist rhetoric was suspiciously silenced, and he disappeared from the face of the earth. This murder should be another case to be reopened and carefully examined, for it bears substantial evidence against the notoriety of the State Security controlled communist prison system.

*   *   *

In June of 1982, the Sixth directorate discovered that East German intelligence "Stasi" AVH, had provided false identity to members of the Italian *"Red Brigade"* and the German *"Baader Meinhof"* terrorist groups and even "mothballed" some of them to an exclusive Sunny Beach resort on the Black Sea. Supposedly, it was the terrorists' recreational retreat to escape a worldwide Interpol manhunt after some of their brutal and senseless bombings and terrorist attacks in Germany, Italy and France. Under the direct orders of Todor Zhivkov, however, an unprecedented secret extraction operation was set in motion. It wisely eliminated any further implications of Bulgaria as a supporter or harborer of global terrorism. To eliminate consequential terrorist revenge against Bulgarian interests, an extraordinary State Security/KGB cooperation with Interpol and the West German BND* evolved into a daring secret operation.

A specialized West German heavily armed commando unit was flown on a chartered jet from Munich to the Bulgarian resort city of Burgas. Two days later, in the middle of the night, the well-trained antiterrorist team apprehended the group of six terrorists, all of whom were at the time semi-sedated from the

---

* Bundes Nahrihten Dienst—West German intelligence agency.

excessive drinking of craftily laced Champaign, without a single shot or resistance. The chartered jet was quickly flown to West Germany, setting the precedent for the communist totalitarian regime's cooperation with western security authorities. A highly guarded and secured trial in West Germany eventually convicted the terrorists of numerous merciless acts against humanity, and assured all of them lengthy incarceration. Details of this peerless arrest have never been publicly revealed, even though the event signifies one of the first examples of effective East-West security cooperation.

Perhaps some members of the Bulgarian leadership realized that the traditionally warm hospitality offered for decades to groups of Arab, Palestinian, radical and leftist West European terrorist groups and leaders, including many notorious terrorists such as *"Carlos the Jackal"* Ilich Ramirez Sanchez, would inevitably one day surface and gravely discredit and compromise communist governing practices.

COURAGE FOR FIGHT

MOLE IN THE HEART OF THE COMMUNIST SYSTEM

For almost ten years, out of my fifteen years working as an operational officer for the communist State Security and KGB, I calculatedly and conscientiously made transparent the security, military, diplomatic and intelligence institutions of the Soviet Union and the Warsaw Pact countries to the government of the United States of America. I watchfully planned and duly exploited any opportunity that arose and opened many heavily guarded doors, safes and secret files. It was my silent but deadly cat-and-mouse game, set off in my childhood and time and again nurtured by my family's deepening incongruity and mistrust with communality.

Over the twentieth century the Soviet KGB and the surrogate State Security evolved into ultimate masters of communist deception and totalitarian malevolence. Since the early 1950s Andrey Zhdanov became Stalin's architect of global communist expansion. His stratagems were instrumental in leading communism against western democracies by instigating, supporting and guiding the world's intelligentsia to stand firm behind the banners of the communism. He thus uncompromisingly led the proletariat to destroy the aristocratic and bourgeoisie values of consumerists and capitalist society. The Soviet leaders fully embraced the revolutionary concepts of Lenin and Marx and promoted on a grand scale the export of socialist theories and utopian communality, all the while blindly believing in virtually unattainable socio-economic miracles.

Not surprisingly, many leading academicians, poets, scientists, writers, artists, composers, architects and sculptors inexorably lost distinction and moral identity by transforming their creativity and intellectual quests into mere socialist propaganda and short-sighted communal endeavors. The vivid example of Diego Rivera, Gabriel Garcia Markec, David Alvaro Siceros, Frida Cahlo, Pablo Neruda and many more multiplied, emphasizing the promising allure of the utopian democratic centralism.

In this highly manipulative environment of totalitarianism and social trickery, I officially authorized for years, often surpassing State Security and the Communist Party management, international travel to the west for academicians, scientists, doctors, architects and intellectuals. Some of these brilliant individuals never returned or craftily defected to the West, greatly embarrassing and discrediting the ruling communists.

In early 1978, State Security unanimously elected me a Member of the Communist Party Committee of the Ministry of Internal Affairs. My responsibilities covered the selection and training of new communist party members among the young State Security officers. This political appointment, in addition to my main operational duties, came as a crafty adaptation to my ongoing fight against the communism.

The late 1970s and early 1980s were distinguished with a steady decline in the centrally planned economic sectors. A lack of competitiveness, productivity, quality, and technological innovations gradually eroded the foundations of the developed socialism. In this environment of growing dissent, the Central Committee of the Communist Party realized that the country needed urgent revival.

Along with the unmatched fanfares and propaganda was introduced the "New Economic Mechanism", a theoretically well endowed idea created by a team of academicians led by the Secretary of the communist party, Todor Bozhinov. It was a lengthy document designed at motivating the proletariat by introducing new forms of socialist achievements and greatly emphasizing on the imaginative future prosperity of the "Developed Socialist Society".

It was no wonder that the grandiose project became an economic disaster and charted the beginning of a colossal and irreversible destructive process. The culmination of this fiasco came with its multiplication, leading to the ultimate disintegration of the East European socio-economic system. Even the radical reforms initiated by Michail Gourbachov's *"Perestroika"* during the second half of the 1980s would fail to revitalize the Soviet economy. In essence, the totalitarian Iron Curtain had veiled East European society and economy for too long from the real necessities for productivity, quality and technology innovations.

*   *   *

The State Security's Party Committee asked me to present an analysis of the New Economic Mechanism (NEM) to the communist party organization. Fortified with an in-depth due diligence analysis, including excerpts from economic research written by leading economists such as professors Ivan Iliev, Pencho Penchev, Kamen Vlahov and Nedialko Belev, I presented the new mechanism's synopsis to the Sixth directorate party organization. My presentation constructively analyzed and criticized the inefficiencies of the central planning process and eloquently explained that the communist beliefs in economic and social miracles reached into an ethereal realm.

". . . While we should be the first to objectively assess the results and the impact of the new Communist Party initiatives, we should become more responsive in charting and creating a feasible and successful socio-economic future for our country. We should not again and again become just a reactive, often suppressive power' instead, we need to identify and remedy the negative results and the impact of theoretical and ideological blunders made by some of our party and industry leaders . . ."

My closing words prompted an abnormal silence followed by a subsequent wave of mumbling amongst the listeners. I expected critical retorts from the old cohort of communist apparatchiks; however, I was taken aback by the crushing critique of the deputy director General Anton Musakov:

"I have not been exposed to this form of flagrant ideological diversion and subversion since 1944—our victory over the fascism. It is disgraceful to our directorate to accept these treacherous and provocative interpretations of an official document of the Central Committee of the Communist Party, especially in this manner and substance . . ."

As a Soviet Union and KGB educated functionary, Anton Musakov* became in the later 1980s a leading State Security communist party functionary and eventually Chief of the Sixth directorate. After orchestrating a crafty purge against General Peter Stoianov and implicating him of political deception and alcoholism, he continued to be a driving force behind the most sinister State Security operations ever perpetrated against the Bulgarian society.

My straightforward analyses undeniably became the unwitting beginning of my confrontation with totalitarian establishments. Although my study initiated some sincere private dialogues among the officers, the majority considered it a flagrant blasphemy of the socialist reality.

Left alone with my conscious soul, I found myself in virtual isolation; suddenly I was vulnerable and irrefutably predestined to political vengeance. Innumerable professional friends vanished, nowhere to be found in my traditional daily routines; how was my destiny to be different? I grasped that I was facing a *"clear and present"* danger. Lucidly comprehending the reality, my courage and determination allowed me to proceed further. This came as an accurately premeditated, conscious judgment call with stern convictions. For too long, I have been a dyed-in-the-wool covert adversary of the utopian communalism. Time has come the truth to be addressed; the realities soon would start to change.

---

*   Peter Mladenov and Anton Musakov become instrumental in the Soviet Union's ouster (overthrow) of Todor Zhivkov as General Secretary of the Bulgarian Communist Party in 1989.

"FREEDOM OR DEATH"

As a consequence of my profound moral thinking for individual human distinctiveness and the necessity of freedom and pursuits of happiness, in the mid 1970s, I believed that a clandestine—trustworthy and constructive relationship with the government of the United States of America should be established.

Some leading dialogues with friends from the American embassy surveillance department, combined with personal observations and reviews of analytical data, allowed me to compile details about recurring and imminent weekend outings of few American diplomats. Suspected CIA intelligence officers consistently visited the *Kopitoto* and *Zlatnite Mostove* regions of the Vitosha National Park. Targeted diplomats took the *Boiana* lift gondolas to the top of the mountain and were also observed taking long walks through the fabulous hiking trails. Though under tight surveillance, no evidence of espionage activity was ever detected in these settings.

My *Capricorn* analytical mind developed a simplistic plan aimed at establishing clandestine contact with an American diplomat code-named "*the Doctor*" while in the lift gondola. To legitimize my approach I used my son's clear enjoyment with snow sports. In two instances I took him to the mountains to get familiar with the overall settings. Unnoticed, I observed the movements of the American diplomats and the layout of the surveillance around the target.

The night before my approach, I wrote a concise letter in a technical font. Avoiding any graphological or calligraphic clues in case of an unforeseen fiasco, I clearly summarized my firm anti-Communist sentiments and offered few specific intelligence recommendations. Elucidating upon my sincere and genuine determination, I laconically disclosed some specific details about the "*Turncoat*" case known only to a limited few. Wiping away any fingerprints, I inserted the note into an empty cartridge of a developed film.

Early the next morning I wrapped the container in a handkerchief and carefully secured it in a pocket of my winter jacket. At the *Boiana* lift station parking lot I found a secluded parking space and nonchalantly offered my son a breakfast sandwich. The few extra minutes allowed me to wax the snow sled. We then nonchalantly approached the ticket counter. A line of about twenty to thirty people eagerly waited to board one of the two gondolas to the top. With two roundtrip discounted tickets in hand, I dispassionately observed the arrival of a familiar maroon Volvo.

Soon, four Americans blended in with the tourists in line. Ilia Tomov, a former wrestling champion turned surveillance officer dressed in a modern ski jacket inconspicuously joined us. The surveillance directorate lavishly spent western currency and confiscated customs items to craftily disguise a multitude of State Security clandestine activities and operations. It was mind-boggling how much went on behind the scenes at any given time around non-suspecting officials, ordinary citizens, foreign diplomats, tourists, businessmen and western visitors. The totalitarian secret forces were overwhelming, as they functioned with virtually impunity and no budgetary constrains.

The arrival of a cable gondola interrupted casual dialogues and the passengers started boarding. We got in line to board the next descending gondola, joining the four Americans and six or seven tourists. Tomov calmly solicited my help in monitoring the diplomats during the ride and casually slipped to the restrooms. It was one of the most incredibly bizarre and ironic situations in the history of surveillance operations against American diplomats, as *"the Fox was assigned to guard the hens!"*

Once in the air I noticed Tomov's BMW leaving the parking lot. My target, a bearded diplomat codenamed *"the Doctor"* and his petite wife *"the Nurse"* were casually chatting nearby. Our snow-sled grabbed the *"Doctor's"* attention and in a good Bulgarian he began to chat with my son. Taking the initiative, I in English asked the *Doctor* if he works at the American embassy. Surprised that I have identified him as an American, he friendly introduced himself as the Embassy's—First secretary. From a professional courtesy, I introduced myself as a foreign trade specialist at the Ministry of foreign trade.

The breathtaking view of the city emerged far below as the gondola steadily ascended. I almost conspiratorially pointed towards the tallest building not far away in the *Bukston* suburb, and bluntly stated that it was the center for international military studies. The *Doctor* lifted his eyebrows and naively inquired if it was an academy. Whispering, I quietly avowed that in reality it was the building of military intelligence.

The dialogue stalled as the gondola approached one of the most beautiful spots over the steep gorge. My target started taking pictures of the city with a modern Olympus camera. He inconspicuously zoomed at the building I had just depicted, and with a few quick camera shots irrefutably confirmed his interests. The *Nurse* nonchalantly amused my son with a story that was evidently well memorized from her language training. She intentionally drew my son's attention, bountifully offering the opportunity to *the Doctor* to tackle the unanticipated catch.

Maintaining a safe distance, the *Doctor* turned towards me while avoiding the attention of the others.

"How do you know that?" he inquired.

The other American couple was almost intentionally noisy, excitedly discussing the beautiful view far below. A monotonous audio recording conveniently distracted the other passengers with information on attractions visible from the sky cab.

"I work there", I stated boldly.

To prove my point, I reached in my pocket and discreetly flashed my red State Security credentials that were attached to a secure string of a brown polymer cord. The *Doctor's* face blushed at the sudden elevation of the situation. As he looked at my ID card in dismay, he perhaps realized that he was looking at one of the most secret and powerful identification documents in the country. With a slow motion he aimed his camera at the ID in my hand and with my silent approval casually took two rapid shots. The bait was too flavorsome to be left unfinished unless he suspected an elaborate State Security or KGB set-up.

I was concerned that the *Doctor* might reject my cassette as provocation and decided to act as soon as possible to avoid any possible altercations as we approached the top station.

"You are surprised, aren't you? These are trophy shots!" I stated calmly, letting my eyes wonder down the valley.

"It is astonishingly beautiful, undeniably!" The diplomat calmly replied, hugging his wife while murmuring something in her ear.

"I have seen some of the most beautiful pictures taken from these slopes". I extended hand and opened my glove, revealing the cartridge well shielded from casual observers. There was a split second of hesitation by both; then, however, the *Nurse* grabbed the cartridge and promptly inserted it in her pocket. Our eyes crossed, creating an ever-lasting moment of trust.

Out of the blue the improbable struck me. The farce that was ultimately propagated by the KGB, the idea of traditional Western rejection of proposals or materials, especially by American diplomats, was conceivably just "active" disinformation. This cleverly formulated "fact" precluded any unorthodox approach by would be renegades, defectors and future assets to the West.

*   *   *

Three weeks later I visited West Germany, as an official of the National boxing federation during the European championship. The contact with my new American friends set off the constructive beginning of many years of a dedicated fight against the Soviet communism and the sinister security apparatus of the

KGB and State Security. I was initially accepted with caution; however, after freely submitting to a CIA administered polygraph and psychological tests, I became a full-fledged member of a winning professional team. My nights in Colon were sleepless due to lengthy debriefings, operational planning and specialized training.

In early 1977, I was approached by FCD and after an exceptional performance review and a thorough psychological evaluation, was offered the opportunity to join the West European or the North American section. The contingency to the final transition was the necessity of satisfactory passing an advanced English and Russian languages test.

Soon thereafter during my business trip to Kuwait, under the cover of deputy director of the Bulgarian National Soccer Federation, we carefully evaluated the new opportunity with the CIA. My supervising officer, John Mathews came from Frankfurt, Germany and we had lengthy dialogues and planning sessions. Mathews was of Slavic origin and had immigrated to the USA in early 1950s. After serving with distinction in the Marine Corps around the world, he eventually joined the CIA. A fluent Russian, Bulgarian and Turkish speaker, Alex emanated the moderate manners and phrenology of a college professor rather than the "James Bond" astuteness of a spy.

Prior to my departure, the station received an emergency cable from Langley. The Center strongly recommended that all necessary steps should be taken for me to rebuff the pending transfer. I was offered financial compensation for the loss of hard currency income I would otherwise gain working as diplomat stationed abroad. For the first time the CIA acknowledged that I was on its payroll, even though I never have asked, demanded or insisted on any compensation. Besides a bundle of $2000 that was ingeniously hidden and readily available for my specific needs, I never requested or accepted money. In the last calendar year, I had used only about $400 in total.

Deep in my mind I was certain that the US government would help me and my family in the foreseeable future in the case of financial hardship or specific needs. Anyhow, I never truly expected the highly professional and considerate approach of the American government.

In Kuwait I received new enhanced communications equipment consisting of a few advanced technical gadgets disguised as common office elements and others cleverly incorporated into a stereo cassette player AKAI. All of my nights passed by more or less sleeplessly; I was dedicated to intense training by two American technicians in secure, virtually constant communication with the Center. A new Swiss Tag-Hur photo-camera watch complemented my second camera, a unique mini MINOX with 3 revolving discs of highly sensitive film with 60 exposures each.

Returning back to the grimy socialist realities of Eastern Europe was not an easy task. For eight days I had enjoyed the lavish hospitality of the oil-rich Kuwaiti government, and covertly the overwhelming professional attention and camaraderie of my American colleagues. Regrettably, my real "playground" had to match my ultimate authority and incontestably was encompassed by the totalitarian communism.

GRINDING DOWN
THE KGB &
THE STATE SECURITY

SINGING CHAIR

My foreign intelligence job interviews cunningly set off an extraordinary CIA penetration of the FCD, the forearm of the Bulgarian State Security and the Soviet KGB foreign intelligence operations.

During my meetings with General Ivan Gorinov*, I obtained and captured detailed visuals and photos of his and the adjacent offices with my *"Tag"*. FCD visitors were normally escorted and carefully monitored. However, through my Party Committee duties of supervising the young operational officers and members of the communist party, I gained unsupervised visitor status to the party secretary Svetoslav Todorov, and was able to effortlessly probe both shallow and deep ponds of opportunity throughout the most secret directorate.

In the later stages, General Gorinov introduced me to the deputy Colonel Todor Genov and Ganu Ganev**, manager of the North American desk. The interviews went smooth and Colonel Ganev was impressed by my advanced training and substantial experience with surveillance and evasion techniques, dead drop operations, gathering of political and scientific-technology information, recruitment of foreigners and more. Most of these activities encompassed the quintessence of a successful foreign intelligence assignment. Lengthy intellectual and semi-psychological quizzes were thoughtfully carried out, and were consistently crossed with some of my previous testimonials for accuracy and attentiveness. Colonel Ganev finished the interview with a promising smile; he left the office by offering me a solid and friendly handshake.

Calmly waiting for General Gorinov's return, I walked around the room and, taking another chair, invisibly inserted a ballpoint pen cartridge into the chair's soft cushion. This cleverly designed and disguised delivery device concealed in a common looking ball pen assured precise insertion of the tiny cartridge in a desirable direction. The new technology cleverly outplayed metal or radiation detectors and all up to date KGB screening technologies.

Reliable FCD sources and my personal observations confirmed that foreign assignment review boards, senior management operational planning, and weekly

---

*   FCD, deputy director and chief of personnel.
** FCD, resident in Washington, DC 1983-86

127

KGB sessions were carried out at the same office. The offices of General Goriniv and the Director of Intelligence, General Vasil Kotzev, soon to be replaced by Vlado Todorov, flanked the executive conference center.

Coincidently, Langley received priceless benefits from this operation: Gorinov's wife Angelina was the personal assistant of Todor Zhivkov, the General Secretary of the communist party.

She unwittingly became the source of immense political information. In order to suitably collect the gathered information by the ultra modern remotely managed electronic bug, the CIA engineered and set off an elaborate plan, which lasted for almost 18 months.

A stationary center near the FCD building was needed to allowing American experts, dispatched from Greece, Turkey and Yugoslavia, to service and retrieve data. The solution came from the fact that autos were a scarce commodity in Eastern Europe. On my proposal, a Soviet made *Lada* was purchased in Greece and driven to a secure location in Bulgaria by a western tourist. It was exactly the same model, color and optioned car as my personal one, but with a very sophisticated security system and plenty of electronics stashed under the rear seat. All was craftily disguised as an amplifying system for the hi-fi radio-tape player.

From an arsenal of license plates surreptitiously obtained from the surveillance department (SID), I selected two pairs of credulous government and private license plates while Langley experts masterfully copied and developed two sets of registration documents. I designed the security procedure with the explicit knowledge that the FCD counter-intelligence staff regularly checked the surrounding neighborhoods.

The CIA's mobile eavesdropping center erroneously became a legitimate State Security car on official records, with current license plates and registration, in reality non-controllable by the traffic militia. As often as twice a week I drove the car around town by inconspicuously changing license plates. I obtained from the SID a pair of special license plates brackets and installed them on my personal car. The KGB ingeniously designed lever brackets, on which the male portion, attached to the license plate, could shift-slide to the left to unlock, and be pulled up free, and allowed quick and inconspicuous replacement.

The system was secure and advanced and was pre-set to erase all data in the case of unauthorized car entry. An electronic gadget in my pocket indicated if somebody got penetrated inside, or tampered with the locks or the doors. Perhaps the most demanding and inconvenient task became the car's maintenance during the winter months. Government cars were seldom left on the streets covered with snow. For this reason I normally used a set of private license plates. Unnoticed to anyone, I drove two cars as one.

This *magnum opus* intelligence operation continued until July of 1980. On July 11th, just four days before my family's summer vacation, the car disappeared and was never seen again. An almost forgotten mark left nearby my office assured that the car was in secure hands, and an electronic message confirmed the car's extraction, thus nullifying my exposure.

During a commendation ceremony at Langley years later, I learned that more than 3500 pages of top-secret materials and important KGB, State Security and government secret information had been transcribed out of this single successful operation carried out against the KGB and State Security's foreign intelligence. Unknown to me, the CIA had surreptitiously installed a special transmitter in a nearby apartment complex' phone box. This enabled the CIA residency to collect data through a new state of the art electronic burst communication process. Some of the CIA's most sophisticated direct satellite links were ingeniously managed from this location in an immediate proximity to the FCD's antennas and transmitters.

OPERATION "TWINS"

Combined KGB/State Security activities against North America prompted Langley's operational group to blueprint a new and thrilling undertaking: an electronic penetration of the inner sanctum of the American desk. The operation was conceitedly aimed at the nerve center of Bulgarian and Soviet foreign intelligence operations against the U.S.A. and North America.

My direct operational needs in the beginning of 1981 allowed me to convince General Peter Stoianov to request official information from FCD on the research and academic institutions in the USA and Canada of interest to the KGB and State Security. Soon Colonel Kiril Atanasov (A), one of the American political intelligence section managers, and a Science and Technology Section manager, Colonel Lubomir Michailov, informed me that they have hefty literary files* with information.

With the preliminary knowledge of the existence of the operational intelligence files, I asked Niki Pandev (A) while on a secure line, to provide the literary files for my review, instead of creating lengthy written assessments and analysis. Although it was strictly against the security norms and regulations of FCD, Pandev in two instances offered me 4 large binders with files, which I transported to my main State Security office in the black *Volga* limousine of my boss, Colonel Diankov. Pandev was reasonably secretive in delivering the files, for he ingenuously breached the security documentation exchange regulations in his actions. I correctly identified his mind-set as semi-lazy, and therefore suggested our concealed form of cooperation. Niki Pandev graduated from the Moscow Institute of International Relations (MIMO) and besides being fluent in Russian and English had completed an advanced course in Norwegian. Bright and intelligent, although married he was an unabashed womanizer, incessantly engaging in sexual affairs even with minor high school girls. He pathetically seduced his conquests with foreign gifts and a charismatic, persuasive and nonetheless flamboyant attitude. His Moscow years were an endless saga of Russian and foreign student seductions, including, but not limited to, amorous relations with two of his

---

*   Future minister of Internal Affairs and vice-president of Bulgaria.

university professors. In Bulgaria and in the Soviet Union Pandev recreationally practiced judo and karate without achieving any acclaim.

I promptly delivered the North American FCD files one by one to my safe houses. Specially dispatched CIA professionals, besides copying all the files, implanted in the folders' metal frames miniature ceramic transmitters. Langley struck a gold mine; vast information soon flowed virtually day and night. Although I never learned the life span of *"Twins"*, the KGB and State Security "modus operandi" in the USA and Canada have been utterly and irreversibly compromised. Coded communications were essentially broken down and offered the CIA stunning views of the Soviet's most secret global operations. Totalitarian communist intelligence was more than mortally wounded by these intricate subversions.

THE GENERAL STAFF

The USDIA (Department of Defense Intelligence Agency) and the CIA determined that specific intelligence collection should be aimed directly at the General Staff leadership of the Ministry of Defense, thus penetrating the primary southern flange of the Warsaw Pact. Regional NATO efforts were virtually fruitless since the "leftist's" takeover of Greece.

My relationship with General-Lieutenant Tzanu Bakalov, First Deputy of the General Staff of the Ministry of Defense, was more or less a polite and respectful matter among friendly relatives. He worked close with his compatriot and chief of the General Staff, General-Colonel Atanas Semerdzhiev*. We often visited our hunting and vacation retreat in Velingrad, the resort mineral spa town where we maintained our villas.

During a weekend dinner in the resort a few months later, I learned from General Backalov the outline of an "ingenious" debugging innovation. A routine swiping of the General Staff's offices by a military counter-intelligence technical team had discovered a signals generating device in one of the walls of the General Staff. Instead of a radical wall demolition, the military engineers came forward with an unorthodox proposal: They soaked the conference hall wall with a conducting saline solution and introduced a high cycling current of 12,000 Volts AC. The Soviet GRU utilized a new microwave device as well. The general's story went so far as to comically state "the device was so powerful a wave radiator that it was capable to cook people and house pets through the walls of a building." Unsuspecting neighbors had been urgently evacuated for the day of the cleansing.

The intelligence bug inadvertently compromised one of the most sophisticated American operations against the Bulgarian General Staff and the Ministry of National Defense. The CIA's inimitable operation was unfortunately lost, but not before allowing the United States authorities to learn with certainty about the deployment in Bulgaria (Samokov, Karlovo and Jambol region) of the new model SS20-22 *"Scud"* Soviet intercontinental missiles, capable of delivering nuclear and biological warheads to any target in Europe and the Mediterranean region.

---

* Intelligence Directorate of the Ministry of National Defense

Revealing dialogues with Generals Backalov, Petkovski and other members of the General Staff during a few hunting outings inadvertently revealed Bulgaria's military readiness; top-secret polygons were to be armed during the early 1983 with the "START-2" prohibited SS 23 nuclear warhead missiles. The secret polygons in the Strandzha region at Jambol's "*Kabile*", and Stara Zagora's "*Zmeevo*" were diligently compromised by the offhand remarks of Generals in seemingly friendly company.

The Soviet Union's leadership cunningly imposed this decision as a viable Warsaw Pact deterrent from the south, and specialized air force engineering units were trained in Azerbaijan and Kazakhstan in precise delivery of nuclear missiles.

The United States government received conclusive evidence about the series of grave violations committed by the Soviet Union and by the Warsaw Pact communist leadership. Despite the official declaration in front of the UN, by the General Secretary of the Bulgarian Communist Party, Todor Zhivkov, that Bulgaria would be maintained free from nuclear weapons, the country was eventually transformed by Moscow into one of the south-most nuclear protuberances of the Warsaw Pact. Bulgaria and the Soviet Union were in gross violation of international agreements and regional bilateral and multilateral norms and treaties.

Every year a team of Air force engineers was dispatched to Kazakhstan's top-secret center "*Kapustyn Yar*" for advanced training and preparation in launching intercontinental missiles armed with nuclear warheads. The Bulgarian missile flange was declared in the beginning of the 1983s the most accurate and combat ready among the Warsaw Pact's fraternal forces.

These dreadful findings, offhandedly gathered from the elite, eventually triggered overwhelming concerns among NATO experts. Within a month I was ordered to pursue another urgent task: the penetration of the apartments of the Chief of Staff, General-Colonel Atanas Semerdzhiev's and the Chairman of the Military foreign intelligence-RUMNO, General-Colonel Vasil Zikulov.

OPERATION "MAY DAY"

In a dark secluded lot on *Marin Drinov* street, just across the Fifth regional (militia) directorate, is located a classy, dark gray, well maintained apartment building of four floors. Colonel Michailov, chief architect of the Ministry of Defense, eventually persuaded the top brass of the Defense ministry to appropriate the well located lot from an executed tsarist general and designed and built a functional apartment complex. The elite of the Bulgarian military moved in, and Colonel Michailov secured a flat for himself on the third floor. The attic was developed into a few comfortable studios inhabited by the young generation of executives.

Through Michailov's daughter Mania, a close friend of mine, and her cousin Nikolai Michailov, I obtained keys to the building's entrance and utilized one of the attic studios as a "safe house" to clandestinely meet some agents. It was a well-situated studio, marvelously wood carved by the renowned artist Lubomir Nedev. The free spirited intellectuals' place radiated a wonderful ambiance for unrelenting parties, offered refuge for liberal amorous pursuits and unimaginably facilitated very intricate intelligence endeavors.

The existing house phone-intercom system and the dwelling of Colonel Michailov allowed an American technical team to successfully bug the flats of Generals Zikulov and Semerdzhiev. Virtually undetectable, the sophisticated transmitters in one of the wood carved roof columns served Langley's strategic interests for many months. An American diplomat living nearby collected the gathered intelligence directly from his flat. Some very sensitive information relevant to the Bulgarian and the Soviet Union's missile defense and nuclear offensive strategies and capabilities were gathered by this operation and warranted the decisive failures of the Soviet Union at a few successive UN negotiations.

The information gathered on Atanas Semerdzhiev allowed Langley experts to profile the general-colonel as a shockingly controversial, pertinently schizophrenic individual. A particularly questionable enigma emerged of Semerdzhiev's professional conduct and objectionable relationship with the Minister of National Defense, Army-General Dobry Dzhurov. His hidden eccentricity and excessive sexual quests were successfully exploited later on by a stealthy American asset and a prominent journalist.

General Zikulov's practice of continuously discussing, for hours every day (on his VCH phone), high priority foreign military intelligence matters was considered a major break-through in the long considered impenetrable, GRU controlled Bulgarian military foreign intelligence directorate-RUMNO. Some information was related back to me in an attempt to gather additional, missing or specific details. The new approach of RUMNO in getting actively involved in Science and Technology intelligence, under the umbrella guidance's of the Soviet KGB's T directorate, became clear. Thievery of western know-how, high technologies, embargoed systems and scientific research also became a new integral duty of the military foreign intelligence. The successful transfer and prompt implementation of advanced military technologies developed Bulgaria during the 1980s into one of the major weapons manufacturing, armament trading and smuggling countries in the world. A plentitude of military works mushroomed throughout the country, greatly contributing to the false and misleading sense of economic success and prosperity of developed socialism.

OPERATION "WINDFALL"

The State Security duty officer on the directorate or departmental level was entitled to access the keys of all rooms and in most instances even to the keys of each operational officer's safe. This loophole opportunity enabled the CIA to obtain room key imprints, safe keys, and safe security stamps and communications keys. Samples of letterheads, State Security top-secret stamps, military communications codebooks, surveillance codebooks and much more were obtained without the slightest trace of qualms or detection.

The spoils of conscious insider's deceitfulness and his "life or death" commitments gradually and imperceptibly eroded the inner sanctum of power and secrecy of the KGB and State Security systems. Many rooms of the Ministry of Internal Affairs, the KGB Center and State Security became readily accessible and susceptible to infiltration, eavesdropping, bugging and routine content review by CIA operational and technical teams.

This pathetically potent operation gravely compromised the strict security of the Minister of Internal Affairs, General-Colonel Dimitar Stoianov, the office of the Chairman of State Security and First Deputy Minister of Internal Affairs, General-Colonel Grigor Shopov, the office of the Director of the State Security archive, General-Major Nanka Serkedzhieva, the office of the KGB Director, General Ivan Savchenko and his deputy Colonel Vladilen Feodorov, the Sixth directorate KGB advisor, Colonel Levon Galustov, the office of the Chairman of Sixth Chief Directorate, General-Lieutenant Petur Stoianov, the Deputy Minister and Chief of Foreign Intelligence, General-Lieutenant Stoian Savov, General-Lieutenant George Anachkov, Director of Second Main Directorate-counterintelligence, General-Lieutenant George Purvanov, Director of the Fourth Directorate, General-Major George Milushev, Director of the Information and Analysis Directorate, and countless others.

The CIA's specific methodology of penetrating, monitoring, collecting and activating or deactivating programs is left untamed on the reasonable presumption that much of the technology utilized and the human capabilities involved was very advanced and perhaps is still active at the time of this writing. On the other hand, the latest KGB moles in the CIA and the FBI (in the intelligence game, an agency is never clean), may have learned about these staggering operations and perhaps have already compromised them. To the best of my knowledge, the CIA does not monitor the newly emerging Bulgarian democracy, as it is already a promising NATO partner. However, it has become a clear prudent duty of the new East European governments to never allow the return of devastating totalitarian communism.

* * *

A moment of historical significance in the American intelligence's triumphant fight against totalitarian communism was the first penetration of the Sofia Ministry of Internal Affairs by a CIA operational officer. The OTS, Langley's technical directorate, reproduced virtually undetectable copies of official KGB and State Security ID documents. Real names and artistic photos of SCD operational officers and KGB representatives were utilized, and an elaborate security and escape plan was set off in case of unforeseen failure or detection.

It was a late evening in November 1979 and 30 minutes earlier I had finished a young communist's leadership conference on the third floor of the Party committee. From the darkness of my office I quietly monitored two CIA officers (fluent Bulgarian and Russian speakers) approach the courtyard's fountain garden after coolly entering the otherwise impenetrable security bastion from the north entrance. A beeping sound on my pocket calculator had earlier indicated their drawing near and my prompt response code confirmed the mission and my positioning. A casual hand wave of one of the walking figures confirmed the communiqué and set a momentous visual contact. The two collectedly crossed the courtyard and casually following my instructions entered the main building using the side door next to the medical and dental offices.

For almost 2 hours the CIA professionals roamed freely through the office of the Minister of Internal Affairs, General-Colonel Dimitar Stoianov, and the KGB center. Completing the eternal journey through the "corridors of power," they eavesdropped on the main surveillance command and control center "Tzeko & Bore". Astute CIA operations were tapped into, and even the newly relocated office of the sole American surveillance section on "Tsar Simeon" Street was found to be craftily infiltrated and thereafter dully monitored.

It is an indispensable fact today that the nonviolent social cataclysms and the ultimate disintegration of the communism throughout Eastern Europe and the Soviet Union in the early 1990s was to a degree ascribed to the silent and dangerous work of few dyed-in-the-wool professionals. These daring individuals extensively grinded down and consistently undermined the strength and capabilities of the notorious KGB and State Security apparatus, and in essence crippled the main vitality of the totalitarianism, its "secret services."

Since their inception, these revolutionary proletarian institutions of national security, historically aimed all of their assets and defensive efforts outside the gamut of real vulnerability. The reds felt a consistent "White Scare," and always believed that subversive westerners were nearby, waiting and watching. The real threat of internal degradation, crippling morals, and lost hope was ignored. The KGB and State Security, similar to the Shutz Staffel (SS), grew vague, split, and peripatetic. Slowly they have become ineffective, mercilessly oppressive and nonetheless self-destructive as *"Governments inside Communists Governments"*.

My grandfather Tzolo Dimitrou in 1947, he was one of the wealthiest Orhanie farmers and entrepreneurs before the ruthless communist nationalizations of 1945-52. He was regional leader of the Agrarian party and well-respected community maverick.

(Courtesy of the author)

My mother (at left-standing) and her family in 1951. One of the last photos depicting the well-to-do family. Soon the final waves of the communist appropriations would take away our remaining land, machinery and livestock in the name of the Proletarian Revolution. I am just eight months old, cuddled by my grandmother.

(Courtesy of the author)

At ten years of age I became a member of the Young Communists. Ironically, their motto was "Always ready"—Vsegda gotov, the nom de plume given to me by the KGB in 1977. *(Courtesy of the author)*

I was one of the youngest State Security and KGB operational officers in 1970. *(DS archive)*

Rebecca and Dania, two Jewish girls, saved by my father from extermination in the Nazi's concentration camp Treblinka. He drove them to safety in a tank through the fascist blockade in 1942. My father's uncle D. Peshev, a Member of the Parliament, saved thousands Jewish families from deportation. *(Courtesy of the Peshev's archive)*

With fellow students at the State University "St. Climent of Ohrid". The man wearing glasses became successful illegal agent in Iran and Turkey. The one directly above him became State Security chief of the dominantly Turkish region of Kurdzhaly. *(Courtesy of the author)*

Leningrad, 1971 in front of the St. Vasilii basilica. I am with Soviet, Polish, and Bulgarian security officials and judo players. Kneeling is soon-to-be KGB officer and future president of Russia, Vladimir Putin.

(Courtesy of the author)

Munich, Germany 1972. I am in pursuit of Olympic glory in Judo.

(Courtesy of the author)

Hunting in the Rodopi Mountains with the General Secretary Todor Zhivkov, Kostadin Giaurov (Bulgarian ambassador in Mongolia), and Colonel Topkarov. Topkarov as chief of the Pazardzhik security prison was responsible for the strangling of the dissident Boris Arsov. *(Courtesy of the author)*

Cologne, Germany 1975. I was a counterintelligence officer of the Bulgarian national Judo team during the Europe tournament. *(Courtesy of the author)*

Visiting Bulgarian historical sights in 1973 with General-Colonel Alexey Bureniok, Chairman of the KGB Academy. At far-left is General Stoilov, Sliven Regional State Security Director. *(KGB/DS)*

Sofia, 1973. Kim Philby and KGB officials with the foreign intelligence Chairman Vasil Kotzev and his first deputy Luben Gozev.
(Courtesy of the author)

Kim Philby and Rufina Puhova in Sofia, 1973. Visiting the State Security Academy (the College) with bodyguard Lev.
(Courtesy of the author)

Ministry of Internal Affairs in Sofia. On the ground floor is the State Security archive. Second floor quarters the office of the Minister, General-colonel Dimitar Stoianov. During the Cold War the CIA, monitoring the stealthiest exploits of the totalitarian communism, clandestinely infiltrated them.

(Courtesy of the author)

A picnic with the State Security leaders of the Surveillance directorate, 1974. *(Courtesy of the author)*

The First Chief Directorate's building, the utmost KGB foreign intelligence arm. The thirteen floor quartered the North American section, where all operations against the United States of America were carried out. Since 1977, the CIA clandestinely penetrated this "sanctum-sanctorum". Illegal technology transfers and smugglings, political and economic disinformation, among a plentitude of underhanded operations against the west were craftily monitored for years and many cleverly thwarted.

(Courtesy of CIA and the author)

The State Security's, Second Chief Directorate, the KGB controlled counterintelligence monster. Fourth floor (fifth) quarters the American section, with external air conditioning available only to its chief. All devious State Security and KGB operations against Americans, the American Embassy and the Ambassador's Residency were craftily pre meditated and surreptitiously carried out from this juncture since 1960.

(Courtesy of CIA and the author)

My father (center), crossing the Bosphorus Strait during a daring State Security and KGB operation. Simultaneously, he is delivering weapons to rivaling Iran and Iraq. After my betrayal by the CIA's Aldrich Ames, my father was cruelly and lengthily investigated. Thereafter he was deliberately murdered by the State Security. *(Courtesy of the author)*

March 1983. A surreptitious surveillance photo catches my tail cleaning procedure in front of a major supermarket. Prudently, I aborted the clandestine meeting with the CIA. The KGB had ordered my apprehension. I was 72 hours away from freedom, or certain dead.
(State Security/KGB DOR "Nemesis" archive)

A surreptitious FCD photo taken moments after the completion of my intelligence assignment in Istanbul, Turkey, in 1976. Operating without diplomatic immunity, I had risked lengthy and harsh confinement in the name of the utopian communism. *(FCD archive)*

The Honorable Edward James Van de Velde. He was credited with saving my life from the KGB assassins in Antwerp, Belgium in 1987.

(Courtesy of the author)

There are tears in my eyes as I learn abou the collapse of the Soviet Union in 1991. Photo taken by a CIA colleague in the Paris Excelsior Hotel.

(Courtesy AvL)

With Jessie Jackson in the 1990s. We discuss operational details of his imminent mission to the warrnig Yugoslavia. As a result of Rev. Jackson's cunning endeavor, the Serbs freed the American prisoners of war.

(Courtesy of the Author)

Long Beach yacht Club, 1994. I prepare for sailing on the *Intrepid* with President Bill Clinton's ISAC advisors John Callos and Stu Kitz.

(Courtesy John Callos)

At my Friendly Hills, Los Angeles home in 1998. My wife Dominique and I entertain Thing Ben Han, CEO of GBM (the largest Chinese electronics manufacturer) and Tian Lei after completion of a multimillion-dollar motion technology business venture. *(Courtesy of the author)*

Rio de Janeiro, 1995. My inspirational wife Dominique and I leisurely celebrating my successful mission at the World Economic Summit in Sao Paulo, Brazil. *(Courtesy of the author)*

Hangzhou, China 1998. I am celebrating with the former General Secretary of the Chinese Young Communist Organization, Liu Wean, the first regional Chinese-American business venture. We are seated at the historic table that had hosted President Richard Nixon and the Chinese communist leader Mao Zedong in the 1970s. *(Courtesy of the author)*

Los Angeles, California 1998. As a General director of the largest west coast distiribution group, I meet witht the Vice President of the Philippines and a JAKA executive. We negotiated amultimillion-dollar business, transforming the "Clark" Air Force Base into one of the largest "Free Trade Zones" of the Pacific. *(Courtesy of the author)*

My wife Dominique, navigating the *Intrepid* with the aid of our daughter Larissa. We are entertaining visiting family along the Long Beach shores. *(Courtesy of the author)*

My inspirational family. Alex Jr., Larissa, Isabelle, and my wife Dominique as we happily welcome the 21st century. *(Courtesy of the author)*

DCI William J. (Bill) Casey, 1983 in Langley, Virginia. An incredible man, he considerably influenced my life. *(D. Brack)*

New York, April 2001. Months before the monstrous 09/11 terrorist attack against the World Trade Center, I attended the UN session on Global Economic Cooperation. *(Courtesy of the author)*

SOVIET INDUSTRIAL ESPIONAGE, TECHNOLOGY TRANSFER AND SOCIALIST PROSPERITY

SCIENCE AND TECHNOLOGY THIEVERY

B y the mid 1970s the KGB had developed a stealthy network of international semi-legitimate enterprises that were blessed by the highest Soviet officials. Endlessly pursuing thievery and smuggling of western industrial know-how, high technologies and scientific research and development, many of them achieved enormous success. Building up and sustaining a prosperous socialist economy by illicit means, however, was inevitably a short-lived communist paradigm. In reality the Marxist-Leninist ideological warfare evolved into grossly misleading propaganda and disinformation about the economic prosperity and the industrial capabilities of *"Developed Socialism"*. The growing western economic prosperity transformed the Kremlin's totalitarian apparatchiks into failing cheaters at home and sinister masterminds of global instability by indiscriminately selling armaments to hot areas of the globe.

My clandestine work with the United States government in painstakingly unmasking and exposing many of the Kremlin's intricate science and technology thievery and the illegal transfers of COCOM embargoed western systems and technologies became one of the most deplorable consequence of the Soviet communism. The unconventional Soviet leadership's decisions that the Warsaw Pact military, navy, air space, bio-chemical, pharmaceuticals, machine building and many more industrial sectors of the economy should be developed through elaborate, although illegal diversion and thievery of western technology, science and know-how was perplexing. These malevolent totalitarian communist acts were equal, if not even more destructive to the West than the East European government's sponsorship of leftist terrorism and radical religious movements. Undeniably shameful was the fact that the Warsaw Pact countries became deliberate perpetrators of international malice and socio-economic polarization under Soviet communist guidelines.

The answers to this appalling totalitarian approach should be undisputedly linked to Lenin and Stalin's hard-line beliefs that: *". . . Only through revolutions and annihilation of the world's richest democracies, and their imperialist and capitalist establishments, can a prosperous socialist society be established and inevitably made to flourish . . ."*

The Soviet Union's twofold standards towards western prosperity, including the prominence of Japan, Hong Kong, South Korea, Singapore and China, were the driving force for the creation of the most powerful science and technology intelligence institutions in modern history. These institutions, through their covert criminal undertakings, inevitably emerged as a main catalyst of the short-lived and misleading economic prosperity of the developed socialism.

Working with the Soviet KGB and Bulgarian State Security's Science and Technology Intelligence since 1976, and managing the academic and scientific exchange of scholars, scientists and academicians allowed me to deeply penetrate the *"sacrum-sanctum-sanctorum"* of the Communist leadership responsible for the economic and industrial growth of socialism.

*   *   *

In July 1976, Ognian Doinov, a member of the Central Committee of the Communist Party, and Prof. Ivan Popov, Chairman of the Committee for Science and Technology Progress, outlined in front of a secretive working group the new Soviet requirements of aggressively pursuing western high technologies and know-how, embargoed systems, scientific developments and research. The Communist leadership had just appointed Ognian Doinov as coordinating and controlling communist apparatchik of the scientific and technology *"revolution"* of the new socialist economy.

During the following few years working with Doinov, I on many occasions visited his two offices. The one at the State Council was equipped with a French manufactured safe that resembled the vault of a major bank and was Doinov's favorite, while the Central committee office was more or less an official party setting. Doinov's peculiarities were inimitable; when speaking, he never allowed interjections, even though most of the time he was a constantly smoking, never smiling listener. Behind his chair was his secret crypt of scientific and technology secrets, meticulously maintained by his advisors: Colonels Stoian Evtimov and Peter Hristozov—science and technology intelligence officers, Ivan Manev, Plamen Nikolov, Petar Tzankov and Luben Petrov—S&T senior specialists. Well-maintained red, brown and green folders concealed immeasurable information gathered from different sectors of the Soviet and the ComeCon economies. It was a succinct record of the needs, problems and anticipation's of the vital Soviet, Bulgarian and the Warsaw Pact countries' ministries and industrial sectors.

At Doinov's office I often encountered Colonel George Manchev, an old family friend and soon to become a general and chief of the Science and Technology intelligence directorate. In 1979 he replaced Colonel Dimitrov as leader of the S&T foreign intelligence, conceivably with Ognian Doinov's intrusion. Doinov possessed a strict secrecy code of ethics, which was maintained for all of the years

I worked with him and his staff. He was a naturally born conspirator, a former State Security agent; he had jumped up in the hierarchy to become in reality a strategic controller and guardian of his own former mentors.

By 1979 Ognian Doinov almost totally replaced Professor Ivan Popov from most of his responsibilities as Chairman of the State Committee for Science and Technology Progress, and set a precedent with his skyrocketing government and communist party carrier. The General Secretary Todor Zhivkov was intrigued and craftily lured by Doinov's in-depth knowledge of the Japanese's shrewd techniques of utilizing stolen American know-how, and unrelentingly supported Doinov. The macro and micro economic theories became Zhivkov's obsession and propelled the new multiplication management concepts of the developed socialism.

Doinov's operational principle, learned during his work in Japan was that any endeavor could be attained, even cunningly pulled off with money. It was a well calculated political and government decision catalyzed by Doinov's personal willingness for business and intelligence adventurisms. Todor Zhivkov, Army-General Dobry Dzhurov—Minister of Defense, Tano Tzolov—Chairman of the Science and Technology Progress Commission and Ognian Doinov made the most "industrious" decisions in peculiar and strict secrecy. In early 1980s Andrey Lucanov became integral member of the powerful group, joined in the early 1980s by the KGB's Science and Technology resident at the Soviet embassy in Sofia, Dr. Valentin Terehov. These political leaders perceptibly understood and realized the gargantuan consequences of their covert and ultimately criminal undertakings. The serious international and legal ramifications in case of even the slightest public disclosures or ominous intelligence failures would illustrate to the world the gravely deepening moral failure and illicit and reckless nature of the Soviet totalitarian socialism. Thus, so many operatives have been left to function "out in the cold" without any viable ways of government protection and security. Typical was the case in 1982 with Penu Kostadinov, a science and technology intelligence officer, grossly compromised through an incompetently carried trade craft of gathering Know-How in New York.

However, the future of developed socialism and the necessity of economic growth and the anticipated socio-economic prosperity was not a serious political and nonetheless financial gamble to be considered by the East European leadership. It was a given. To the communist apparatchiks, Stalin's revolutionary slogan was simple and clear:

"... *with all means fight the capitalist and imperialist main enemies, to defend and help the socialist motherland to prosper* ..."

The flagrant thievery of industrial, military, aerospace technology, components, research and development papers, scientific discoveries, embargoed industrial automation and computerized systems, chemical and bio-chemical products and many more, represented in actuality the vital necessity for sustaining and growing the Soviet and East European economy and industrial capabilities. No moral, ethical or legal norms could be obstacles or impediments for the KGB and State Security to fulfill the Soviet goals to economically and socially overtake the developed capitalist West.

By priority, Ognian Doinov's "secret chamber of wealth" soon became of enormous importance to the United States intelligence and the NATO's strategists. It contained some of the most secretive KGB and GRU assessments on western products, technology and equipment needed for rapid industrial implementations.

During late 1981 or early 1982, George Manchev introduced to our operational group an analytical KGB report describing the annual equivalent in US$ (convertible rubles) of the implemented western programs into the Soviet economy by industrial sectors. We were overwhelmed by the stunning figure of almost 3.7 billion dollars of annual savings accomplished by the Soviet Union. Doinov's adviser, Ivan Manev almost naively asked what the comparable Bulgarian figures were. Manchev, known to most of the participants under his cover as Director of the Science and Technology Institute, hesitantly turned to Doinov. Retrieving a red leather folder from the safe behind his chair, Ognian Doinov with a devilish face spelled out our illicit undertaking: for 1980, $538,000,000; and for 1981, by September alone, it totaled over $594,000,000. The dollar amount represented the cost Bulgaria should have paid to western institutions and corporations in order to obtain the broad spectrum of high technologies, military and industrial equipment and know-how. The figures blatantly represented information already stolen and implemented by State Security.

George Manchev further assessed that the Soviet Union for the period of 1979-1980 had utilized advanced technical information and equipment mostly from the USA, equal to more than 63% of total stolen tech. Around 11% was acquired from West Germany and from the United Kingdom and France around 8% equally. Once a leading provider of the Soviet industrial and technology espionage, Japanese miracle had slipped in the early 1980s to less than 2.5%. In the same period of time the KGB's "T" Scientific and Technology Intelligence directorate had obtained more than 3,200 scientific secret documents and more than 850 industrial samples from the West. As a result, 60 major industrial projects were initiated and more than 750 had already been completed.

Ognian Doinov's comparative disclosures to the group a few months later assessed that the State Security's Science and Technology intelligence (NTU) had acquired in the similar period of time roughly 486 secret documents from the West, consisting of more-than 40,000 pages and more-than 100 strictly embargoed industrial samples. By priority, most had been utilized in the development of the innovative sectors of the Bulgarian microelectronics, information storage and micro-processing industries. The military industrial complex alone had utilized substantial technologies and know-how, illegally obtained from the West, assuring business and economic opportunities.

In a stealthy rivalry with his closest friend Andrey Lucanov, a deeply rooted KGB asset for his Machiavellian secret connections with the Political Bureau of the Communist Party of the Soviet Union, Ognian Doinov developed a pragmatic relationship with Leonid Smirnov, the Chairman of the Soviet Union's High Military Industrial Commission, with Alexey Shokin, minister of electronic industry, with Ivan Silaev, Deputy Chairman of the State Council, and with many other high-ranking Soviet officials, including but not limited to senior Department of Defense officials. With Soviet help and consent, Doinov had derived and set in motion an equivalently powerful group in Bulgaria.

At this time I learned that KGB and GRU efforts had obtained and in production secretly utilized modern American military jet technologies, navy destroyers and even aircraft carriers designs. From the multi-purpose military transportation "Boeings" to the strategic B1 bombers and the F-16 and F-18 attack jets, not to mention AWAX radar and communications interceptors, the Soviet KGB and GRU had bluntly penetrated the most secretive western military institutions, industrial facilities and research centers. It should be known that the KGB's fraternal State Security cunningly conducted some of the best of these thieveries.

The creative "criminal" gambles and attempts of Warsaw Pact countries to overcome the western embargoes in reality were elevated to unofficial government policies. Many specialized international trading and research institutions were established and many western-manufacturing facilities were acquired with the sole purposes of facilitating the Soviet strategies and necessities. Towards the end of 1982, for example, a State Security intelligence agent in Great Britain successfully obtained the most secret aerospace software of "McDonald-Douglas" in the USA and a fully-fledged CAT-CAM computerized modeling and guiding system of "VAX 750".

With Ognian Doinov's growing semi-criminal inventiveness, and as a result of his remarkably growing political power and influence, the State Security's Science and Technology Intelligence received an almost unrestricted budget for operations, even though our group ironically generated and saved much of the government's money. Soon, however, Andrey Lucanov emerged as a contender to Doinov's free cowboy rides through the West. With palpable Soviet pressure, Lucanov was installed as a key money manager of the vast sums generated through Doinov's never ending channels of ingenuity and business development acumen. This was not a happy outcome for the General Secretary Todor Zhivkov, for since early 1981 he had been forced to obey any Soviet requests and recommendations.

Through my deepening contacts with General Savchenko and Colonel Ferov, it became unmistakable that Soviet leadership was growing concerned not only by the unorthodox "cultural diplomacy" of Ludmila Zhivkova, but also by Todor Zhivkov's alleged independent orientation of the Bulgarian economy towards cooperation with West Germany and Japan. Doinov was perceivably destined to sooner or later lose influence in favor of the stealthy Soviet and perhaps even western asset in Andrey Lucanov. During this time I received unsubstantiated information from the SCD that Lucanov was developing stealthy relations with western intelligence agencies*.

The "VAX 750" was promptly reproduced by "Izotimpex" at the "Industrial Technology Factory" in Sofia and sold to the Soviet Union's Central Missiles Control and Guidance Center. To the great intimidation of the senior Soviet scientific community, Bulgarian experts had greatly surpassed their efforts.

Although this acquisition alone saved the Soviet Union virtually immeasurable costs, the fact that State Security had offered to "Big Brother" one of the most desirable and necessary tools for successfully competing in the never ending militarization game with the West had more than symbolic effects. In many instances the greatly deceived and intentionally misinformed western intelligence underestimated the superior capabilities of State Security's foreign intelligence. To them, it was the Soviet Union's iron fist that controlled Warsaw Pact governments and directed countless illicit enterprises aimed at stealing western high technologies and ingenuously surpassing COCOM restrictions.

These secret multilateral dealings became a serious concern of the leading western democracies, especially after some of my detailed information reached the desks of two American Presidents and reaffirmed some earlier staggering findings by French intelligence.

In early 1980, one of my analytical reports to the CIA was accompanied with a few cartridges from my cleverly disguised "Minox". Through a successfully persuasive stint I obtained for review two of Ognian Doinov's "top-secret" folders in preparation for an academic exchange program in the USA of Professor Peter Gladkov, Dean of the Physics Faculty of Sofia State University. Two top-secret Soviet reports from the office of Leonid Smirnov, Chairman of the Soviet Union's Central Military Commission, unequivocally confirmed the illicit and destructive totalitarian approach towards pluralistic western democracies. As a senior CIA official proudly explained a few months later in West Germany, these particular

---

* Major K. Evgeniev, SCD—American section, disclosed in 1980 an ongoing investigation of Lucanov's contacts with a CIA officer in Sofia and his contacts with the CIA's Len Thomas in Switzerland during the late 1960s.

documents were of "explosive nature" and promptly reached the desk of American President Jimmy Carter in a special PDB* report.

* * *

Langley received evidence from the Sofia residency, that Ognian Doinov's office and the offices of other leading government members were electronically monitored. Through my Party committee liaison at Fourth Independent department (FID), Liliana Vasileva (a divorced and sensual young lady who spoke fluent German, English and Indonesian), I obtained substantial information on the inner workings of the special section of the Telephone Central designed to monitor the main government, military and party institutions of the capital. This information apparently allowed the CIA residency to successfully eavesdrop on the most secretive communications center since early 1981.

Vasileva acknowledge that Sixth department monitored Zhiivkov's son-in-law Ivan Slavkov, Chairman of the Bulgarian National Television and Ludmila Zhivkova's contacts with British socialite Peter Uvaliev. Vasileva was not privileged to know at that time that just a few years earlier I had personally worked on the Uvaliev's case.

The FID's operational feedbacks made me reevaluate my relationship with Ludmila Zhivkova and other high-ranking government officials. The necessity of an effective penetration and monitoring of Doinov's office and Dimitar Dimitrov's American desk were evaluated through different filters in order to allow the CIA to devise the most suitable methods. Furthermore, some new developments connected the Israeli Mossad and the KGB's special interests with Doinov and his connections with Armand Hammer and Robert Maxwell.

For the upcoming monthly meeting with Doinov's group (which occurred on every first Thursday of the month) I scheduled an appointment with Dimitar Dimoitrov and Ivan Milushev, the science and technology adviser of General Secretary Todor Zhivkov. A technical bugging team penetration was ruled out and only my personal commitment to the endeavor became a feasible solution. With caution and accuracy, and assuring ultimate concealment, I two weeks later implanted the remotely controlled devices during one of our meetings. Soon the information that was gathered prevented multi-billion dollar illegal transfers of embargoed high technology from the West.

In addition, a highly sensitive political liaison was unraveled between the KGB and the Israeli's Mossad that was ingeniously perpetrated through Doinov's

---

* Presidents Daily Briefing. Top-secret daily intelligence assessments for the Presidents of the USA.

deepening relationship with Robert Maxwell. In many instances the implanted microelectronics transcribed the secretariat's IBM typesetting. This allowed the CIA a direct glimpse at most typed in the office papers. It took me almost five years until I learned the magnitude and complexity of this thrilling endeavor that was perpetrated directly in the vital operational center of the totalitarian communism.

CLEVER SLOVAKIAN JEW

In recent Soviet and East European history, Ognian Doinov, a member of the Political Bureau of the Bulgarian Communist Party, should be credited with orchestrating the shrewdest totalitarian schemes for making hard currency through elaborate weapons and drugs smuggling channels and western technology thievery. His set-forth endeavors triggered unprecedented economic and industrial growth throughout the Soviet Union and Bulgaria that surpassed even the greatest expectations of Moscow. The man was not truly exposed to the Soviets until they forcefully installed the Soviet born party apparatchik Andrey Lucanov to oversee the Bulgarian financial operations with hard currencies, transferable Rubles* and the highly secretive *Program for hard currency reserves*.

A deeply rooted KGB asset, Lucanov divulged to Kremlin the mind-boggling stratagems of Bulgarian economic and industrial accomplishments. Western high technology thievery and cunning embargoed smuggling achieved by the State Security was promptly implemented in the promising sectors of the socialist economy.

Concurrently, Moscow's preferentially priced supplies of metals, coal and oil to the Soviet's *Sixteen Republic**, was continuously refined and sneakily re-exported by Bulgaria to the West, even as far as South Africa. Hard currency reserves in billions of dollars were set in West Germany, Switzerland and the United Kingdom, in essence without affecting the planned national resources. Various western companies were acquired and proprietary shell corporations with silent foreign partners were established in order to utilize Bulgarian and Soviet chemicals, pharmaceuticals, technology, products and partially assembled machinery. Thereafter, lucrative sales of western made products, automation and digital systems, CNC controlled machinery and metal cutting robotics equipment and commodities abounded.

---

*   Within the SIV (East European equivalent of EEC) the Ruble was used as a common currency for intergovernmental transactions and was pegged to the price of gold.

**   Common reference to Bulgaria as integral member of the Soviet union of socialist republics.

Ognian Doinov developed through the KGB and our State Security group exclusive contacts with leading western entrepreneurs, scientists, politicians, bankers and even civic leaders. Patronizing the xenophobic Ludmila Zhivkova's *"1300 Years Bulgaria"* and *"Banners of peace"* initiatives and wholly unchained by State Security interests while printing and promoting Todor Zhivkov's memoirs, Ognian Doinov established a mystifying relationship with philanthropists, media, finance and industrial moguls, such as Armand Hammer, Robert Maxwell, George Soros and Rupert Murdock.

Doinov's cronies Blagoi Ganev and Petar Tzankov went so far as to make an unsuccessful attempt in the early 1980s at liaisons with the Rockefeller group in New York. The eventual rebuff came as the result of serious implications that Hammer had led his group towards imprudent business and socio-political innuendoes with the Soviet Union. Behind Brezhnev's grayish Soviet communist apparatchiks and the senior KGB operatives of Yury Andropov cunningly hid a bunch of corrupt criminally inclined political chameleons. In the long run after the crumbling of the Soviet empire in 1991, they surfaced in the global business arena as filthily corrupt multi-millionaires.

Parallel contacts were developed with myriad leaders from Africa, Latin America and Asia. Doinov's acumen at successfully working with cross-cultural issues propelled him as a stealthy KGB liaison with the Jewish *saianims* * around the world. During the late 1970s he became an intermediary and introduced the KGB General Nikolai Leonov** to Robert Maxwell who was setting off an illicit Mossad business undertaking in the Panama Canal Zone.

The conniving pro-socialist Jew built up a local network of Russian Jews with the help of the KGB and exploited their stealthy relationship with General Omar Torijos. The same perfidious Mossad and KGB controlled network became functional far to the north in Nicaragua, where it provided Columbian drugs to the Sandinistas as well as the Contras. Ironically, both rivaling groups managed to collect money from smuggling drugs into the United States***.

The roles of the Soviet KGB, Bulgarian State Security, East German Stasi, as well as rather perplexingly the Israeli Mossad in this dirty trafficking of narcotics throughout Central America and into the United States should be closely reexamined. The role and activities of the shady "Doctor" Leonov, the KGB station chief in Mexico City, were dully documented and unequivocally confirmed Soviet attempts to callously erode and steadily destroy the moral

---

*   Jewish (Mossad) secret collaborators around the world.

**   High ranking KGB General and Deputy KGB Chairman, former director of information and
     analysis.

*** Court documents from the trail of Manuel Noriega in the USA, 1997.

values of the American society and nonetheless grate Mexican and some Latin American veracities.

Maxwell's *enigma*, as Doinov in chorus with Andrey Lucanov often referred to the British tycoon, should be explored further, for it illustrates his boundless business greed, stealthy acumen and nonetheless questionable affiliations, which inevitably led him to his ultimate demise.

By the early 1980s a small circle of highly connected KGB and State Security and party officials had dully utilized Petar Uvaliev's prominence in London. With devious KGB stratagems, they focused on few endowed Jewish targets, including but not limited to the left oriented British socialite Robert Maxwell and the Hungarian born George Soros in the United States. Years later, Soros became not only a compelling philanthropist and leader of the "Open Society" foundation, but also the foremost investor in Bulgaria and the Russian Federation. His vision and business acumen transformed vast former Soviet military industrial conglomerates into civilian, consumer oriented manufacturing enterprises.

Meanwhile, the Czech born Robert Maxwell recognized Ognian Doiniov's promising business wisdom. Greedily utilizing Doinov and Andrey Lucanov's vast business and political connections, Maxwell would embark on an East European quest that linked him in the early 1980 with the most powerful circles throughout the Warsaw Pact. However, Maxwell managed with the communist apparatchiks not only his personal wishes, but also mostly Mossad orchestrated stealthy agendas. An affluent and prominent man, he became the most powerful political link of Israel with the vast East European and especially the Soviet Jewish community. The most brilliant Soviet minds were of Jewish origin, but even so the Soviet leadership on contemptuous political, social, ethnic and religious grounds viciously and deliberately has been shattering the bond. From Szacharov to Shcharanski and Solzenitzin, the intellectual, scientific and academic brain of the Eastern European nations were grossly deprived and brutally subjugated by the totalitarianism.

As a messiah, Maxwell undertook the role of a moderator, craftily trading western secrets, western technology and political influence for pulling strings in respect to Israeli interests. Robert Maxwell's mission was far more than humanitarian and patriotic to his motherland Israel, where he was buried in the end of 1991 with the highest state honors.

Ognian Doinov and Andrey Lukanov worked in tandem at developing opportunistic undertakings with the help of Maxwell. Although I remember one of the first Uvaliev* assessments on Maxwell as categorically classifying him as a flamboyant *"buccaneer"* and a devious *"Jewish conniver"*, Doinov powerfully decided

---

*   Petur Uvaliev a.k.a. Pier Ruff, British intellectual of Bulgarian ancestry.

to override the unreliability findings. Not surprisingly, for at that time, Ognian Doinov had already been controlling Scientific and Technology intelligence (NTR) and fulfilled KGB's complex demands and guidelines behind the back of his closest adviser Colonel Stoian Evtimov.

Through the governmental and party connections craftily set forth throughout Eastern Europe, Robert Maxwell envisioned endless opportunities. Astutely cherishing the top communist brass, he stealthily bribed his way through lucrative and long-term business deals and commitments. Doinov and Lucanov set fort a specialized duo, managed by Colonels Lubcho Michailov and Vladimir Terehov, to stage-manage and control Maxwell's sudden infatuation with business opportunities in Bulgaria and the Soviet Union. With substantial hard currency payments from reserve accounts in Western Europe (especially Switzerland and Great Britain) Maxwell like a ghost craftily provided high technology and equipment (strictly embargoed by COCOM) to bogus British, Holland, German, Israeli and Greek companies.

Robert Maxwell should be credited today for helping Andrey Lucanov and Doinov to artfully develop the top secret programs *"Don"* and *"Neva"**, by providing computerized technology and equipment for data memory storage systems factories in Bulgaria and the Soviet Union.

Although the original project was developed by Doinov in mid 1970s with the help of Japanese experts and modeled on American technology utilization, by the early 1980s Maxwell's cronies, who were in reality Mossad agents, had helped NTR in surpassing the western embargo. They obtained microelectronic systems directly from the United States and Great Britain for similar undertakings in the Soviet Union's cities of Penza and Rostov on Don. These programs' implementations allowed Bulgaria to initially become a leading provider of memory devices for the needy East European industries and the burgeoning developing markets.

During the late 1970s the Science and Technology resident in Japan and in the 1980s in Singapore was Vlado Moskovv. Despite his Far East assignment, Moskovv was a frequent Doinov visitor, often departing with an armored briefcase crammed with more than a million US dollars. Vlado Moskow's work was well admired by Doinov. The culmination was his success in convincing *Mitzuy* executives to secretly send Japanese electronics experts to train and develop the new microelectronics plant in Pravetz, the birthplace of Todor Zhivkov.

At some point in January 1980, Ognian Doiniov calculated that NTR investments encompassed through Japan over five years had surpassed the one

---

* Bulgarian-Soviet joint programs for manufacturing of semiconductors and disc memory systems.

billion US dollars mark. However, the gross return had been more than $4 billion*. Analogous with Andrey Lucanov's stealthy Soviet interests, "*Izotimpex-InCo*" became a key center for electronics industrial espionage and computerized technology pirating under the astute management of the former Italian Science and Technology resident Asen Stamenov.

Doinov in the early 1980s appointed Ciril Mednikarov as General Manager of the new highly secretive enterprise "*Techinvest*", a company specialized in illegal transfers, thievery and the witty pirating of advanced Western machines and digital/CNC controlled systems. Mednicarov was Doinov's boss at "Balkancarexport" during his work in Japan, and under the new reversed roles embarked on a grand scale pirated machine-building endeavor, including a joint venture with the British conglomerate "*Lancing*", facilitated by Maxwell. By the mid 1980s, more than 17000 specialized machines were manufactured annually, primarily as exports to Western Europe, the U.S.A., the Middle East and Latin America.

Almost on a barter trading sting, Maxwell helped Doinov along with Lucanov to build up relationships not only with leading western companies, Soviet apparatchiks and shady gray industry leaders, but also with a plethora of left oriented and non-alliance movement African and Asian groups. No sooner had some promising business undertakings started to materialize than State Security discovered that hushed KGB interests and Israeli Mossad backed innuendoes had been craftily set in motion.

At that time I realized that a special interests bond was developing between Andrey Lucanov, Ognian Doinov and Robert Maxwell. The "*Siberian winds and the wolfs*"** have emerged as a strong and reliable partners.

Andrey Lucanov reticently mentioned during a hunting trip to Satovcha in the Rodopa Mountain that Maxwell had been associated with the monstrous Russian Jewish Mafia. What was he referring to was in reality a grand scale deception, craftily intermingling totalitarian criminal pursuits with western intelligence services interests and Israeli Mossad undertakings by the KGB and State Security. Political and economic information, as well as diverse technology and commodities, secretly exchanged hands as poker cards under the table, solidifying each group's financial interests and building a devious network of camaraderie and "socialist" prosperity.

---

*   Through Japan NTR has been purchasing technology and systems, difficult to acquire in the west. Substantial funds from this period are controlled today by *Masanobu Seya* San in Tokyo, Japan.
** Reference of the powerful underground Soviet Jewish organization, helping the "*Gulags*" victims and prisoners.

"... *We need the global Jewish networks in order to generate business and establish reliable contacts. They (Maxwell, Soros, etc.) are wealthy, although greedy for money, though they need assistance with Soviet and East European Jewish issues...*" Ognian Doinov sardonically assessed in May 1981 upon his return from a trip to London.

From the publishing, printing and media benefits of serving the First family of Todor Zhivkov, and the foundations *"1300 Years Bulgaria"* and *"Banner of Peace"*, Maxwell embarked on the lucrative exportation of Bulgarian made chemicals and pharmaceuticals to the west in a few years. Astutely manipulated by Ognian Doinov and the minister of Chemical industry, George Pankov, Maxwell got deep into the development of a pharmaceuticals (antibiotics) factory in Razgrad, Bulgaria, and facilitated embargoed French and Belgium technology and strategic substances for more than ten million dollars. In a big publicity stunt years later, Robert Maxwell, pretending to be a leading western philanthropist, donated two planeloads of medications to Bulgaria in exchange for the opportunity to set a multinational business development arm of his Maxwell Communications Co. in Eastern Europe. Linking three Bulgarian banks with a western style management training facility and numerous business and industrial enterprises, Maxwell *de facto* set a stepping stone in Bulgaria and the Balkans that dominantly served western and Israeli strategic interests. Furthermore, substantial western funds have been artfully siphoned trough the new Bulgarian bank from Russian enterprises to Switzerland and UK, thus setting a government sponsored money laundering channels for Maxwell. Investments made in Bulgaria by Maxwell to these undertakings totaling US$ 2.5 million were traced to the Israeli—Mossad controlled *Safra Bank** in the UK and Switzerland by a joint KGB and State Security team.

During a staff meeting in early 1983, Doinov perceptively outlined his uncertainty with Maxwell's ventures. However, overwhelmed by Maxwell's humble Jewish background and a *Phoenix* like ability to recover from business and financial failures, Doinov described him on a mystic pedestal of human triumph. Perhaps devious supplementary planning was in the making, for in mid 1985 his strongman status gradually eroded under mounting Soviet allegations of western favoritism and nonetheless rumors of financial divergences. Perhaps, by that time Doinov already had become a rather uncomfortable witness of Andrey Lucanov's undertakings not only with the KGB, but most importantly with some secret British interests.

By the second half of the 1980s, it became clear that Robert Maxwell was functioning as a bankroller for multiple Mossad operations around the world,

---

* Republican National Bank of New York.

nonetheless assuring and developing viable secret liaisons of Israeli officials with the new breed of KGB generals and the shady Russian Jewish Mafia.

My sealed bond with the KGB center revealed growing Soviet interests in Ognian Doinov and his activities. Perplexingly, secret information discussed at operational meetings with Doinov started surfacing in the hands of General Savchenko and Colonel Ferov in June 1979. Casually, but most often during prearranged clandestine meetings with Ferov, I was asked to analyze specific strategies, details, goals and intents of Doinov.

Strikingly mistrustful, the KGB grew suspicious of Doinov's extensive knowledge of vital Soviet industries and the possibility of relating top-secret information to the west through his contacts. With the acquisition of western know-how and embargoed technology, Doinov and Lucanov ingeniously set forth the development of modern companies in the Soviet Union, and not without astutely utilizing western assets such as Robert Maxwell. Thus the KGB unraveled the operations of Doinov, Lucanov and Maxwell by gradually linking their success to an apparent flow of restricted information, money laundering and closed links with greedy and powerful Soviet communist and industry leaders, as well as prominent (former Soviet) Jewish interests abroad.

On February 12, 1983, Ferov disclosed to me a secret KGB document recounting Maxwell's perplexing connections with former Soviet Jewish immigrants in Israel, Hungary, the United Kingdom, Africa and especially in the United States (New York in particular). The document clearly outlined that Maxwell had set up more than 360 companies worldwide with the help and participation of Russian Jewish immigrants, most of them with illicit inclinations. The KGB code name of Robert Maxwell was *"Philanderer"*. With his gregarious attitude and conniving mind, Robert Maxwell should be designated a *Godfather* of the Russian Red mafia (greatly dominated by astute Soviet Jews) and sensibly associated with the most potent and capable business and financial circles around the world. Murat Balagura, boss of the Russian mafia in New York, and his counterpart in Moscow and Israel, Semion Mogilevich, were described as secret Maxwell contacts and liaisons with Russian-Jewish criminals and the *Safra bank* in Zurich and New York. With the same gregarious impudence, Maxwell nonetheless craftily has been developing and manipulating Ognian Doinov and to some peculiar extents Andrey Lucanov.

By the mid 1980s Maxwell became a vivid collector of East European art through the KGB/State Security company *Multiart* managed by Ilia Pavlov, son-in-law of General Chergilanov, Chief of the Bulgarian military counterintelligence. Ilia Pavlov, a reputed Bulgarian crime lord and president of *Multigrup* became a leading East European billionaire in the 1990s. Cunningly exploiting Maxwell, Doinov, Lucanov and Zhivko Popov's connections and stratagems, he was murdered years later by the never forgetful Russian Red mafia assassins. The faultless sniper shot had followed the public execution of Andrey Lucanov, former Bulgarian Prime Minister. Both had apparently bridged off contractual agreements with the energy giants *Gasprom and Topenergy*, which were astutely managed and controlled by the Russian Mafia.

*　　*　　*

After the collapse of communism throughout Eastern Europe, Ognian Doinov silently escaped persecution for embezzlement and corruption and out of the blue became the East European Director of Maxwell Communications Corporation in London, managing even his old cronies Blagoi Ganev and Ivo Janchev. Maxwell's stealthy interests with Russia's shady economy and developing African nations received fresh blood through Doinov's high level political and business connections and never ending shameful initiatives.

Linking Robert Maxwell with Grigorii Luchiansky's *Nordex* and Hodorkovsky's *Jucos Enterprise* allowed Ognian Doiniov to deeply immerse himself in the sanctum sanctorum of the Russian Mafia and the shrewd regional Jewish interests. The energy and metallurgy sectors of the Soviet Union overnight became ingested with western and local—gray economy cash that was craftily and semi-gregariously delivered, laundered and invested by Maxwell and his cronies.

On September 19, 1991 with the exceptional help of the British Secret Service, we organized my casual reunion with Ognian Doiniov during his lunch break in downtown London. Approaching *Indigo Jones* restaurant near the Bow Street, I made myself genuinely stunned to face my former boss through the windowpane. Visibly aged since our last meeting eight years earlier, his shoulders had crooked even further under the heavy burdens of invisible physical and perhaps excruciating physiological burdens.

"... You are in exile, so am I ... No attachments to the old system ... ?"

Doinov murmured the metaphorical query with a devilishly composed face, demarcating his uncertain status as a formerly powerful man that had been gruesomely persecuted by his own communist cronies. The lunch came as a more or less wonderful opportunity to assess our current and past projects. Doinov sounded content with the British prospects and was thrilled by Maxwell's promising business endeavors. Immediately after his extrication, he had received an invitation to become an advisor to the cabinet of the Mozambique's President Francisco Caravalo, but Maxwell had swayed him away by doubling his salary and craftily signifying the future utilization of the African region for new business.

With Doinov's astuteness, Robert Maxwell invited President Caravalo to London and, shrewdly surpassing the British monarch's protocol, had developed the African nation into a viable media business partner. Doinov proudly assessed that he had developed business for Maxwell Communications Holding and

Mirror Group newspapers in Mozambique, Kenya, Zimbabwe and Nigeria. He was conceited of these achievements and gaudily attributed them to his latest wage increase. Agitated, Doinov mentioned growing Jewish contention in the London financial district as the main impediment to his and Maxwell's business goals. He eloquently expressed distress that Maxwell Communications' Holding company, Mirror Group (MGN), which had recently gone public with its IPO, had become a victim of grand scale market manipulations. At that time, Doinov was evidently not aware that Robert Maxwell and his main holding company were already deeply in debt, facing not only sinister enemies, but also hordes of conservative bankers. However, Doinov firmly expressed belief in the unlimited virtues of the maverick *Captain Bob* and his sons Kevin and Ian. He sounded deeply battered by Andrey Lucanov's insinuations and treachery as a short-lived Prime Minister, and intensely puffing his cigarette, more or less vengefully whispered:

"*. . . Do you know that Andrey was a conduit with the CIA in Rome**? He balanced the KGB's plans for Zhivkov's overthrow with the same CIA guy who tipped the KGB off about your defection . . .*" A shiver jolted down my spine; disgustingly foreseeing a devilish stratagem, I soon calmed to realize that Doinov was forthright.

"*. . . Information about your work with the CIA in the United States came to the Polit Bureau four years ago directly from the KGB Chairman. They had information from a senior CIA asset working for the KGB in Italy . . . and Zhivkov . . . oh, he was perplexed and dumbfounded for months . . .*"

Ognian Doinov was forthcoming yet more or less secretive, for he knew well how to serve many masters. Perhaps he already envisioned future cooperation with the CIA. By all means he was disturbed by the fact that Robert Maxwell had hired Andrey Lucanov as Maxwell Communications' Russian and Bulgarian operations counselor, in essence limiting his responsibility. The former Bulgarian Prime Minister had already arrived in London with his family and received a lavish accommodation. Backed by powerful Russian interests and anxious to take over most of the stealthy operations, Lucanov had emerged as an imminent hindrance to Doinov's job.

At this juncture Doinov lowered voice and calculatedly whispered:

"*. . . I lately helped Maxwell clan (referring to Robert and his son Kevin) to raise capital through Montagu Bank, injecting his stock net asset value; however he is going down, desperately in need of cash . . . perhaps for this reason Andrey was catapulted here so fast . . .*"

---

* Ironically Andrey Lucanov's American contact in Rome was Aldridge Ames, the KGB moll inside the CIA.

Doinov also mockingly referred to the vast dollars reserve Lucanov controlled in the past:

"... *Andrey helped Bob (Maxwell) to meet secretly with Vladimir Kruchkow* in Split, setting off the Israeli support for the coup d'etat against Gorbachov. As a result of some new relaxed Jewish immigration policy that was instituted by Moscow, he expects 500 million dollars from Israel as a pay off to Kremlin. However, he needs the cash to save his companies from business restructuring ...*"

Ognian Doinov stealthily tipped me, and thus the CIA, about something as controversial as the collapse of the Soviet communism and the terrible Jewish Gulags in Siberia. He assessed the developments in the Soviet Union as flummoxing, stipulating that Lucanov's *"muzhiki"* (mafia) and KGB connections had been craftily transformed into a powerful global network. Talking without restraint about his role in guiding Grigorii Luchanski to build *Nordex* into the largest diversified Russian conglomerate, Doinov delineated Maxwell's entrenched ties with the Red and the Jewish mafia and his control of more than 70 companies established already throughout Russia.

The meeting was somehow cut short, for Doinov had to sustain his workaholic demeanor. After we agreed to get together for a dinner the following evening at the *Jerrold's Pub*, he hastily crossed the street. I expected to extrapolate more about Robert Maxwell and his and Andrey Lucanov's London and Russian endeavors; however, the *"hunchback"* locked his destiny in secrecy.

The next day dinner was more or less a courteous settlement of our first dialogue. Doinov was very concerned with his impending indictment in Bulgaria, and perhaps even more with my sudden show up. Delineating my American government (CIA) connections, he laughably rebutted his old comments about Bulgarian former Prime Minister, for he was uncertain who Lucanov's real masters were.

*　　*　　*

A few weeks later in the beginning of November 1991, Robert Maxwell drowned near the island of Tenerife, from an apparently incidental fall overboard his luxury yacht *Lady Ghislaine*. Short of receiving the multimillion-dollar savior payment from Israel, he left Maxwell Communications Corporation grossly depleted of pension funds and the Mirror Group indebted of 2.3 billion Pounds.

Back in Gibraltar, in the midst of deepening investigations *Lady Ghislaine* lost its trusted yacht butler, a former Soviet Jew, to apparently merciless wharf

---

*　Chairman of the KGB.

muggers. Ognian Doinov was indicted for totalitarian crimes by his compatriots in Sofia, and after guiding the new Russian barons and few entrepreneurial Bulgarian gangsters to business stardom, was coldheartedly discarded, soon to succumb to cancer in relative obscurity in Vienna, Austria.

The CIA maintained a stealthy and courteous relationship with Ognian Doinov and his brother Emo in Vienna for a certain period of time and receiving needed information and assessments. After Doinov's funeral in Sofia, his older son Rumen elected to rebuff our warnings of behind the scenes life and was deviously silenced; however, prior to his death he reveal two secret Swiss accounts to a band of heavyset Russian sambists*.

Former PM Andrey Lucanov and his disenchanted Russian wife Lillia returned to Sofia, and upheld a stealthy relationship with the same group of powerful Russian executives who had cunningly utilized Doinov beforehand. Machiavellian and deceitful, Lucanov with few of his cronies grossly compromised a multibillion dollar Red Russian Mafia energy business in Bulgaria and Turkey, and as a result was gunned down in the mid 1990s, notwithstanding diligent CIA attempts to save his life.

---

*   Sambo—self defense without weapons, Russian martial art sport.

RUSSIAN ROULETTE

T he Fourth Directorate, located on the outskirts of Bankia near Sofia, was one of the most secretive KGB and State Security institutions in the Balkans. It received a modern new building during the 1970s, equipped with some of the most powerful computers and communication equipment in the entire Warsaw Pact. The director, General-Lieutenant George Purvanov, maintained his main office on the second floor of the Ministry of Internal Affairs, near the KGB center. His secretary Lydia was a beautiful and vivacious young lady, married to the alcoholic driver of General Kostadin Kotzaliev, the Director of the Main Investigative Directorate. I regularly visited Lydia Boneva's office to collect information on scientific and technology broadcasts and publications of Radio Free Europe and the BBC that was jammed by the directorate's powerful transmitters. My flattering attention gradually developed a trustworthy relationship with Lydia, who assisted the KGB center with translations and administrative support as well.

In the beginning of October 1977, General Ivan Savchenko invited me to a private celebration of the 60th anniversary of the October revolution at the KGB villa in Simeonovo.

On a warm Friday evening a few days later, I rang the front door of the secluded villa at the heavily guarded compounds of the State Security academy. Snezha Ovcharova, Savchenko's main assistant, kindly opened the door and I soon found out that I was the only State Security officer invited. The atmosphere was relaxing; a corner table in the main living room was full of tasty dishes, and an adjacent bar offered a variety of drinks next to a cozy, wood-burning fireplace. Patriotic Soviet music accentuated the event, as a solid oak table was skillfully set for the dinner.

Before long the patriotic sentiments faded away, as gradually captivated Soviet "Chekists"* encircled the sizzling young ladies on the dancing floor. A playful Russian harmonica permanently replaced the patriotic hymns, contributing to a jovial exhilaration. A Cossack fur hat started flying from head to head, allowing

---

* KGB operational officers' name from the period of—Felix Dzherdzhinski's (Che Ka) *Chrezvizhainaia Komisia.*

the playful men to change dancing partners in motion. A stealthy fraternal family celebrated the revolution which 60 years earlier had set forth the beginning of the Leninist proletarian communalism.

A little past midnight Natalia Primova, Colonel Ferov's assistant, guided General Savchenko to the door. As time progressed he had become semi intoxicated. Assisting him with the overcoat, Natalia devilishly rotated her big blue eyes and extended a long middle finger behind his back in a weird gesticulation.

The group loudly acclaimed the wily courage, as the general silly lifted eyebrows before heading for his villa in the darkness of the night.

Vladi Ferov merrily embraced his sensual secretary for a tango. The rhythms soon changed to the revolutionary *Katusha* and the tempo augmented to a joyful elation. The harmonica player artfully stepped forward, mixing Russian *kazachok* with Bulgarian *ruchenik**, making us truly immersed in the celebration. With the final accords, Ferov's secretary unbuttoned her blouse and genially removing her wet bra wiped the Colonel's red face, at the same time casually displaying a beautiful torso. Laughter and claps exploded as the Colonel blubbering rubbed his nose in the damped bra. Natalia tied the blouse ends and her nipples sensually popped out.

After few dances and a growing euphoria, meaningfully the main candelabrum was dimmed. Pulling Snezha Ovcharova near the diner table, Lidia handily cleared glasses and plates and removing shoes they easily ascended on the tabletop. Natalia excitingly started clapping hands as the pair seductively started a slow body dance. Soon, Vladi Ferov buoyantly and gregariously drew a bill and inserted it inside Snezha's blouse. A gracious stacking of bills in the blouses and the bras of the dancing girls followed.

I nonchalantly inserted a bill in Lydia's bra while she invitingly smiled. The exhilaration mounted when Vladi squirted the dancers with a bottle of Champagne and calming the yelp, he stoically requested them to one by one remove their clothes. We eagerly continued putting money down, as Vladi rolled a new bill and inserting it in Snezha's skirt, slowly but surely dragged it downward. The table exploded in amusement as he kissed her necked thigh. Bills and clothing soon covered the table as the ladies audaciously continued dancing necked. Natalia shrewdly distorted the sleazy daze, and unbuttoning her shirt, resolutely demanded that all man get undressed as well.

Vladi Ferov removed his shirt and with a commanding gesture made us follow. Everything evolved so hastily and went far beyond my slightest expectations without any feasible ways out.

---

*   Russian and Bulgarian folklore dances.

Two of the naked ladies pulled Vladi Ferov up on the table and playfully finished undressing him. Embracing and dancing with Snezha, the Colonel seductively started exploring her promising body. Coming behind me, Lidia elatedly finished unbuttoning my shirt, encouragingly bonding her wonderful chest to mine. Discreetly pulling me to a chair, she conspiratorially whispered: "I like to be with you. But they have surprise for you. Be careful!"

Somebody calculatedly placed a chair on the table and the naked Vladi promptly found refuge for his excitement. With an unexpected surprise Natalia covered his privates with a creamy slice of the Revolutionary cake. We exploded in hilarious laughter, and encouragements hit the roof when Natalia with a long tongue tasted the cream. Snezha, meandering forward, seductively licked away some of the cream covering the Colonel's privy, revealing her natural treasures. Slowly she mounted the Colonel's laps and without delay he slowly and gaudily penetrated her. An invigorating copulation continued for a while, though the creamy substance ludicrously and palpably enhanced or perhaps tarnished the act.

"... Come inside! Inside! Come inside ...!" Natalia sung the popular Visotzky's whimper, as Major Valery Dubinin embraced her from behind, playfully holding her breasts and cheering at the Colonel's patrician play. It was stunning to observe the serious, powerful and impersonal Colonel Vladi Ferov in this act of frivoling Roman orgy. The seductive atmosphere and the rhythmic music were electrifying and everyone poignantly fulfilled their innate Freudian human wishes for pleasure. Lydia eagerly held me, shivering in anticipation and growing passion, when Natalia suddenly rolled between us with a bottle of Champaign. She elbowed Lydia and possessively hooked a hand around my neck. Rubbing her breasts on my chest, she hastily jumped; locking legs on my waist and with refined motions assured my excitement. Perfunctorily shored up by my hold, Natalia blissfully invigorated my vitality.

Although semi-blinded by the spotlights, I noticed Vladi Ferov retiring to a nearby room. A large mirror on the adjacent wall was in dissonance with the interior. Next to us Valery Dubinin unbearably hugged Lydia and smoothly sat her on his laps. His hold emerged inexorable, for singing the *Cavalry* march of Budiony* he soon trotted his rider, manifestly controlling her gorgeous body.

My pleasurable encounter with the famous former Soviet national gymnast champion and KGB officer slowed with Vladi's return. Natalia unceremoniously jumped onto the floor and handed me the Champaign. Filling up the glasses, I lowered the bottle and squirted some sparkles on Lydia's chest. Shrieking, she instinctively moved aside, revealing the mighty toy she was coddling on. Dubinin

---

*   Famous Russian Cossack, legendary marshal.

foolishly displayed his impressive givens and blatantly swearing, emptied the bottle onto his privates. Disappearing in the kitchen, Lydia came back coolly holding a few large towels and a robe. She contentedly wiped us and then the floor.

On the other side of the table, the chair was moved to the floor and a new horse riding game was unleashed with a full swing. Zhenia Aneva was in a trivial pursuit of getting a bout of Chekist's hormones from Ferov's deputy, Major Oleg Artiomov. She was inebriated, uncontrollably and powerfully swinging in attempts to please or to be pleased.

Wrapped in robes, Natalia and Lydia cleaned the table and the floor. Coming close to me, Lydia earnestly pushed me on a chair, lightheartedly taking away my waist towel. With a resolute and controlling movement Lydia mounted me, letting her robe off her shoulders. Undeniably sensual, she made us the center of attention as Ferov vanished behind the walls of the secret chamber. Joyfully exhausted, a few minutes later I tied the towel around my waist as Lydia palpably disappeared in the kitchen.

Oleg Artiomov slowly rotated Zhenia at the edge of the table and his tiger hold resolutely glided him towards her anus. Perceptibly uncomfortable, Zhenia attempted to defy; however, no matter how she tried, she was sadistically sodomized and triggered the Russian's euphoria.

I was innocently unaware of the traditionally opulent Russian orgies, though stories about the licentious Russian "naked dancing" and "spousal swapping" abounded.

It was perplexing how these drinking binges and unrestricted sexual encounters made everyone equally communal, followed by stern rules of submission, discretion and deadly silence. The Italian *Omerta** was reincarnated by the communist plutocracy; it assured a silent and bonding fraternity, ranging from licentious behavior and nepotisms, to enormous material, economic and political interests.

*   *   *

Early in the morning, semi-dog-tired, I drove Lydia to her apartment near the national investigative service, my tape recorder clearly catching her chatter:

". . . Snezha's story is too long for today! However, be aware that her husband was an operational officer of our directorate in Paris, but . . . he is not anymore . . ." Displaying signs of getting inebriated, Lydia depicted Ovcharov's Paris affairs ranging from sex liaisons with embassy's political officer, to a Russian socialite, a French intelligence agent and even few French prostitutes. As a result of

---

*   Sicilian Mafia oat of silence.

Ovcharov's transgressions, the French *Securite** had eventually approached him with a recruitment pitch that had gone awry, and promptly recalled to Sofia, he was consequently fired from State Security in late 1977.

While the Bulgarian embassy cipher officer Ovcharov worked on various "glamorous" fields in Paris, his wife Snezha worked as a translator at the Fourth independent department, listening and transcribing State Security radio-electronic and telephone taps. During a joint KGB operation, she had eventually befriended Colonel Ferov, and soon after became his secret lover and was transferred to work at the KGB center.

For years, top-secret information flew from Lydia's overstuffed basket and her confidential sincerity. Grossly mistreated by her abusive husband, she found sanctuary and comfort in my comradeship and considerations.

---

*   French counterintelligence agency.

OPERATION "UNRESTRAINT"

T he windows of the KGB Secretariat glowed in the dark courtyard of the Ministry of Internal Affairs. Lydia and some of my eternal friends were still working this early March 1980 evening. Warm spring winds had gradually started to melt the last winter snow.

An early call from Lydia revealed that her boss, General George Purvanov, had departed to the club *Slavianska Beseda's* celebration of the upcoming women's day. Forgetting to pay tribute and consideration to a special lady asset, friend, lover, agent or a wife was considered a grave misdeed and normally was a long haunting mistake.

Through stealthy connections at the diplomatic Duty Free shop of BODC* I purchased gifts for my invaluable female assets. I stealthily secured the secret loyalty, attention and indispensable cooperation of more than two dozen intelligent and powerful women that vitally connected with the operations of the totalitarian government. ** I additionally effectively controlled 39 male secret agents. All of my clandestine assets, under the auspices of assisting the KGB and State Security, in reality diligently fulfilled the CIA's and NATO's specific goals and interests.

The women's never ending seductive work abilities became a paradoxical trend for the operational recruitments. One of my classmates and friends, Vladimir Nikolov from FCD-foreign intelligence, department fourteen (cultural and historic heritage), sinisterly assessed once:

---

*   Bureau for services of the diplomatic corps.

**   Four sources at the Ministry of Internal Affairs & State Security (Lydia, Natalia, Snezha and Liliana Vasileva from Fourth Independent Department), two at Kintex and Metalchim (Zdravka and Nely), one in RUMNO-military foreign intelligence (Svetla Daskalova), two at FCD-foreign intelligence (Ventzyslava and Iskra), two at the Central Committee of the Communist Party (Anelia P. and Sashka). One at the State Council (Clara M.), two at the Ministry of Foreign Affairs (Antonia and Rosytza), one at the Foreign Passports Department (Stany), one at the State Security Archive (Katia), two at the Ministry of Education (Christina and Stanka) and the esteemed offices of Ludmilla Zhivkova and Stanka Shopova.

"... I do not need male agents! I need beautiful and intelligent women, whom I can legitimately select, develop, control, recruit and most importantly ... have plentiful sex with ..."

Indeed, the required conspiracy and the thorough investigations of the selected targets allowed the operational officers to become great manipulators. We were in position to learn specific details about the personal and professional life of a potential target, including but not limited to strengths and weaknesses, preferred approach to life, family and carrier practices and etc.

All meetings I conducted were in safe houses that allowed security, discretion and more than open association. These well-exploited and psychologically justified practices during our KGB trainings, became a driving force for the KGB and the East Germany's HVD—Stasi's staggering success in the west. Women possessed, in addition to their seductiveness and dedication, a wonderful sense of secrecy and conspiracy, which very often was overlooked and underutilized.

*   *   *

My fashionable French perfume gift to Lydia was incredibly appreciated and after sipping aged *Euxignac* from Purvanov's reserves, we soon indulged in a congenial craze.

However, instead of relaxing in a patrician satisfaction, I had an intricate mission to fulfill. As Lydia cleaned the sofa and arranged her ever-immaculate look in the darkness, I comfortably took General Purvanov's solid leather chair. Relaxing my legs on the desk, I casually veiled my undertaking. My ball-point pen calculatedly aimed at the leather seams of the armrest. The silicon treated surface of the cartridge slid easily into place and allowed me to wipe with my shirt's elbow any residues and fingerprints. With a documents folder in hand, my shadow soon vanished off into the dark corridors.

"Hi comrade Natalia! I have materials for Colonel Ferov, can I stop by to deliver them?" My voice sounded suitably official.

"... You surprised me comrade, Colonel Ferov took Snezhka to the big party and I am alone! Did you take notice? Alone!!!" Natalia was fuming.

I put the gift bag inside my briefcase and locked the office. Walking in the hall I grew anxious, for I had just observed Natalia playing with the electronic keypads on General Savchenko's door and then on Ferov's door as well.

Natalia's casual clothes tonight, as often before, accentuated her peasant upbringing. She smiled apathetically as I handed her the folder; however, the elegant gift made her childishly happy. Conspiratorially pulling me outside the office Natalia kindly expressed her appreciation and in the darkness rewarded me with a passionate kiss.

"I cannot invite you inside. I just activated the alarm. Ivan Ivanich (Savchenko) believes that Sixth directorate is monitoring his office." She mumbled, pushing me in the chest with her pointed finger.

I had to act; it was imperative to the success of the overall operation to activate both devices simultaneously, in order for an electronic shield to be set off against interception and jamming.

"Please, I want you! You cannot be alone tonight! Go and open and if you are asked, you can justify everything by delivering my folders . . . Leave the outside door open and I will be back in a few minutes." I left her without a chance to rebuff.

A visit to the nearby restrooms made me uneasy. What kinds of traps perhaps had been laid out for me?

I deposited my safe keys at the duty office and walked back through the gloomily lit corridors, realizing that it was a rather spooky setting. Approaching Savchenko's office, I noticed the slightly opened door and entered without hesitation. Natalia sat shivering in the darkness, slightly illuminated by the courtyard lights. The inner office door was slightly opened and Natalia's desk was brightly lit.

Removing my overcoat and blazer, I silently mimicked her to go and lock her door. Fretful and slightly tense, I took the general's chair while armed with my second priceless ballpoint pen in hand as Natalia more or less reluctantly left the office. My exploratory touch with difficulty found the appropriate leather seams, for they were on the outer side of the armrest. Half way in I hit an unexpected hard object or a carpenter's nail, and almost biting my tongue of anxiety forced the device's entry with two hands. My cotton sleeves casually wiped away any traces of force while my heart bounced, for the office could be video monitored.

Natalia locked the main office and stupidly turned her lights off. Finally she came in the sightless darkness and gave me a seductive hug. Her sporty body twisted with excitement as I passionately embraced her. The desk top comfortably accommodated us and her gymnast's flexibility became more than invigorating. After a few lengthened and silent minutes of passion our bodies quivered in joyful contractions. Finished, Natalia arranged the room and I put on my overcoat and moved to the office door, firmly holding my operational briefcase. Natalia soundless locked General Savchenko's office and gently entered a six-digit code, which I easily recollected later on.

The code 913931 was an ingenious triangular clue for dummies.

We made a brisk arrangement to meet in few minutes on the parking lot of the nearby Sports palace.

Warming up the car, I recognized from distance Natalia's elegant walk and Russian mink coat. She entered with a pleasant smile, and as we drove towards the American college, I smelled her new perfume. Natalia stylishly crossed her legs and tenderly held my gear-shifting hand, silently expressing her appreciation. Besides being a well-organized and meticulous administrator, she possessed unique vivaciousness and gallantry, uncommon for her obscure Siberian upbringing.

A few provocative questions prompted Natalia's sincere affirmations that Vladi Ferov had become her lover with some big promises just before coming to Sofia. He had received recently divorced from his estranged wife and was expecting recall to Moscow, unless he was promoted to replace General Savchenko after his pending retirement. Most recently, however, he had been inundated by an ongoing sleazy affair with Snezha Ovcharova.

My beautiful Russian companion showed deepening jealousy, which if left unrestrained could set off some unpleasant calamities even for me. With all of my persuasive and manipulative clout, I gradually swayed Natalia to forget Colonel Ferov's current indiscretions. Playing her narcissistic wisdom allowed me to shrewdly use her age, mesmerizing beauty and sensuality as unyielding comparative advantages over her married archrival.

The most unexpected and puzzling information from Natalia was her disclosure that embassy technicians had discovered potentially unauthorized entries in Savchenko's MIA office. Assuming that the Sixth directorate on behalf of the KGB's Fifth Chief Directorate monitored him, had made the General more or less alarmed. His unsubstantiated complaints had eventually been thwarted by the MIA's administration by changing the janitorial services schedule. However, the inherent paranoia of KGB officers from Beria's perfidious era was extreme and unnecessary. On the other hand, General Savchenko should have perhaps been apprehensive, for a CIA team, perhaps the most unanticipated visitors have visited his office in the past.

Natalia easily spelled out that Savchenko and Ferov received science and technology information, similar to the one from my office, every week in a special folder from FCD—foreign intelligence. Minister General-Colonel Dimitar Stoianov briefed them twice a week on all aspects of intelligence, counter-espionage and police work. Attempting to probe George Markov's assassination in London delineated Natalia's limited knowledge, though she recalled that General Stoian Savov* was a frequent guest to Savchenko's office and they had even traveled to Moscow together.

Intentionally delineating information about my work with Ognian Doinov and Andrey Lucanov's offices and the substantial contribution to the local economy we had generated, turned out to be of great interest to the astute KGB officer. Deep in her convictions, Natalia remained a Soviet communist apparatchik and a dedicated professional.

---

* MIA, Deputy Minister, overseeing State Security's foreign intelligence operations.

We showed credentials to the guards at the Academy's gate and were allowed inside. On the left was the white building of the Science and Technology Directorate. Passing by, I intentionally provoked Natalia, mentioning that much of our work started or ended there. Glimpsing at the building's lighted entrance, she solemnly mumbled: "Comrade Dubinin spends most of his time here, with his team of scientists and Ph.D's."

Alleviating any casual bystanders, I stopped on the main parking lot and reluctantly rejected Natalia's invitation for a cup of Russian tea.

Driving back, a few surveillance detection and evasion techniques assured me that I was alone. In front of the SCD-counterintelligence directorate, I parked at the *Kosharite* (The Barn) restaurant and while stretching my body walked to the edge of the park and positioned a red lipstick mark on the entrance sign. Ironically, the confirmation sign just across the SCD was clearly visible to passing by cars visiting the diplomats' hospital.

BULGARIAN CONNECTION

I n early May 1983 on the American TV prime time NBC *"Nightly News"* the renowned journalist and international affairs analyst Marvin Kalb reported to the nation and probing world viewers that CIA Director William Casey had "... Changed his mind and now believes that there may not have been a *"Bulgarian Connection"* in the plot to assassinate the Pope ..." Just a month earlier I had submitted to the DCI my findings and assessments on the attempted assassination of Pope John Paul II.

Six months before, from the lush and picturesque Tuscany countryside of Italy, Clair Sterling had published *"The Time of the Assassins"* in a bold attempt to convince the world of "the Bulgarian State Security and the KGB's complicity to the Crime of the Century."

Bulgaria had long been declared not only the European bridge to Asia, but also for more than three decades had pathetically been named and perceived as the Soviet Unions' Sixteenth republic. It was in reality a *dyed-in-the-wool*, supple and well-integrated satellite state of the Kremlin's political and economic interests. Bulgarians and Russians alike were bonded for centuries by indistinguishable ethnic, cultural and religious heritage. Since the 19th century Bulgarian liberation by Tzar Alexander II Romanoff from five centuries of ruthless and degrading Turkish-Ottoman yoke, both nations worshiped a lasting brotherhood. In the most recent 20th century history, a highly deceptive Red Army's bloodless victory in 1944 over the Bulgarian fascist monarch Boris III, Saxe Coburg-Ghota's government, combined with the Teheran and Yalta Allied Conferences years earlier, destined the fate of the Balkan nation. Thereafter, the Bulgarian government, the communist party and the military and security institutions were placed under total Soviet and KGB control. The binding relationship between both nations until early 1990 was determined by the Kremlin's totalitarian policies and priorities.

On May 13, 1981, Mehmet Ali Agca, a deranged, right wing, Turkish extremist, a convicted murderer and escapee from the *"Maltepe"* maximum-security prison in Istanbul, attempted to assassinate the world's Catholic pontiff, Pope John Paul II, on the Vatican's "St. Peter's" Square. The stunned global community and believers and the leading western democracies almost instantaneously pointed fingers at the tall red brick walls of the Kremlin in Moscow.

Pope Wojtila's (John Paul II) never ending moral and spiritual support of the Polish people, his native Poland's labor unions and especially for the "Solidarity" movement at Gdansk's shipyards, in the beginning of 1980s was perceived by many western institutions as a legitimate and sinister reason for the Kremlin's totalitarian leadership to orchestrate and perhaps perpetrate the pontiff's elimination. The Pope's strong condemnation of the Soviet Union's military and bloody intervention and suppression of the Hungarian and the Czechoslovakian anti-communist revolts and the never-ending repressions became a *stumbling stone* for the Polish Communist government of General Voicheh Jaruzelski. Despite the strong and resolute Soviet requests for declaration of a Martial law in Poland and cruel eradication of the "Solidarity" labor movement, the growing apprehensive Polish leadership had long delayed any actions, greatly influenced by the Pope's call for a peaceful solution.

The swiftly ageing Soviet leader Leonid Brezhnev was not entirely thoughtless to the representation of his nation on global scale. His eventual descendant Yuri Andropov, Chairman of the KGB, was not so insensitive to through his almighty apparatus perpetrate such a blunt, palpable and malevolent act that would stonewall and isolate the Soviet Union from the rest of the world.

Many hypothetical studies and some pseudo-analytical circumstantial conclusions were conducted, aired and written all over the world after the attempted assassination. Fundamentalist religious movements, terrorist organizations and communist security services were implicated and some even incriminated in complicity to the matter. The greatest allegation ever that pointed directly to Moscow was the Bulgarian State Security services' implication in involvement and advanced undeviating awareness of the stratagem. The fact that after escaping from Turkish high-security prison Mehmet Ali Agca had spent more than a month (March and April, 1980) in Bulgaria, under an assumed name, was sufficient circumstantial evidence. Enjoying the warm treatment at sunny Black Sea resorts and the opulence of the Bulgarian capital had convinced the Italian magistrates and the international media, such as the prominent Clair Sterling and many others, of an alleged *"Bulgarian Connection"*.

Although DCI Bill Casey for some period during the 1981 and 1982 had become convinced that Clair Sterling's facts-finding disclosures and analysis "bore" logic and convincingly truthful evidence of a Soviet and Bulgarian complicity, he eventually decided to form his final judgment solely on reliable human intelligence. Instead of relying on convincingly persuasive journalistic writings coincidentally backed by sudden baffling and divisive confessions of Mehmet Agca in the mid 1982, the DCI Casey commendably elected the most professional approach to solving the crime of the century.

Under the escalating global political confrontation and the shameful communist complicities with the West, especially after the controversial, though believably implicating reports of Clair Sterling, in October 1982 I received a high priority "*Urgent Attention*" request from the CIA. I had to promptly collect and assess reliable intelligence from any State Security and KGB sources on the matter of the Pope's assassination attempt.

A month earlier, in September 1982, the grotesque assassin Mehmet Agca started confessing from his "*Ascolly Pichenno*" jail cell. He ingenuously implicated the Bulgarian State Security and the KGB in the alleged assassination attempt on the life of Pope John Paul II. The Cold War against totalitarian communism gained a bizarre catalyst in the chilling confrontation with the West.

Although the western media greatly accentuated on an embryonic Soviet connection to the Pope's assassination attempt, in reality the free world's much wider spread battle with totalitarianism had just began.

*   *   *

My diligent efforts and reliable intelligence collection, duly disclosed to the American government in November 1982, eventually convinced and changed the standing of DCI William Casey, the States Department and the White House on the Pope's assassination attempt. In essence, these findings defended the credibility and integrity of the Bulgarian nation.

The State Security defector to France, Vladimir Kostov, painted a blatantly misleading picture of grand scale Soviet-Bulgarian complicity in the Pontiff's attempted murder. Although possessing limited operational intelligence, as he worked as a journalist, Kostov utilized his creative wisdom to "disclose" a few anti-communists "bomb shells". Not surprisingly, he was backed by clever, although logical sounding insinuations by another disgruntled Bulgarian defector, in reality a common criminal, from the military counter-intelligence, Lieutenant-Colonel Stefan Svredlev, who had escaped criminal persecution in Bulgaria by embarrassingly defecting to Greece and thereafter contentedly settling in West Germany. Furthermore, an affluent and vocal group of avid anti-communists in the United States implicated virtually overnight the communist State Security in close cooperation with the KGB in perpetrating the "*Crime of the century*".

The prominent Reaganite Michael Laedeen, Bulgarian emigrants Cyril Black and Alex Alexiev of the Georgetown's Center for Strategic and International Studies, and John Paniza of Readers Digest became strong proponents of the "*Bulgarian connection*" and masterfully contributed to the growing western hysteria against Soviet communism. However, their publications and journalistic work were in reality irrational and irresponsible professional standings.

I had four weeks to assess any reliable information and intelligence gathered in order to prove the State Security and KGB complot, or to justify the contrary. An old friend of my father ranked first on the list of reliable professional sources.

Colonel Veselin Bozhkov was a well-known and highly regarded former deputy chief of SCD's Turkish counterintelligence department. His success against Turkish espionage in Bulgaria had catapulted him to chief of the Turkish (Muslim) department of Sixth directorate. I worked with Bozhkov in the early 1970s against Turkish diplomats in Sofia, and most recently against some of the major Turkish scientific institutions. Exploiting legitimate operational tasks, I contacted Colonel Bozhkov directly. The outcome of a few meetings with him and his trusted former deputy Lieutenant Colonel Nedialkov clearly indicated to me that Mehmet Agca was a State Security target DOR *"Nemesis"* (one who is under an Active Operational Investigation) of SCD's (counter intelligencea) fourth department. Sofia's State Security's city administration initially had gathered information on the whereabouts of Agca through eavesdropping on Turkish executives living and habituating at hotel *New Otani a.k.a.* Vitosha. SCD thereafter had learned from a secret agent that the inconspicuous Indian citizen Singh that often shared rooms with other Turkish or Arab guests at hotels Vitosha, Sofia and Moscow, was a notorious Turkish terrorist.

State Security's Sofia directorate—Major Vasil Kotzev had obtained information from a reputed Turkish criminal and State Security informer Osman Nabil a.k.a. *"Jester"* that Joginder Singh a.k.a. Mahmut Aga was truly cherished by the powerful Bekir Chelenk for his ultra-right nationalism and Islamic fundamentalism. As soon as the questionable identity of Mr. Singh and details of his participation in the murder of the renowned Turkish journalist Abdi Ipekci, editor of *Milliyet* newspaper were related to Colonel Bozhkov, he had ordered Mr. Sinfh's active investigation.

The potent export/import trading group had a spider web network of successful traders and distributors, as well as smugglers, of weapons and hard drugs, such as heroin and hashish, from Asia across Western Europe and throughout the Middle East. Bekir Chelenk and his long trading partner Abuzer Ugurlu (suspiciously abducted in Sofia during March 1981 by Turkish intelligence and smuggled to Turkey for trial) became a front arm of the Bulgarian trading companies: *Kintex, Agroimpex, Hranexport, Electroimpex, Metalchim and Rodopaimpex.*

In 1980, the military took over the Turkish government. *Vardar Impex'* trading and smuggling business in Turkey and the Middle East was dramatically impacted by new stringent rules, enforced laws and the arrests of corrupt Turkish ministers and officials. Among the arrested Turkish government officials were four high-ranking military officers, stealthily developed by the KGB and State Security into moles inside the Turkish military and NATO. Although a semi legitimate business enterprise, Chelenk's group survived and steadily continued operations throughout the Middle East, Turkey, Austria, Switzerland, France, Belgium and Germany.

Omer Mersan, one of hotel *New Otani's* frequent guests, had offered unregistered accommodation and money to Mr. Singh in Sofia. He was *Vardar Impex'* senior partner, running operations from Munich, Germany and managing as a Godfather the notorious Turkish right extremists *"The Grey Wolfs"*. Mersan, code named *"Dingo"* was recruited as a secret agent of FCD—foreign intelligence while in Bulgarian custody, craftily arranged on drugs smuggling charges. His information eventually confirmed the questionable link to the real identity of Mahmud Aga a.k.a. Mehmet Ali Agca to Colonel Bozhkov's SCD officers. Lieutenant-Colonel Zhivko Nedialkov and his officers prudently had conducted a complex investigation of Mr. Singh, and discovered in the process that Agca was on the arrest-warrant list of Interpol and other western nations. Furthermore he was on the top of the "most wanted" list of criminals in Turkey.

The investigation had unraveled Agca's close affiliation with two notorious Turkish criminals: Mussa Cheleby and Oral Chelik. Cheleby was leader of the *"Federation of the Turkish idealists" (The Grey Wolves)* in Switzerland. He had provided Mehmet Agca with money and had graciously given him a US$15,000 gold Rolex watch as a gift. Nedialkov rationally had contemplated that it was an upfront payment for Agca's wolf-pack brotherhood loyalty and fervent commitments to a future sacred Islamic martyrdom.

Colonel Bozhcov was truly the first individual during these meetings to spell out that the Islamic fundamentalism was emerging as an ominous menace to the developed world. As an effective measure, during Singh's ongoing investigation, Bozhcov had imposed on him international travel restrictions, through the State Security's controlled KPP—border control center. Any attempts by Singh to leave the country, would have guaranteed his detention at the border.

Through Wilhelm (Willy) Betz, Managing Director of *Betz Trucking* in Austria, a secret agent of the Bulgarian State Security's Second Directorate's (transportation) department eleven, *Vardar* group had emerged as one of the most efficient, versatile and well-connected international trading groups in Europe. Despite of being a wicked criminal enterprise, *Vardar* executives consistently have received the KGB and State Security's protection and secure channels of operation. Lucrative trade and foreign intelligence interests prevailed, making the Soviet and Bulgarian totalitarian leaderships stealthy collaborators of unending strings of war crimes, weapons and narcotics smugglings all over Europe, the Middle East and Asia.

In the early 1980s, the egotistical Willi Betz was not prudent enough to realize that the State Security and KGB were steadily developing him into a special interests marionette. The Central Committee of the communist party had secretly authorized the development of a strong international transportation arm, serving the new government operations of lucrative trade, logistics and smuggling of embargoed technology, restricted commodities and weapons. Soon thereafter

Betz's half-brother Bobby received an almost exclusive contract by the Bulgarian Ministry of Foreign Trade for export of the globally controlled psychotropic substance *Captagon,* considered the most powerful motivational drug.

Despite the presumed efficient State Security control, a *Betz* Turkish TIR driver covertly had furnished Mr. Singh with a new identity, that was cunningly provided by the Turkish *Grey Wolfs* in Germany and Switzerland.

The smugglers spider networks have been invisible to the self-content State Security. Reliable information had started to intentionally flow through the stealthy Turkish criminal fraternity. Mohamed Iorgiz, an inconspicuous Turkish businessperson, undisturbed by the meticulousness of the communist border authorities, had departed Bulgaria, traveling throughout Yugoslavia and Austria to Germany, Italy and Switzerland.

Colonel Bozhkov and his operational officers through this act have lost one of the most wanted terrorists and criminals in Europe, or perhaps intentionally had let him slip through the border's loopholes instead of jeopardizing and compromising the lucrative Bulgarian international trade, smuggling and intelligence gathering operations that were ingeniously perpetrated with the help of the Turkish mafia. However, perhaps senior KGB and State Security officials, carrying much heavier epaulets than Colonel Bozhkov's, should have approved this intricate undertaking.

The State Security and KGB utilized Betz and SOMAT trucks for a plentitude of secret operations across Europe and the Middle East. SCD Colonel Ivan Petrov was in charge of the overall management and supervision of these complex operations. Through this mind-numbing process, Petrov became a life testimony of the corrupted official; he virtually extorted favors, gifts and hard currency payments from TIR drivers in order to get some of the preferred and lucrative routs of smuggling and trade operations. For a decade Colonel Petrov was one of the few State Security officers who drove a Mercedes-Benz car. In this secretive environment of corruption and protection, gifts and sleazy nightlife, briberies and racket, secret intelligence exchanged hands like street-bought drugs.

Colonel Bozhkov was instrumental in analytically outlining most aspects of the question: *"Why was there not a real Bulgarian or Soviet Connection in the Pope's assassination attempt?"* despite the overall beliefs to the contrary. After losing to political and religious circumstances and even to assassinations a few reliable Lebanese, PLO and Arab trading connections in the Middle East and Western Europe, key Bulgarian foreign trading companies, most of them fronts of foreign intelligence interests, had approached the ninth department of SCD. Their proposals for development of preferred trading partners with some of the new breed businesspersons from Turkey and the Middle East delineated viable opportunities. Colonel Bozhkov eloquently confirmed that State Security and KGB could not only develop, but could also successfully recruit leading Turkish, Lebanese and Palestinian merchants and export/import dealers, mostly on criminal and *compro* basis. Some of these secret assets lived permanently in Bulgaria and consistently reported information on Turkey and the Middle East gathered through their networks. Substantial data relevant to the Turkish and Arab countries' secret operations throughout Bulgaria and Western Europe was generated consistently.

Hence, Colonel Bozhkov clearly stipulated that neither he, nor his operational officers, nor their Turkish assets, nor even Arab ones received any information or gathered evidence of organized or advanced preparations of Mr. Joginder Singh a.k.a. Mohamed Iorgiz, or Mehmet Ali Agca related to the assassination of Pope John Paul II. Colonel Bozhkov's highly professional assessment was that the Islamic world was highly deranged by the Pope's visit to Turkey during the 1979 (assessment of some of the leading Bulgarian Islamic leaders as well). Religious Islamic fanatics, such as, but not limited to Mehmet Ali Agca had eventually perpetrated the assassination attempt in Rome, solely to fulfill an Islamic martyr's call and to slow the Pontif's unrelenting global unification efforts.

An Islamic canon that guides martyrs of the prophet has been utilized in utmost secrecy for centuries. Perhaps, the rather common Islamite Agca had been gradually developed and transformed by the secretive and fierce neo-fascist *Gray Wolfs* into a chosen one, a "martyr", one who waited the call of Allah for a holy war and ever-lasting venerable sacrifice. Same forms of extreme religious sacrifice would become years later devastating mayhems for the Israelis and tragically even for the Americans. Events, leading from the Lebanon's Marine Barracks destruction in the 1980s to the World Trade Center 9/11 tragedy in 2001, never could be forgotten.

*   *   *

I indefatigably made the most of my reliable contacts at FCD in gathering operational intelligence on the Pope John Paul II's assassination attempt. The communist indoctrinated and manipulated mind of the operational officers was somehow a burden in alleviating their sentiments and geo-political assessments. It did not matter how logical and convincing some of them sounded, I needed real intelligence that flowed through raw operational channels. My party committee duty allowed me endless added dialogues with State Security officers, but was of no significance in tracing down any reliable clues.

Colonel Vandov, the former State Security resident in France and Turkey, for example believed that the group for special operations *"Star"* managed by General-Colonel Slavcho Trunski, was involved in the assassination attempt with the KGB support. He had two years previously voiced the similar opinion of the assassination of the renegade writer George Markov. However, Colonel Vandov was a master of deception, and thus deliberately shot some "traceable" blanks.

Captain Dimitar Meranzov, a former Bulgarian athletics champion and a friend, exploited his powerful uncle's nepotism to become an operational officer of the foreign counter-intelligence department in the late 1970s. We maintained professional contacts by investigating Italian and Swiss foundations that attracted Bulgarian scientists and intellectuals. Among some of the main targets of our joint interests were the Vatican's Library, the Institute of Theology and the Vatican's Roman Catholic Bishops Council. With time running short, I initiated legitimate contacts with Meranzov. From a counter-intelligence standpoint, he perceivably possessed reliable information on the Pope's assassination attempt.

Under the KGB and the Polish Security services' request I was already working on the case of two Polish Catholic professors from Poznan University that trained and managed the Bulgarian Catholic church in Sofia on "Tsar Boris" street. The Polish academicians were prepared for the Vatican's annual theological conference and I craftily penetrated their inner-circle through a professor at Sofia State University, "Clement of Ohrid".

On November 04, 1982, I visited the Swiss-Italian section of FCD. While discussing the Vatican's operational strategy with Meranzov, I casually mentioned my work and knowledge from the past of the KGB's Italian asset *"the Lioness"*— Alexandra Melnikova and her deep penetration of the Italian Labor unions. A few carefully stipulated details easily opened the secretive Pandora's Box of the Italian section and we soon discussed in detail the Pope's legacy.

Although time has elapsed since the attempted murder and Mehmet Ali Agca was at a secure prison in Rome, the Italian magistrates' implication of Bulgarian State Security and the KGB had just begun. Agca's elaborate confessions provided seemingly irrefutable evidences of a "Bulgarian State Security and KGB connection" behind his martyr inspirations.

Meranzov eloquently disclosed that Colonel Marchaiev, the KGB's FCD advisor, had expressed Moscow's concerns about the unsubstantiated Italian accusations. As a result, an in-depth assessment by the FCD was conducted in June 1982, and indicated the lack of evidence corroborating any Bulgarian or Soviet involvement. The comprehensive analysis had pointed at radical Islamic and neo-Nazis groups in Italy, Turkey, Germany and France, and even circumstantially had implicated the Libyan Jamahiriya.

*　　*　　*

The assassination attempt has set off stringent security and surveillance measures by the Italian and other West European special services. The Italian security agency inadvertently had uncovered the closely guarded collaborator of *the Lioness.* Luidgi Scrichiollo and his wife Paola have been unmasked as secret communists and State Security controlled KGB agents. They were uncovered as an operational couple that shuttled between the State Security and the KGB's sinister interests in Italy, Western Europe and even the United States of America. The Scrichiollos were charged with stern acts of espionage: infiltration of the Italian Labor and Union movement, sabotaging the Polish Labor movement *"Solidarity"*, collecting scientific and technology intelligence from Italian, West European and especially from American universities, providing legitimate documents and working records for KGB and Bulgarian illegal agents, and recruiting students with leftist orientation as future communist spies. Most damagingly, they were indicted on charges of collaborating and perpetrating acts of sabotage and terrorism in conjunction with the notorious Italian *"Red Brigades"**.

In my mind a few times came the devilish inspiration that I should intentionally misinform Langley of the East's papal innocence and discredit the communist fraternity of Bulgaria and the Soviet Union even more. However, I realized that the outcome of any of my insinuations would be gruesome not only for the totalitarian leadership, but mostly for the Bulgarian people.

My personal feelings were a strong catalyst of my anti-communist activities; however, I was not ready to sell short the destiny of the Bulgarians. I had to find the truth, and only the truth was to determine what I divulged to the American government. The outcome became an astonishing tutorial of ethics, morality and conscientiousness, and I came forward unblemished by my personal feelings and detestation of communism.

A few days later Meranzov informed me that the FCD chief of station in Rome, Ivan Donchev, had returned to Sofia, literally escaping arrest by the Italian magistrates. He had hurriedly escaped Scrichiollo's scandal in Italy and the disclosures of his confessional incriminations that Donchev not only had controlled him as a communist spy for years, but had also discussed with him a plot to assassinate the Polish *"Solidarity"* leader Lech Walesa during an official visit to Rome in January 1981.

Meanwhile Mehmet Ali Agca continued the string of strange, fabricated confessions and further implicated the Bulgarian resident Donchev, not only as the master Bulgarian spy chief in Italy (in accord with Scrichiollo's confessions), but also as one of his mentors and co-conspirators in the plot to assassinate Lech Walensa. In due course, he had confirmed Scrichiollo's confessions**. Meranzov's assessments, backed by FCD and Italian documents, explained Agca's sudden implications of Bulgaria in the Pope's assassination plot. However, the lacks of

---

*   Avanti and Corriere de la Sera—07.83 transcripts

**   La Repubblica, March 1983 transcripts.

any counterintelligence data in the FCD's Italian and Vatican files strengthened and corroborated my findings that the *"Bulgarian Connection"* did not exist. Instead, it sounded like a one-dimensional, malevolent, Italian or international conspiracy aimed at damaging and eroding Soviet communism and Moscow's East European fraternity.

*   *   *

The operations director of hotel *Vitosha-New Otany*, Ilia Pavlov, I developed into a reliable professional contact and gradually he became a close friend. Utilizing my cover as Director from the Ministry of Finance, and with his approval, I received direct access to the recreational facilities of the five star hotel and even rented modern ski equipment that was reserved for only affluent and rich foreign guests. Often, I make use of hotel rooms or suites for clandestine meetings with agents, foreigners or secret collaborators. Through my frequent visits, I became more or less an insider with the hotel operations, receiving priority service and ultimate attention from waiters, the telephone center and front desk management. I also became familiar with most of the frequent foreign guest, and walking through the hallways at the restaurants, the casino or indulging in the spa, some of the permanent and frequent Arab and Turkish guests would habitually greet me.

At the lobby bar more than 18 months earlier, Pavlov casually had introduced me to the Turkish businessman Mussa Cheleby. Same evening I shook hands and spoke some Arabic with a long faced, gypsy-like young man in Cheleby's company. A man who's face the world will remember later from the newspapers and the TV as the Pope's assassin. In fact, I was one of the only few State Security officials who held the frail hand of Mehmet Agca. Luben Levitcharov, the man responsible for the operational and eavesdropping security of the complex, became an indispensable source of information. On the eleventh floor, State Security maintained an office equipped with a switchboard concealed behind an inconspicuous electric board panel that allowed instant audio and video monitoring of any hotel room. Levitcharov was familiar with all eavesdropping and investigative operations against hotel guests. Thus he unquestionably held information about Agca and his Turkish fraternity. Intricately manipulating Colonel Bozhkov's information, I shrewdly probed Levitcharov about Chelenk's group.

Since the Italian government opened the official Bulgarian investigation, Bekir Chelenk and some of his Turkish partners, all of them residents of hotel *Vitosha-New Otani*, were swiftly whisked away to a government villa in Boiana and put under house arrest. Luben bluntly categorized the group as dangerous international smugglers that were deviously sheltered by the KGB and FCD. He identified Boian Traikov, the Bulgarian government spokesperson, as the main coordinator of the group's isolation and impending investigation.

The group was apparently under SCD investigation for an alleged role in the Pope's assassination plot. Levicharov described Agca and Mersan by names as "religious nuts" that bragged about undergoing guerilla training by the Palestinian Fattah movement in southern Lebanon and by the Russian "green berets" in Jordan. He was unambiguous in that no clues of the Pope's assassination had ever been intercepted or recorded by the Fourth department, who has been electronically eavesdropping on most of them. They have reviewed and studied lately all old tapes fruitlessly for any clues to the matter. One of State Security's operational officers that was in a critical position of possessing knowledge of Bulgarian, Soviet or Turkish preparation and complicity to Pope John Paul II's assassination attempt unequivocally confirmed that State Security and the KGB had nothing to do with the *"Crime of the Century"**.

I needed credible facts from FCD; lucky for me, the breakthrough came in a most unforeseen way. During a meeting with Ognian Doinov and his assistant Atanas Atanasov, we charted a shrewd technology-training program for *"Wurtz"* robotics systems in West Germany of an exchange professor that worked with the Soviet Ministry's heavy machine building. The door opened without announcement and Andrey Lucanov sheepishly popped inside.

I was surprised, for Doinov was a member of the Political Bureau of the Communist Party, the highest governing body and the disrespect was more than apparent. Inquiring about the technology transfer, Lucanov swiftly changed the subject and asked about the Italian "innuendos". Doinov shook head and explained that the Reagan administration had a lot to do with Agca's confessions and that the KGB chairman was soon planning to offer Sofia a helping hand. Then Lucanov almost egotistically reaffirmed *". . . Alexander Haig should be blamed for setting off this Italian crusade! At least that's the latest assessment from Moscow . . ."*

Exiting the State Council building, I was ecstatic. Two very powerful party and government officials that were well connected with State Security and KGB had confirmed that they did not possess even the slightest clue of any Soviet or Bulgarian involvement with the Pope's assassination.

Down the street I entered the office of Plamen Despotov, director of international affairs of the State Committee for Science and Technical Progress. He was ready to depart to Beijing, China on a FCD cover diplomatic assignment. For years I have worked with Despotov in charting the international exchange of scholars and academicians. He was one of the most pragmatic foreign intelligence

---

* Audio tape #10/11/82/4 confirms Levicharov's assessments and testimonials.

officers I have ever known, audacious enough to critique in private some of the policing practices and activities of the counterintelligence.

Plamen greeted me kindly and we soon sipped the strong cappuccino of his secretary Lilliana. Charting the possibilities of future academic exchange with the Far East Asia and Japan, I intentionally mentioned the just concluded meeting with Doinov and Lucanov. Knowing that Despotov was one of Ognian Doinov's earliest considerations for an adviser, I shrewdly provoked his comments on the Italian ignominy.

Lilli secretively popped her head into the room, announcing that "friendly" visitors wanted to join us, as two familiar FCD officers popped behind her back almost hastily. George Denichin, a jolly fellow, was an old friend working under cover as First secretary of the Bulgarian mission to the United Nations in New York. His companion, a remotely familiar face with a long brown leather jacket and a short grayish hair, displayed a despondent and prematurely aged complexion. His outer jacket's pocket inconspicuously displayed an edition of the Italian daily "Corriere de la Sera". Our warm greetings with Denichin set off a wonderful comrade's environment, as Despotov introduced me to the guest named Dontchev, diplomat, recently returned from a foreign assignment.

I was astounded, for perhaps the most sought after intelligence source has come before me. If any information on the Pope's assassination was available, Donchev unquestionably possessed the keys to the sinister undertaking. Unexpectedly, the alleged mastermind, or perhaps, the unjustly accused diplomat and covert intelligence professional has turned up in front of me. Ivan Donchev was initially an almost ashamed and disinclined participant in our meeting. He unflappably opened his Italian newspaper and wordlessly sank in the old leather sofa, sipping his coffee. Boldly stipulating some of my operational goals and long term planning at the Vatican, I prompted Donchev to point at the newspaper, resolutely affirming: ". . . it appears that the Italians are intentionally orchestrating Agca's fabricated confessions, virtually cutting us off . . . off of any feasible opportunities in Italy and the Vatican for a long, long time . . ."

Despotov academically and diplomatically delineated the Orthodox issues of Patriarch Maxim with the Bulgarian church in Rome, as I frankly continued; asking Donchev about Clair Sterling's convincing accusations against the KGB and State Security.

". . . Obviously she has been paid big to write these plausible stories . . . For this rationale, her writings are so adamantly good and logically convincing to the public. It is, however, a blunt "active measure" operation composed and craftily fed up to Sterling by the CIA and the MI6, nonetheless ingeniously reconfirmed by her favorite Israeli Mossad. By the way, she became famous in the West long before writing on the Pope's assassination, for her book "*The Terror Network*" had a significant impact on western political life . . ." Dontchev was sharp and egotistical, an arrogantly self-centered man, and although I despised his attitude immediately, I played my high regards and sycophancy in order to reach the substance of my real interests.

"... Speaking of active measures ..." calmly got involved Denichin: "We should be very thankful to your neighbor Blagoi Platchkov*, for so thoughtlessly eliminating this crucial department. Today it would have been the driving force for convincingly proving our innocence ... to the world ..."

I stood silent, acknowledging his statement more as a rhetorical play of words. Without admonition, I pitched Donchev on the "*Lioness*" and the KGB/State Security's relationship with the Italian Labor Union movement. For the strictly compartmented intelligence officer, even though he was the Italian resident, it was astonishing that I knew Melnikova's stealthy transgressions. Theatrically shaking the newspaper, he condemned the Italian press of disseminating incriminating information about the bogus Bulgarian spy operations in Italy on behalf of the KGB. "... We can handle international scientific and academic exchange, we can control the pomacs (referring with sarcasm to the Sixth directorate handling of the problems with the Turkish minority in Bulgaria), but we cannot handle international intrigues of this proportion and magnitude. They are in the hands of the CIA, and could overnight destroy our credibility for any of their sinister geo-political reasons ..."

The implication of Donchev's diatribe undoubtedly confirmed that religious Islamic fundamentalism played a crucial role in Agca's undertaking. Especially, knowing that he had been extensively trained in guerilla war tactics by the PLO radicals and not without the strong fundamental influence of the crafty Iranian Pasdaran**. Almost lightheartedly Donchev stated that in Italy he had heard so many stories of Libyan fanatics pursuing the Pope, that if it was not for Agca, perhaps it could have been one of Khadafy's "Green book"*** brain washed martyrs that committed the crime: "... *That Turkish bastard was until three years ago just an uncomplicated and unadulterated Anatolian peasant boy. With his unstable aiming at the Pope in Rome, and with his fabricated confessional stories, he has recently attempted to destroy centuries of hard work between global religious movements and cooperative governments* ..."

It was an openhanded and unsolicited intelligence assessment and a credible synopsis of the Italian political drama. The covert record of the entire meeting became one of my stealthy attestations to the affair. Because of Ivan Donchev's

---

*   Bulgarian foreign intelligence resident in Vienna, Austria—1960s and Teheran, Iran—1970s, FCD DD—1980s.

**   Iranian Islamic foreign intelligence services

***   Libya Premier, Muamar Khadafy's writings on Islamic believes and virtues. 1977

aggressive espionage activities in Italy, not only linked to the Pope's assassination attempt, but also to the cunning and lasting perpetration of the Italian political establishments, within weeks he became target of an international arrest warrant from the Italian judge Ilario Martella.

Plamen Despotov made known that the KGB Chairman Victor Chebrikov was stalwartly unsettled by the over-blown "Soviet-Bulgarian connection". In order to assure the world of the orderly relationship of the fraternal security and intelligence services, the Chairman had announced his intentions to visit Bulgaria shortly.

The same afternoon George Denichin visited my office and reconfirmed Donchev's position. With the head of the North American section of the Central Committee of the Communist Party Dimitar Dimitrov, Denichin had evidently participated in the FCD assessments and the preparation of the latest report for the government and the KGB. Digging through thousands of pages, their secretive group did not find any State Security or KGB documentation that led to the planning or the perpetration of the assassination attempt on the Pontiff.

*　　*　　*

The rainy and gloomy season of 1981 proved uninviting for tennis outings with my KGB contacts. Walking out to lunch one day, I saw Colonel Ferov crossing the inner court. Exiting through the side gateway, I aimed towards the main entrance, eager to join him for a walk. Through our shrouded gatherings, and by providing him with complex intelligence on a variety of subjects, I had gradually befriended Vladi Ferov to the extent that he has started to provide me with information that was unconceivable by any KGB standards.

"... Accurate preparation is reassurance of accomplishment," states Berzin's* axiom, inscribed on the walls of the KGB Academy in Moscow.

Accurately timing myself, as soon as I walked by the entrance, Ferov emerged from the building. Warm handshakes put us in an instantly gentile environment and we agree to lunch together.

Inquiring about the health of General Savchenko, I prompted one of Vladi's peppery, comic jokes about the aging man's growing insanity. My excellent Russian always seasoned our intelligently veiled words in secrecy. By nature, Vladi was a born schemer, who shrewdly exploited any opportunity to gather information, or to calculatedly deceive. Entering the club-restaurant, I presented my credentials

---

* Jan Carlovich Berzin, one of the founders of the Bolshevik's communist Ceka (Special Commission) in 1917.

with two red lines that authorizing access to any State Security facility and we were cordially invited to the executive's section.

After ordering, I inventively grumbled about the growing calamities with the Pope's assassination attempt and the problems I was facing in sending secret assets to the Vatican Theological Academy's annual council.

Vladi Ferov smiled somberly and referring to Agca's missing shots cynically affirmed: "... Apparently the Seljuk* was not a good gun for hire ... or perhaps somebody gave him too much *Captagon*** ..."

The implication was more than palpable. Playing an attentive apparatchik, I remarked, "... Providentially, the Pope survived, leaving us time and opportunity to talk the Polish comrades into taking over the Lech Walensa's union ..." Subtly suggesting that the pope's elimination would have been a triumphant act against the anti-socialist movement in Poland and that the Pontiff's growing enigma would have been wiped out naturally set off Vladi's retort. With perfidious dignity, he looked around and then while fixing me with his intense blue eyes unflinchingly declared: "... Comrade Andropov*** never would have authorized this kind of operational dullness and sacrilege against the Vatican and the Pope. We have many other ways of influencing the Catholic Church, not to mention the Vatican's inner workings, as we have been doing so for decades ... the Pope is not George Markov ..." Vladi Ferov was firm and convincing, although he made a perplexing correlation to the case that had baffled Western Europe for two years.

Instead of continuing on about the London incident, I calmly bluffed disinterest and accentuated on Papal political rhetoric. Among the few valuable added bits was Vladi's conviction that the Pope had become too antagonistic, freely traveling through divisive domains with doubtful standings on the Christianity, Judaism and even the Islam. At this juncture, the superb Sony recorded with remarkable clarity Vladi Ferov's description of the KGB's concluding assessment that the latent origination of the plot was Iran and its notorious *Pasdaran**** supported fanatic Islamite. His inadvertently spelled out insight on George Markov's murder later proved to be an invaluable corroboration of the KGB complicity in the matter.

---

*   Turkish tribe, notorious with its viciousness and savagery.

**   Strong motivational drug.

***   Yury Andropov, former KGB Chairman, and General Secretary of the Communist Party of the Soviet Union.

****   Iranian secret intelligence organization.

TURKEY TIME

The loading of an ingeniously spacious dead drop with secret materials completed my final preparations for an incognito trip to Stockholm, Sweden. A prearranged visit to a safe house where I maintained a secure suitcase stacked with western cloths, astute disguises and common paraphernalia, permitted me to realistically alter my look to match the CIA's set of dependable travel documents.

The day before Thanksgiving 1982, Sofia International airport was exceedingly inhospitable to travelers. Heavy fog and intense rain gradually stalled all flights. My plane from Istanbul landed in Plovdiv and all Hungary and Sweden bound passengers had to be transported there by bus. At the Plovdiv airport, an out of the ordinary twist of fate caught me by surprise: One of my colleagues, Ivan Stanchev, deputy director of our analytical department, emerged unexpectedly from the restricted departure area accompanied by visiting Hungarian State Security guests. Even more perplexingly, a friend, Professor Anna Pencheva from the Academy of Social Studies at the Central Committee of the communist party, approached me and kindly remarked that I bore a close resemblance to a friend of hers. She spoke English, obviously noticing my British periodicals popping from my pocket.

"I beg you a pardon madam, wrong person . . ." I mumbled with a well-trained Scottish dialect, and moved on with a smirking face.

Just prior to boarding, a group of officers from Sofia's airport border administration (KPP), unexpectedly surfaced in the departure hall of the airport, and prompted the unforeseen symptoms of my imminent arrest. I had carelessly taken with me a pocket calendar loaded with top-secret information. Most of the innocuous notations were hidden and calculatedly distorted; however, if cracked, they warranted my execution for high treason. Although with my sound identity papers and exceptional disguise it appeared that I was not susceptible to be unmasked, a vacillating numbness swamped my veins with adrenalin.

Nonchalantly perusing a magazine, I swiftly peripherally dissected the surrounding through my new bone frame glasses. A large, western style leather bag attracted my attention, for it had side pockets that invitingly offered refuge to my "priceless" calendar. A bulky Swede stood next to the bag with a green topcoat flipped in his hand. I indifferently accosted the traveler and subtly prepared to transfer the lethal evidence.

An announcement indicated the departure of a Moscow bound plane and the ticking noise of the information board momentarily gripped everyone's attention. With a smooth downward move towards my bag, I inserted the agenda into the stranger's bag pocket and stood up with my tickets in hand. Even the closest bystanders missed the transition, for it was more or less an invisible pocket picking trickery.

Soothing my excruciating angst, the chatter of two unfamiliar border officers nearby revealed their impending training in Budapest. Shortly, a new announcement let me follow my unwitting carter to the business section of the plain, as our tickets matched colors. At the third row of seats, the Swede placed his bag and overcoat in the overhead compartment and with a relief, heavily took his lounger. Offhandedly rebutting the flight attendant's proposal to hang on my raincoat, I folded it over the two travel bags and retrieved the calendar and then inconspicuously placed it behind the bags. For the next two hours I vigilantly screened the Swede and the activities in the main cabin. At the Malev's Budapest International airport, I relaxed in the cabin while most of the continuing travelers to Stockholm took a walk on the terminal.

I had to treat the situation as if I was still in Bulgaria, for close cooperation existed between the Bulgarian and the Hungarian secret services. Once in the air again, my evaluation of the circumstances revealed flaws and mistakes which I never should have made. I should have traveled through different, less vulnerable paths. Years later, I with dismay discovered that the CIA paths I had taken were in essence the most secure and reliable ones. *"The back yards are strictly controlled, however, the front doors have been left unlocked . . ."* by the totalitarian security system.

More than four hours of delay had inadvertently bemused my Stockholm contacts, for no one was waiting for me at the predetermined kiosk. I had alternative arrangements and contact phone; however, I suspected that the KGB's technical outfits were perhaps monitoring it. A shuttle bus from Arlanda International to the Old Town's Sheraton Center allowed me to enjoy the darkening sky that was intriguingly illuminated by the Arctic Circle's *"mid-night-sun"*. In front of the bus the lights of the burgeoning city gradually emerged.

The neutral Swedish parliamentary monarchy that in the 1970s and the 1980s ingeniously implemented a mixture of capitalism and socialism was a prosperous, socially stable and wise industrious nation. Colorful streetlights, garlands and beautifully decorated homes soon replaced the darkened pristine countryside, keeping me in the warmth western Christmas spirit. I came from behind a dark, senselessly veiled by an "Iron Curtain" society, where similar centuries old festivities had been condemned for the last three decades by a merciless socialist doctrine.

The Stockholm's Grand Hotel was classy, chic and accommodating. After a warm and stress relieving bubbly bath, I craftily disguised myself and headed to the main lobby's restaurant. Grilled Nordic salmon with freshly steamed vegetables, topped with walnuts, capers and buttery lemon sauce shortly re-energized my fatigued senses. A chilled white burgundy matched the delicious dinner, as my thoughts followed the reflective lights of Skeppsholmen Island through the partially frozen canal across the street. The domains of the Swedish National Museum, the Museums of Far East Art and the Modern Art came into sight on the lit sky as dark, monstrous medieval dungeons.

As a security precaution I preferred to stay away from the obscure populace of the hotel's main lobby. Walking out of the restaurant, however, I found myself in the seductive company of two beautiful Russian girls. The Grand Hotel with its affluent clients from all over the world was undeniably a "promising stage" for their exclusive talents. However, the sensuous prostitutes were taken aback by my silent rebuff and glimpse-less stride away in revulsion.

The relatively liberal, free and neutral Sweden has over the years conventionally entertained many international intrigues, covert intelligence operations and nonetheless pleads of well-diversified entrepreneurs. After Vienna, Stockholm emerged as the second most convenient KGB espionage center in Europe. Few will deny Stockholm's pearl as the worlds most beautiful and civilized capital. Initially set as an island defense fortress, it had spread to nearby islands and mainland. The *"City on the water"* delights visitors with its mesmerizing waterways, green parks, friendly people and superb city planning.

I was an American businessman of Greek origin, specializing in the export/ import business with scrap metals. This dull cover allowed me to conceal my Central European accent by conveniently blending Greek with English and German. Warmly dressed, I walked out of the hotel. The clouds attempted to snow but the deep cold hampered it. The arctic winds blew the snowflakes through the icy canals and drove the temperature far below freezing levels. Shivering, I hired a passing taxi and directed it to the Central train station. Reading the schedules, I simulated gathering data and wrote a note card message to my contacts at the American embassy. From the North terminal, I took another taxi to the USA embassy on *Strandvagen* Street. As the driver waited in the cab, I inconspicuously handed my card-note to the marine sergeant on duty and returned to the center of the city. I deceitfully satisfied the Arab driver's curiosity by expressing my frustration with the cumbersome process for a Greek of obtaining an American visa. His English vulgarity eloquently sketched out a deeply rooted hatred and religious prejudice against the United States.

A little past midnight, John Curtis, the first secretary of political affairs at the American embassy, called in my room, apologetically explaining the eventful mishap with my arrival. After more than three hours of patiently waiting, John had followed the arrival of a Balkan airlines plane. However, the announcement was not clear enough in that the plane had arrived from Oslo on a return flight to Sofia, and the waiting team was deceived even further and waited in vain for another two hours at the gathering point.

Although the mishap was over with, I was perplexed by the blunder of my professional hosts. I received a vivid warning that the establishment was annoyingly sloppy and inefficient. Exhausted from the lasting endeavors, I finally found a soothing refuge in my bed.

The next morning, Thanksgiving 1982, members of the local residency picked me up and we drove to a conveniently located safe house in the peaceful neighborhoods of Ostermalm. After brief greetings and introductions and some clarifications surrounding my arrival, we prepared a tasty bachelors' breakfast of sunny side-up eggs with bacon and hash browns. We soon transformed the table into a dynamic operational center with a plethora of supreme Columbian delight.

The Stockholm's Directorate of Operation (DO) Station chief, Rich Miles, was a professional diplomat and highly respected intelligence officer with successfully completed assignments from Moscow to India and the UN in Geneva. We diligently discussed and analyzed all data and relevant findings on Pope John Paul II's assassination attempt. With consistency and attention to the smallest details, we worked nonstop for almost five hours. Rich's Russian fluency was commendable, for it helped us evaluate closer some details when my English proficiency hindered. Around 2:30 PM we concluded the project with a joint statement of assessment, accompanied by the relevant findings, and duly formulated it into a document to be immediately transmitted to the center in Washington DC with the special designation "D1", for immediate attention of DCI William Casey. This designation normally guided the DCI analytical staff to compose an assessment statement for the United States President's Daily Briefs—the PDB's.

The weather turned to a warm, sunny afternoon and Rich invited me to a Thanksgiving lunch in the nearby park-restaurant. The roasted "American delight" turkey special was very appetizing. Not surprisingly, the spot was crowded with American and local patrons, as well as members of our watchful security team.

Back at the safe house, I worked with technical experts for a few hours on ongoing operational issues and new reliable methods of communications. Two emergency escape plans were developed and activated in case of imminent danger, unanticipated exposure and even apprehension. My imagination at the time couldn't sufficiently envision that within two years, one of these plans would cunningly bring me to freedom, and in essence save my life from certain execution.

The 1982 Thanksgiving holiday weekend turned into prolonged working hours for us. With John and Alex Mathews, who arrived for our meeting from Frankfurt, we went through endless pages of specific information that needed my examination, breakdown and clarification. One of the crucial documents that we worked on was the rather convincing secret document, but obviously fabricated intelligence on Pope John Paul II assassination that was offered by the Bulgarian defector Stefan Sverdlev.

I possessed detailed information on Sverdlev's escape to Greece in the early 1970s and was convinced that any information he disseminated recently was more or less flagrant disinformation. Evidently, Greek intelligence had craftily manipulated data and boldly intended to compromise the Bulgarian authorities, the Warsaw Pact's south flange strategies and the KGB's intelligence and political interests. Lieutenant-Colonel Sverdlev was a deputy director of the Pernik Regional Directorate of MIA responsible for military evacuation matters. A former military-counter intelligence officer responsible for the Petrich border troops regiment, he criminally misappropriated funds during the construction of his private villa. Facing officer's dismissal, expulsion from the communist party, the loss of his government pension benefits and certain prison, Sverdlev stunningly defected to Greece. During a family outing at the Greek-Bulgarian border crossing Kulata, unwittingly facilitated by his former reporting officers, Sverdleev boldly and comically crossed into the Greek section of the border bridge on the Struma River with his personal car and entire family.

The fact that Sverdlev was not an active State Security operational officer was sufficient corroboration of his "kitchen blending" of information on intelligence matters. Risk assessments after his defection revealed that the highest damage he inflicted to the State Security was based on his unauthorized removal of a military emergency and evacuation plan from his directorate. Using data, logic, professional assessments and analysis of Sverdlev's disclosures by cross-referencing it with my knowledge and facts, the CIA clearly determined that he was a pawn in an overly deceptive game. Sverdlev was a common criminal, playing *Zorba* with false Greek and German rhythms.

My last dead drop load was promptly recovered and the plentitude of audio, photo and secret documents, on the spot assured no deviations on some of the matters. Evidently the Pope's assassination was of tremendous importance to the CIA and the United States government, for I became subjected to a surprise polygraph test at the end of my trip. I was not intimidated, for I understood well the necessity of preventive measures in assuring indisputable trustworthiness. Passing flawlessly made me a proud CIA professional, without any signs of mistrust and intimidation. In a similar manner, during my first test a few years earlier, the examiner found slight deviation only when answering the question about the psychological conditions of my wife. In reality, she suffered from a serious hereditary mental disorder that every so often made her act disturbingly.

Because of the ominous *"Bulgarian connection"*, many CIA people missed the traditional Thanksgiving family holiday. Several traveled thousands of miles for the meeting. Clyde and Katy Bedford, my embassy contacts, arrived from Sofia through a Romanian round trip, in order to discuss at length our imminent operations. Clyde and his wife became my good friends in Washington D.C. years later. When they departed on a challenging diplomatic mission to Cuba during the mid 1980s, Clyde circumvented U.S. regulations in order to supply me with a few boxes of exceptional *Cohiba* stogies.

Bulgarians also should celebrate Thanksgiving of 1982. The day changed the position of the United States government on the assassination attempt on Pope John Paul II, and therefore the view of the world. The circumstantial speculations and harsh indictments of Bulgaria in the *"Crime of the Century"* were eventually permanently removed on March 23, 1983.

During 2002, Pope John Paul II visited Bulgaria as the official guest of the new democratically elected government. Eloquently and convincingly, the Pontiff addressed the world from Sofia and with the gracious hand of a Saint removed once and forever the veil of suspicions and accusations from Bulgaria as the main perpetrator of his assassination plot.

Despondently, in the end of 2004, months before his death, Pope John Paul II somewhat loosely delineated in his book *"My prayers and my life"* the Vatican's findings and beliefs on who attempted to assassinate him. Thoughtfully alleviating strife between global believers, the Pontiff caringly withheld gross accusations against the fanatic Islamism. This act of goodwill prompted an avalanche of unsubstantiated new insinuations and renewed charges against the former (communist) Bulgarian State Security and the Soviet KGB by sensations hungry Italian magistrates.

DEVIOUS KGB ASSET

T he steady and somehow relentless camaraderie offered to me by General Ivan Savchenko and his deputy Colonel Vladi Ferov was veiled in an air of secrecy. Plainly, the KGB kept our gatherings extremely private, conveying the necessity of unquestionable discretion to most channels of communication. On the other hand I constantly sensed behind their exceptional approach General Bureniok's solid authority and a plentitude of Kim Philby's positive vetting and analytical assessments on my personality and professional capabilities.

It was not long before Colonel Ferov offhandedly asked me to check a few individuals through the State Security register and archive after conveniently suggesting that he preferred to stay in the shadows. When the results came back to me I was surprised, for I was almost set up, digging the closest associates of Ludmila Zhivkova. From Emil Alexandrov's assistant to George Jordanov and Andrey Lucanov's secretaries and three other government officials, the KGB center disclosed to me some of their sensitive and rather unorthodox interests. Perceivably my KGB *"friends"* incorrectly assumed that they had successfully conscripted me as a fraternal asset since our October revolutionary party or perhaps much earlier, when general Savchenko had casually asked me for information on some government and party officials. This first information to the KGB I almost jokingly signed *"Vsegda gotov"*, or *"Always ready"* a.k.a. *Semper Paratus*.

It was paradoxical for me to see how the KGB pursued exceptional assets inside State Security. To protect and justify some of my stealthy activities, I opened in my safe a literary file entitled *"KGB and Science and Technology Cooperation"*, where I diligently but unofficially filed most of the KGB inquiries and tasks.

Vladi Ferov surprisingly implied another time, that he knows about my connections with Ludmila Zhivkova and forthrightly asked if Ludmila works with any of the senior State Security officers. Reasonably informative, I disclosed the facts that general Ilia Kashev, Colonels Emil Alexandrov, Zhivko Popov and Dimitar Murdzhev, Jaroslav Radev, George Jordanov, Alexander Fol, Todor Radulov and Kosta Chakurov were in reality Zhivkova's only real contacts with the world, the State Security and State Council. On communist party issues, Ludmila worked consistently with Milko Balev and Todor Zhivkov. I did not omit the fact that Ludmila had grown into an obsessive paranoid, a rather introvert megalomaniac and nonetheless a crafty conspirator alike her father.

Many questions were methodically explored by the KGB in reference to Zhivkova's secretive initiative *"Cultural Heritage"* and the build up of foundations *"1300 Years Bulgaria"* and *"Banner of Peace"**. Ferov was surprised to learn that the staff of *"Cultural Heritage"* was composed entirely of State Security officers, assigned personally by General-Colonel Mircho Spasov and Colonel Zhivko Popov. Endless inquiries by the KGB residency followed on the outcome, intents and especially the long term planning of Ludmila's events and how the entire extravaganza was budgeted with millions of dollars in hard currency. Shortly after these meetings, Ludmila Zhivkova was abruptly replaced as Chairman of the Committee for the celebrations of the *"1300 Years Bulgaria"* by her father Todor Zhivkov, an unorthodox move that was perhaps politically inclined and skillfully devised by the Soviet leadership.

In an almost deliberate hookup Ferov mentioned once that he knew my favorite retreat in Samokov, just few miles from the government residency *"King's Bistriza"* at the mountain resort Borovetz. By inference, he accentuated on the restored 17th century *"Stoilov's"* residence*, the guesthouse of the Committee of Culture and one of Ludmila Zhivkova's favorite retreats and the fact that devious forces have been in place assuring this transparency. It became evident that the KGB was working on a complex program aimed at shedding light on Ludmila Zhivkova's milieu, as well as her contentious initiatives. Although the KGB never surveyed her moral profile, it emerged that Zhivkova's ideological and psychological silhouette was a legitimate substance of trepidation for the Kremlin. Savchenko, rather seriously delineated allegations behind her unorthodox revisionism, proclaimed Ludmila's deviations from the Soviet internationalism as deliberate "Slavic xenophobia" and megalomaniac "Pan-Bulgarian chauvinism". Listening to some of the KGB testimonials, I was growing concerned about the inevitable outcome, nonetheless even about my own wellbeing.

The KGB residency interests with western Know How, Science and Technology issues and the Bulgarian political elite grew immensely. Almost with whispers were discussed growing issues of reliability and loyalty of the members of the communist government of Todor Zhivkov and the leadership of the Soviet Union. Colonel Levon Galustov, a KGB Fifth Chief Directorate representative started appearing surprisingly often at our directorate's operational meetings.

Natalia, stealthily provided me with details as she was the typist and the editor of Galustov's intelligence reports and was deeply disgusted by his arrogant Georgian demeanor. Perhaps, others disliked the dark skinned, grayish Caucasian

---

*   The KGB was monitoring Zhivkov's family through Colonel Dimitur Murdzhev. Code-named "Beregovoi". In 1982 Todor Zhivkov believed that Murdzhev had tampered Ludmila's medications, contributing to her KGB orchestrated dead.

as well, for he never showed up at our KGB private gatherings. Eventually, it became a common denominator for representatives of the "political police" from the KGB and the State Security to be viewed by other directorates with extended suspicion and repugnance.

In early 1981, I helped Natalia with a secret document assessing information collected on Ivan Slavkov, Ludmila Zhivkova's estranged husband and a renowned playboy. Slavkov was one of General Savchenko's tennis playmates in the past. However, besides the communality of their first names, they had no compatibility or mutual sympathy. Assisting with the translation, I came across a stunning Sixth department top-secret document. It detailed the ongoing monitoring and investigation of *"Panjandrum,"* Ivan Slavkov, and 7 high-ranking communist officials, covertly identified only by pseudonyms and numbers.

Taking one of our traditional walks through the Liberty Park with Colonel Ferov, he one day unambiguously spelled out the weighted dislike of Ludmila Zhivkova by the Soviet leadership. Undoubtedly, and perhaps intentionally he made me a silent partner of an impending *coup d'etat.* The drift had started apparently a few years earlier, when Ludmila Zhivkova had personally met the critical evaluations of her global cultural diplomacy of the Soviet ambassador to the United Nations, Anatoly Dobrinin. Thereafter, most of her unorthodox initiatives have irritated the Kremlin, for they intentionally have been disregarding the Soviet democratic centralist principles as the guiding philosophy of socialist communality and global unity.

My KGB friends almost impatiently guided me into infiltrating Ludmila's Buddhist and yoga spiritual circles and her stealthy entourage. Astonishingly, one of Ludmila's instructors in Asian martial arts, an old associate of mine, Dr. Hincov, was soon indicted on ideological subversion charges by the Sixth department. An invisible, suffocating noose, stage managed from Moscow, slowly encircled Zhivkova. She perceptively distanced herself from Colonel Murdzhev and grew restlessly paranoid of her surroundings. Examples were her suddenly changed relationship with Kosta Chakurov and soon thereafter with Emil Alexandrov. The epitome of Zhivkova's shifting mentality, or perhaps sudden realization of political rejection, was her swift extrication of Zhivko Popov from the helm of the "Cultural Heritage" program.

The KGB stealthily traced Todor Zhivkov's orders for secret transfer of substantial amounts in hard currency to the United Kingdom, West German and Swiss bank accounts. Vladi rhetorically attempted to implicate Ognian Doinov as Zhivkov's surreptitious mentor for ingeniously transshipping Soviet commodities, including but not limited to oil, coal, oar and weapons to western and especially developing nations to generate illicit billions. Through this veiled in secrecy process, the KGB believed that billions of dollars had never been returned to Bulgaria by Zhivkov's cronies. I noticed that Vladimir Ferov deliberately avoided any clarifications on Andrey Lucanov, despite the fact that Lucanov worked very close with Doinov since early 1977 on most foreign financial and industrial opportunities and was for certain period of time Ludmila Zhivkova's closest friend and even a deviously persistent wooer.

My information on Zhivkov's far-sighted relationship with the Chairman of the Bulgarian National Bank and the Bulgarian ambassadors to Switzerland and Austria aimed the KGB queries into looming hard currency diversions by Ognian Doinov to copious western banks and companies. In reality, I personally observed how easily Doinov virtually unaccountably handled sums of US$250,000 from the National bank. Substantial funds were utilized for questionable intelligence operations through the "*Cultural and Historic Heritage committee*"*.

One day during a lengthy meeting in a room at Park hotel Moscow, just across the new Soviet Embassy, Vladi Ferov pointed out his and General Savchenko's ongoing mistrust with the stealthy operations of the Sixth directorate and sarcastically suggested that it should aggressively work against the corruption and misdeeds of the high party officials! He circuitously implicated Ludmila Zhivkova of a deliberate ideological subversion and Ognian Doinov and Todor Zhivkov of financial misappropriations, craftily utilizing even the Jewish moguls Robert Maxwell and George Soros. Doinov's astute NTR cronies throughout Western Europe have become "wealthier than their masters", Vladi cannily concluded, plainly alluding to Andrei Lucanov as the only insider source of his information.

Later on, we took a long walk through the park of Liberty, semi-conspiratorially chatting on the intricate subject of technology transfer and western electronics divergence. Approaching the national stadium "Vasil *Levski*", Vladi indicated that we should avoid public visibility. Unknown to him, I was fully aware of the reasons of his growing furtiveness, as I had craftily set forth an immense trap ahead of him. As Vladi Ferov and Ivan Savchenko steadily cultivated me as an indispensable KGB secret source inside State Security, they eventually have been following a grander scale plans laid by General Bureniok. The old spooks, including Kim Philby, irrefutably positively vetted my vast acumen, complex political and economic insights; however, they grossly failed to identify my implausible determination and the fact that I could stealthy control my KGB gofers.

---

*   Mircho Spasov's clan developed in the 1990s the mightiest economic enterprises "*Orion*" with questionable funds. Z. Popov and E. Alexandrov have been convicted and jailed for embezzlements during the 1980s and early 1990s.

My escalating contacts with the Soviet KGB in the last several years was vigilantly analyzed and prudently guided by the CIA. A ferocious cat-and-mouse game came into the making and my Soviet "friends" could not have been more off the mark as to their traitor. From an acquaintance, I grew to become a close friend of Ferov, all the while in order to run and stealthily manage one of the East's best on behalf of the American intelligence.

*   *   *

During the 1982 Coordinative council of the KGB's Fifth Chief Directorate and Sixth Chief Directorate in Sofia, I became more than an operational liaison between the parties involved. In the final phase I coordinated the joint resolution and the "top-secret" assessment document of both directorates' global operations. The extraordinary document allowed the United States government and the NATO Alliance accurately to pinpoint at few deeply buried and some recent communist penetrations of *Radio Free Europe* and the *Voice of America*. Stealthy KGB assets were as a result cornered, and Soviet illegal officers well planted inside the Polish *Solidarity* movement, who posed as western supporters of the labor unions were exposed.

In early 1983, Vladimir Ferov became a general, replacing the ailing Ivan Savchenko as the KGB Chief of Balkan's operations. Ferov was perhaps the first person to read a top-secret Moscow cable that had implicated me as an eventual American secret asset inside the vital communist institutions. I did not receive any warnings from Natalia or Snezha Ovcharova about the imminent KGB investigation, and believe that they have been prudently proscribed from specific top-secret KGB communiqués.

I can imagine the steel faced expression of the newly epauletted General Vladimir Ferov while reading the inexplicable information. In the perfidious intelligence game of deception, he categorically has been asking himself with a grate doze of fear and concerns:

"Who in reality served who? Who calculatedly managed this intricate intelligence game? How was the mighty, perceivably impenetrable Soviet KGB craftily subjugated to the extent of becoming an ineffective bureaucratic monstrous totalitarian string-puppet?"

Ten years earlier, General Alexey Bureniok had steadily attempted to nurture me as his likely son-in-law; he had resourcefully associated me with Kim Philby and inevitably entered my name in the secret KGB's rosters. General Ivan Savchenko thereafter, gregariously bonded me with his *"Chekist"* group in an anticipated ever-lasting secret fraternity. The General selected me as his primary tennis playmate and unambiguously used my assistance to dig through the secret

State Security archives to conduct intelligent and sheltered research. In due course the veiled brotherhood had shared an immense plentitude of forbidden fruits: delightful philandering and drinking orgies, secretive liaisons and nonetheless enormous political and social clouts.

In the final annals however, it had turned out that one of these secret brothers deviously has long deceived the fraternity's political rostrum. Even worst, he had cunningly infiltrated and gravely grinded down the KGB brotherhood's grotesque veracities.

PROVIDENCE

CHARTING THE FUTURE

After years of thrilling anti-communist activities and self-sacrificial conscious fight against the sinister totalitarian security institutions of the KGB and State Security, the United States of America became my country. This splendid land of unlimited opportunity became my patriotic devotion, land of my pride, my new family and thorough human happiness. My self-contained approach was not an assurance for success; however, my focused, clearly directed actions have been the only venues available to me, successfully carrying on my silent war against the monstrous totalitarianism and the destructive consequences of the growing socialism.

In any of my stealthy undertakings, there were risks; however, I wisely minimized them whenever possible. Yet to avoid risks completely was the greatest risk of all. I realized clearly that my actions could always bring the possibility of failure and defeat, however if I have stand still, obedient to the socio-economic and ideological injustices of the communism, my spiritual and moral defeat and human failure would have been certainly greater than my family's lost prominence and wealth to the totalitarian communality.

In early 1983, I received a transfer, most likely as a result of my nonconformist political standing and the jagged criticisms of the communist party policies. Undercover as a senior councilor at the State Committee of Higher Education, I became responsible for all foreign scholars and students in the country. Although, it was a high civil servant position, in reality it was an unambiguous derailment of my professional career. At the time, I was not envisioning justifiable professional implications, nor was I attempting to find serine comfort and refuge, while evaluating the situation in the remorseless shadows of the reality. What mattered; was what I have achieved, and perhaps; what else can I do effectively, without failing or being defeated?

Sixth department (the political police) of our directorate unquestionably has started investigation of my work as member of the Party committee and a parallel due diligence review of my operational activities. Furthermore, and perhaps deadlier: on March 01, 1983 the First Deputy Minister of Internal

Affairs and Chairman of State Security, General-Colonel Grigor Shopov*
eventually had authorized my top-secret investigation for espionage, on request
of the KGB.

---

*   Information revealed to me by T.Shopov, former senior State Security official, during my first
visit to Bulgaria in 2001.

DOUBLE AGENT'S MISDEEDS

During the late 1979 I successfully recruited as a secret agent George Filipov, an Associate professor of biochemistry at the Sofia state university. During his studies in Moscow, he boldly had approached the KGB and offered his cooperation. Unknown to State Security, the KGB had exploited Filipov's proposal and had recruited him as an "*agent in place*", instructing and guiding him to collect information on foreign and Soviet students in Moscow and later on to work on specific targets in Bulgaria and East Germany. Eventually, the KGB had instructed Filipov to accept my recruitment pitch on behalf of State Security, imposing however a strict secrecy on his affiliations with Moscow.

Dr. Filipov* was a bright, intelligent and eager to be trained and directed spy. He grew up as a surprisingly effective secret agent, successfully passing even few elaborate tests of trustworthiness. We gradually developed him as a science and technology expert, capable of obtaining secret and advanced research on bio-chemical, pharmaceuticals and bio-technological subjects from the developed west. Based on his German fluency, we arranged through the West German embassy in Sofia and the Ministry of chemical Industry a research exchange program at BASF in Leverkusen, West Germany. The KGB and State Security considered the German conglomerate BASF, a primary science and technology target, for it manufactured key components and materials for the western chemical, military and air-space industries.

I was scheduled to attend the upcoming annual ITA, trade show in Cologne, West Germany and at the same time had to relate a clandestine meeting message to an American contact through the IREX office of Mr. Carlson in Washington, D.C. To eliminate any counter-intelligence suspicions, I had designed an emergency communication program as a normal procedure on behalf of the Committee for Higher Education, pursuing new assignments of Fulbright scholarships. Agent Filipov was instructed to send a letter to the USA after his arrival in Germany, attaching a light sensitive** adhesive address label to the letter

---

* The author obtained secret State Security and KGB information on Dr. Filipov during 2002, corroborating the matter.

** Within minutes of exposure to light the address on the adhesive sticker was designed to fade away and to be replaced by the correct recipients address

at the mailing, by simply removing it from a small pouch hidden inside his leather photo camera case. This was designed to train Filipov in handling complicated technical methods of secret communications.

Two weeks later, no Americans showed up at the prearranged meeting, nor did anyone respond to my emergency mark near the famous Cologne Cathedral. Waiting in vain, in the end I had to use an alternative and risky channel to relate to Langley important military information.

After Filipov's return, he gave me a somewhat contradictory assessment, especially about the exact procedure and the timing of sending our letter. Yet at this time, he was still a trustworthy source, providing overwelming scientific data on specific bio-technological developments.

In July 2001 we learned, that my plain letter had not only intrigued, but also had strongly convinced the KGB of my unusual and suspicious activities, and had warranted my thorough investigation. Filipov apparently had noticed the heliolater characteristics of the mailing label and duly had reported the facts to his KGB masters.

UNDER FIRE

By late March 1983, I felt the chilling wisdom that my professional career was steadily spiraling into a blind alley. I started noticing atypical surreptitious activities, nonetheless, distinctive symptoms of infrequent surveillance coverage in areas in which I was present. Maintaining extreme caution and a cool mind, I found conclusive evidence that my home was searched and my car penetrated. The American section of SCD inadvertently provided me with the most suggestive forewarning by unilaterally canceling two prearranged meetings. A forthcoming scholar to the USA, an agent of First detachment, they have instructed to stop all contact with my office. I steadily started recognizing the shady nuances of a treacherous labyrinth and the nonetheless stealthy traps that have been cunningly laid ahead of me.

Conspicuous verification of an ongoing secret investigation came to light during my approach to a clandestine meeting with my American contact in Sofia. Our skillfully planned and seldom rendezvous were in the vicinities of the Liberty Park and the Pioneers palace, whereas we had even two exceptional dead drop sits. Driving through the city assured me of not being under surveillance, although, I knew well about the new methodologies of remote monitoring. I parked near the *Roman wall* ranch market and walking through the abundant venues, purchased fresh vegetables and fruits. Avoiding the crowded and slimy fish and poultry section, I cut short through the vendors' stands and inadvertently stumbled into a surveillance layout.

Less than ninety minutes before my clandestine meeting, I unmistakably identified two surveillance squads. One I recognized as customarily working against the American diplomats, while the other eventually was tracing my activities. The American target was in the vicinities of the market, for when I greeted friendly the team's leader standing nearby, his strap radio emitted few traditional beeps, indicating their target was in motion.

Inadvertently, I grew concerned that perhaps something different from my political dissent had duped me off. My prudent forethoughts directed me to immediately cancel the imminent meeting. I placed the fruits and the veggies in the trunk of the car and nonchalantly drove up the boulevard. In one motion, I checked my pocket calculator; however, no code message was displayed. Accelerating, I passed a familiar maroon station wagon parked in the opposite direction of *Anton Ivanov* Boulevard. Plausibly, the American surveillance team has been unnoticeably following my contact. With a shiver, I realized that the American diplomat's inability to detect the surveillance inadvertently was walking me into a deadly trap. Inserting my ball pen—antenna into the calculator slot, I entered a common geometry formula. A brisk beep instantaneously confirmed my warning message. After repeating the procedure, two beeps concluded my operational call.

At *Jordanka Nikolova* square, I stopped near the small park and as I descended the public restroom stairs casually positioned an undistinguishable ECC* mark that was easily noticeable by a passer by. In the semi-dark, spooky and suffocating odors of my compartment, I within seconds destroyed two rolls of top-secret photo materials, twisting the cartridges until a simple popping sound confirmed the deployment of image erasing chemicals. Down the filthy drains of the totalitarian public sewage, ample top-secret information about their sins was forever lost.

My professional counterintelligence expertise allowed me to recognize behind the complex and insistent surveillance efforts an advanced stage of investigation. Certainly, it was not a result of my ideological rebellion, but perhaps my secret affiliations with the CIA have been compromised and my bona fide intentions vigilantly contested.

The surveillance's angst and the lack of coordination between both units at a particular moment become palpable. An unsettling feeling of my imminent apprehension chilled my brain. Enormous trepidation abruptly paralyzed my movement as two familiar colleagues from the surveillance walked nearby. Utterly sure that incriminating materials could not be found; I cooled and managed to keep composure. However, the adrenalin level in my veins made my heart bouncing. It was a bizarre filing, perhaps never experienced in my life; the crushing stress made my ears whistling, as bursts of red and black circles suddenly impaired my vision. Conceivably an "*easy talk*" drug perhaps has been sedating me, thus I bit my tongue until pain and salty blood taste levelheaded me.

Crossing the street, allowed me to recover from the psychosomatic shock and rationally I entered the corner supermarket. No surveillance lock stepped me while shopping. Purchasing a magazine from the exit kiosk, I noticed a sloppy, concealed taking off my picture** by an unfamiliar young officer. The hourglass of my soul determination and eventually of my own subsistence has been running short of sand, for invisible and destructive cracks perhaps have surfaced.

---

*   Emergency contact cancellation

**   SID (surveillance) employed tailor made blazers for surreptitious snapshots taking through the pinhole buttons.

The Sofia night streets were uneventful and remote, as my mind vividly broth to life wonderful and life fulfilling memories. Content emanated from the cat-and-mouse evening upshot, brightening some of the staggering blows we have silently inflicted on the totalitarian communism. In reality, I was not pursuing just a meager revenge for my grand father's persecution and our family's appropriated wealth. With my unyielding anti-communist determination, I inadvertently have been charting a new better social destiny, which would take over the Soviet communism sooner than anyone had expected.

At home, I made a few misleading telephone calls to the countryside on my certainly monitored phone. I faked the sleepless night as calm and relaxing, certain that a video dot and eavesdropping bugs vigilantly controlled all aspects of my whereabouts. After very careful evaluation, I reached to the conclusion that I have to activate one of my contingency exfiltration plans.

Instead of becoming another victim of the totalitarianism, buried unmarked in the rugged land of my ancestors, after an executioner's bullet had pierced my head, I painstakingly and dignifiedly decided to continue my mission.

Our apartment's restroom was presumably free of video monitoring, allowing me early in the morning to emit a silent message to the Center. A plain beep soon confirmed that the American government was ready to help one of its indispensable assets.

DESTINY

Any intelligence undertaking requires certain level of simplicity, besides professionalism, faultless planning and skillful implementation. Such are normally the assets extraction (exfiltration) plans developed by the CIA's OTS specialists. Two exceptional procedures allowed me with high level of certainty to fade away successfully, even under direct and tight surveillance. No magic applies, but advanced science components, Hollywood imagination and illusion, technical diligence and most importantly—considerable professional determination. Precisely implemented procedures assure that within hours, perhaps days an asset can be far away from the draconian KGB control and the choking hold of the totalitarian security services.

For the upcoming weekends, I organized the traditional build up of wild animal's feeders and winter shelters at the Rodopa Mountains, the main domain of our hunting group. After some diminutive incongruity with my wife, who had deplorably grown emotionally susceptible most of the time, we prepared for the weekend trip to the countryside. Besides, I sought to find out if the surveillance would be bound for the mountains, thus indicating the true level of my investigation.

A month earlier, feeling the tightening, although invisible forces around me, I had made a casual pitch: During an evening stroll, I tactfully complained to my wife Svetla, that the life is becoming more or less miserable and restrictive under the totalitarian communism. Probing her willingness and desire to follow me to freedom clearly indicated that it was an impossible task. She was much too faithful to her own roots of upbringing and in reality was inherent to her mother's dilapidating mental predilections. It was a sadly staggering fact, that unfortunately for my family's future, I had discovered too late in our relationship. Something was painfully chocking my mind when thinking of my two wonderful children Panko and Tsvetelina, which I had to live behind.

The early morning fog fledging the *Tracie* highway did not dissipate through the valleys and made my efforts to spot surveillance fruitless. A freshly brewed coffee at the Vacarel's Duty Free stop revitalized my exhausted perceptions to the point where I suddenly noticed a sloppy surveillance officer. For a "take into custody" operation State Security should not have driven so far from the capital. Calmly assessing the situation new pertinent questions blurred my mind: Would they continue? The answer would clearly determine the level of my investigation and my unwavering deeds.

Convincingly casual, I checked the oil, wiped the windshield and we soon continued our trip. Besieging the morning fog, the sun rose, making the highway clear stage for observation. We were virtually alone, besides a few loaded cars returning Turkish guest workers back home. Entering the Veleca river gorge, I jovially pushed the accelerator up the winding road. The missing surveillance misleadingly let me assume that I was just under a preliminary investigation DOP*. Unearthing an unusually parked off the road *Lada*, dismayed my self-possession. Up the steep rocks, I spotted a man aiming binoculars at us, unflappably finding refuge behind few semi-leafless bushes. It was a peculiar spot and timing for even an astute tourist to admire the nature's solitude and beauty. More or less, the advanced lay out "spot surveillance" allowed invisible observation by spotters of key segments of a target's road. The new finding was indicative of my fully-fledged DOR** investigation.

My state of mind bowed into an eternal sorrowfulness for the unknown future of my family. The trepidations of last few days palpably implied that I was not an "iron man", with lost human filings, concerns and fears. Furthermore, my impending *dead* inevitably was going to bring serious problems and sufferings to so many people I truly loved and cherished.

Recollecting past treacherous steps and devious clandestine operations, I was unable to identify any questionable endeavors that could have tipped off the KGB and State Security of my double play. Tough, it was unquestionably my American fidelity, which has been putt on dissection.

Compassionate family time made the psychological grinding day go slow. At our habitual dinner with relatives, I saw more or less my *"last supper"* with the dearest people I have come to cherish and treasure. I had less than a week for the CIA to validate and design my extraction. Although I had noticed a suspicious car parked in front of Balkan tourist hotel, I did not detect surveillance during the day. The resort was evidently not a suitable playground for full-fledged surveillance, thus the exit roads were definitely carefully watched.

Early the next morning, I took a dirt road behind the mineral spa Chepino, avoiding the main road and soon was nowhere to be found up the winding mountain road. After an hour drive through the beautiful Rodopi Mountains, I joined my hunting buddies at the ranger's station *"Pobit Kamak"*—Standing Rock. For another 4 to 5 miles, we drove on a worn by the storms macadam road. Near an old abandoned timber processing plant, we parked our Russian Jeeps and my

---

*   State Security Operational Check.
**   State Security Operational Investigation.

new *Lada*. Then the group ascended the mountain slope on a narrow mule pat for a mile, until we reached a secluded valley, hauling stacks of hay, tools and lumber. The hunting district required the construction of windbreakers and winter feeders for the wild animals, for during the winter, the area was often inaccessible by rangers. Jovial and camaraderie work further bonded our members, forming a wonderful hunting fraternity of nature lovers and protectionists as well.

Meanwhile, the surveillance, especially in Sofia was getting tight and unrelenting, while our apartment was secretly searched once again, an act dully recorded on foot prints embossed on plain paper from indigo sheets sited under the vestibule carpet.

Following weekend, we completed two additional feeding stands in a ravine, nearby a stream and loaded them whit dry haystacks. On a green and lush meadow, we had our final picnic, facing the mesmerizing beauty of the snow-capped ridges of *Beslet* mountaintop, far to the south. Perfidious feelings that I could never see these marvelous mountains again, my friends and especially my beloved family, filled up with awful grief and soreness my heart. Two days earlier, I have received the CIA extraction confirmation. What kinds of problems were laid ahead for my family as a punishment, revenge and retribution for my anti-communism, or perhaps ... sinister support, because of my premature, accidental death? Overwhelming questions made me feel guilty; however, there was no breathing space for sentiments, for it was solely my "life or death"!

Maintaining a traditional and calm attitude, I recognized that a demanding investigation would soon surround my accidental death. The State Security and the militia (police) investigations could use any questionable traits as circumstantial evidence in order to prove any deviations from my past and customary behavior. Thus, nothing questionable or unusual could be left to dirty or compromise the outcome.

THE SHAFT OF OBLIVION

Our hunting group in two weekends overshadowed more than we had done in the last three years in feeding and protecting the wild animals in the gorgeous Rodopi Mountains. Late in the afternoon on Saturday, I decided I was ready to return to our villa, 60 miles down the road in the mineral spa resort of Velingrad. I gave most of my superb 12 gauge Remington 2-00 and 3-00 buckshot to the members of the group. With true Samaritan joy, I traditionally made this gift giving during the hunting seasons, to the continual appreciation of my friends. For our members, the possession of American ammunition was more or less a "*silver bullet*" in their guns. It was a psychological paramount that assured hunting success and was in some instances the only answer to feeding an entire *Pomac family*.

Around 5:30PM I approached the old mine "*Vurbiza*", where my father-in-law, the Director of Velingrad county management operations Spas Halatchev kept under heavy lock industrial and specialty supplies of explosives for a variety of projects. We routinely used dynamite sticks for lifting wild game out from the bushes and especially to enrage our ferocious tracing and chasing dogs. These unusual game-chasing methods, which under normal circumstances were illegal, made me a pyrotechnic expert, capable of perpetrating a lot of damage if deemed necessary.

Invisible from the main road, I parked the *Lada* next to the abandoned ore separator. From a bushy slope across the road, I for few minutes carefully surveyed the vicinity for any unwitting witnesses. To justifying the short detour I took the opportunity to relieve my natural needs, and when done walked to the mining shaft entrance.

With a surreptitiously obtained set of keys, I unlocked the grated front iron gate. Hundred of yards down the shaft was another solid gate that protected the main depot. My flashlight's beam slid along the jaggedly edged granite walls, reminding me of the mine's recent past; when few years earlier uranium ore was extracted from deep underneath the mountains. Unexpectedly, however, the enriched vein had gone astray, and the operations had ceased within months. One of the Soviet Union's greatest sources of cheap, high-grade uranium ore had gone off track. Ingenious Soviet-Bulgarian geological explorations nonetheless had discovered just 7 miles southeast in the *Syutkya* area another promising uranium deposit of even greater quality. At the new top-secret mining project, Soviet experts for years have utilized an ecologically devastating method of ore extraction. Pumping in specialized acids deep in the heart of the ore vein, they then pumped the oxidized concentrate, efficiently and cheaply receiving desired results.

However, the strategic military and economic interests of the Soviet Union greatly disregarded the potentially devastating ecological consequences and the lasting radioactive contamination of the pristine and picturesque mountains*.

This murky uranium mineshaft was destined to become my presumed grave. It was suppose to bury under thousand, perhaps millions of tons of rocks not only the truth about my life, but also most importantly the truth about how the communist's State Security and the KGB operations in the Balkans had been deeply penetrated, skillfully misguided and for years irreversibly damaged and made dysfunctional.

I had limited time to carry out the grand-scale deception by setting off the stockpile of explosives with a simple time delayed mechanism. It was one of the most feasible solutions for my escape from the choking hold of the totalitarian security apparatus.

Verifying all details, I pulled from the inside compartment of an empty ink-pen two copper blasting caps. One by one, I inserted inside them the ends of two rolls of black ignition cord, and unconventionally squeezed the soft copper ends firmly over the cord with my teeth. Sticking the detonators into packs of Czech made CX explosive was an easy, although chilling task. Profound perspiration clouded my eyes, as my steadily shaking hands hindered the final tasks. Extending the cord ends, I returned the hot bundles into the original boxes and positioned them between a few boxes with TNT sticks. The still air was hot and pungently sulfuric, making me vomit and sweat profusely. I locked the inner gate from outside with a cut out key, keeping my main key chain with all my keys on the inside dead bolt. This was intended to be unambiguous evidence that the gate was locked from the inside at the time of the blast, substantiating my certain death and eliminating any "foul play" stratagems.

A stealthily and traceless escape from the country was the only viable alternative for my life and a horrific accidental dead was the only warranty for the future well being of my family. Facing lengthy and merciless interrogations and inevitably a totalitarian execution was my imminent destiny. Knowing the State Security and KGB's methods, only an unforeseen flaw in my secret CIA operations had triggered the current extraordinary security investigation.

---

* During the 2002 numerous mushroom-growing operations in the Rodopi region had to close, for the harvests have shown substantial radioactive contamination. Italian and EC operators unilaterally had canceled any Bulgarian supplies.

The rolls of black blasting cord were 250 meters long and were certified by the German manufacturer for a 25 to 30 minutes delay. To alleviate any unexpected malfunctioning, I set forth two independent rolls with individual detonators. With a bouncing heart, I checked the time repeatedly, senselessly biting my lips. Igniting the cords, I swung the flashlight into the dark back of the shaft, and semi-blinded locked the main gate from outside with the cut off key. Running in virtual darkness towards the dimly lit contour of the main entrance, I numerous times tripped on the rocks, adrenalin pushing me even when I seemingly strained my right knee.

With shaking hands, I locked the front grate and nonchalantly waited in the entrance cavity. Camouflaged in my dark green clothes, I slipped away into the falling night. I had more than twenty-five minutes to the blast and less than a quarter of an hour to the passing train. The chill made my semi-wet body shiver. I had exhausted much of my cerebral and physical energy, or perhaps the poisonous shaft gases have sufficiently sedated me, for my body convulsed and the remnants of my picnic violently left my upset stomach.

I hurriedly found refuge from the cold in the car. On the back seat, an old military blanket covered my ammunition and the cherished "*Izhevka*" hunting rifle, a gift from General Alexey Bureniok. I pulled it over my shoulders, and removed from my wallet some of the extra cash, stacking my credentials in the glove compartment next to my 7.65mm Walter PPK handgun. Other hunting gadgets, including my Damascus hunting knife, I kept on my belt.

The hard work during the day and the challenging shaft undertaking made me feeble and semi-conscious. For a while, I was totally spent. Almost in a dream, I heard remote whistles trumpeted by the steep slopes. The echoes abruptly announced the end of my comfortable refuge; however, my sedated brain was reluctant to move my body. With a lasting determination, I got out of the car's soothing comfort and locked it for the last time. With the flexibility of a chased animal, I crossed the tracks and watchfully settled behind an old wagon resting at the far end of the abandoned station. Few almost invisible footprints left in the soft shoulder I carefully smoothed and looked around for a last confirmation that there were not any witnesses.

Soon, the steamer approached the crossing with warning whistles and I had to hide craftily from the intense head light. Squeaking breaks and steam release valves disrupted the tranquility of the valley as the train composition gradually emerged. Down the gorge, echoes intriguingly multiplied the noise. Shielded by the night, I easily jumped on the second to last platform and quickly disappeared in the rugged service compartment housing only a mechanical emergency hand brake lever and a folding wooden bench. Virtually an indiscernible phantom I lowered handily the bench, locking the door from inside. Entering the canyon, the steamer accelerated and my mind consciously started praying for a delay of the charge, averting a potential rockslide on the tracks. My subtle prayers worked, for the powerful tremor came almost three minutes later than my calculations. Three or four remote thunders echoed through the mountain, even solidly shaking the train. Although remote tremor, the prudent engineers steadily engaged the brake, halting the train to an almost crawling speed. Whistling few times, the steamer finally accelerated, setting the real beginning of my long and mysterious journey towards reincarnation. I rolled onto the floor, attempting to warm-up in a fetal position. Three mountain stops accommodated just few passengers, and after an hour, the train arrived in Velingrad.

I had serious concerns about the station, for if any suspicions had come up, State Security would have increased the security at this junction. A few intense minutes passed by until the train mechanic checked the resonance of the wagons wheels with well-measured swings of his long hammer. Completing his routine, he whistled at the traffic controller and a green light made the squeaking train composition slowly move forward along the lighted track.

In the darkness of my observation post, I suddenly became terrified as an undistinguished looking female attracted my attention. She was carefully checking the passengers through the windows of the two passenger compartments, nonchalantly holding a handbag over her shoulder. I lowered swiftly and literally slipped under the bench. With a resolute motion I opened my last defense, a narrow and long bladed razor sharp stiletto that was ingeniously designed and disguised by Mossad as a pocket pen. It was one of the most lethal silent weapons, for it could very easily be inserted in a body and with a simple shift in any direction was capable of inflicting deadly internal organ slashing and undetectable massive bleedings. While the virtually invisible penetration slit seldom exceeded 3mm, the crafty weapon was a mortal tool in the hands of a trained professional.

Leaving the station, I resumed my vigilant, tough well camouflaged observations. In the darkness of a warehouse, flanked by the railroad and the highway, I noticed two inconspicuously parked surveillance *Ladas*. With crawling shivers, I monitored the surveillance trap that was narrowly outplayed by my determination and astuteness. Not surprisingly, in a little while, one of the cars speedily paralleled the train's passenger compartments. I lowered my ski mask head and the hunted man instinct pumped my veins with adrenalin.

It was few minutes past 10:00 PM when the train arrived at Varvara, one of the last stations. Vigilantly scrutinizing both sides of the track, I was perplexed to see a suspicious looking couple combing through the passengers of the train. I did not have time to think about defensive strategies, so I promptly rolled under the seat. The few minutes until the whistle of the traffic controller elapsed into eternity, but as the steamer sent a long shrill through the wagons, I momentarily rejoiced. The squeaking noise reminded me of a fading call for hope, proclaiming that perhaps I have another station of opportunity coming in my life.

Before entering the brightly lit international railroad station September, I wiped away any traces of my boots and jumped off the train. I quickly vanished in the darkness of a public park west of the station. Motionless in the shadows of a large pine tree, I became familiar with the settings. A few minutes later, casually walking to a bench, I wiped off the night mist and invisibly retrieved a luggage compartment key that was push pinned under the wooden seat. Flying-by-night drunk, I monitored the surroundings and the two nearby entrances of the station. An old dusty light bulb meagerly lit the west wing that housed the luggage storage section. It was a desolate, late evening, with no passersby. Distant motorcars from a brightly lit courtyard indicated some activities besides few drunken voices from the south flange restaurant.

The spooky station characterized an ultimate setting for a deadly ambush. If pertinent intelligence had tipped off the KGB and State Security about any unusual American activities in the area, or perhaps diligent surveillance had detected and monitored the extraction team's work, I was unquestionably predestined to the gallows.

Dispassionately displaying natural needs, I vigilantly checked the street and the parking lot in front of the station. Blending with the shrubs, I waited motionlessly, scrutinizing the surrounding. Convinced that everything looked secure, I walked unflappably through the station's side door to the storage lockers. Anticipating the rusty hinges to echo throughout the station's corridor, I was astonished to find them well lubricated. Entering the men's rest room across the hall, I carried a soft duffel bag and a similar backpack in hand. Withstanding the unpleasant stench of the service cubicle, I methodically changed my clothes, appearance and identity.

A few extra minutes allowed me to review, remember and substantiate data and essential facts from my travel papers. A specially designed polymer bag with a sealed chemical compartment transformed all my personal documents into a milky substance as soon as I zipped the bag and twisted the chemical chamber. Once the disintegration process slowed, the bag steadily dissolved and the content disappeared down the sewage pipe. A plastic bag easily wrapped my dirty shoes and filthy clothes. After a few final touches to my remarkable disguise, I assertively exited the malice-ridden chamber and confidently headed towards my new life. Nonchalantly depositing a coin, I placed the plastic bag with my old clothes back in the locker for collection.

ESCAPE FROM THE MOTHER LAND

A slightly grayish middle-aged man with casual western clothes carrying a travel bag and a handy dark green backpack entered the sooty waiting area of September train station around 11:45 PM. A few local commuters and unperturbed travelers at 12:15 AM boarded the *Orient Express* train arriving from Frankfurt, Germany with a final destination of Istanbul, Turkey.

The ticket controller glimpsed at my international ticket and slammed the door of my compartment, moving to the next compartment without a word. After a few hours of cross-country travel and numerous stops along the way, the train early in the morning approached the Turkish-Bulgarian border zone. At the city of Lubimets a border patrol boarded the train, indicating that the train has entered a guarded and restricted perimeter. The sentries skillfully walked through the compartments, verifying everyone's identity papers and travel documents. At Svilengrad, the last stop before the border, a group of border officers and customs agents replaced the boarded guards. As a stealthy western asset, mercilessly hunted by the totalitarian authorities, I was a step away from freedom in one of the most unique American operations against the KGB in the modern history of espionage.

A few UNESCO files were visibly positioned on the small table next to my window; a pack of partially eaten Italian cookies and a half-empty bottle of mineral water completed the casual compartment setting. Faking a casual snooze, I carefully monitored the hallway. Besides two noisy Turkish families, there were just a few other passengers in the entire wagon. However, I had with slight concern noticed two of the passengers nonchalantly walk in front of my compartment numerous times.

Sliding door noise and English conversation at the compartment next to mine hastily indicated the border control's arrival. Moments later, my door swiftly opened, waking me up from the nap.

"Passports and travel documents please!" Firmly stated an officer, accompanied by a customs agent.

Seemingly displeased by the wake-up call, I casually yawned and stretched while looking out the window at the rugged hills. Politely handing my travel documents over for inspection, I once again glimpsed outside, slightly veiling my face from the agents.

The neutral European passport with numerous visas and border crossing stamps had a noticeable official attachment identifying me as a scholar traveling to Turkey. My light skin complexion, corrective bifocals and slightly grayish hair convincingly matched the passport photo.

"Thank you! Have a pleasant journey!" Cordially stated the officer, making some notes in a specialized ledger and handing me the stamped passport. No questions were asked by the customs agent the door slid closed behind them.

The train slowly proceeded, then came to a full stop at a modern, well-landscaped Bulgarian border crossing, well guarded on both sides of the train by armed sentries. A few prolonged border formalities followed the engine substitution. Soon, a sudden pull advanced the train and the landscape changed into chilling symbols of totalitarianism. Barbed wire fences linked high observation towers with machine guns and spotlights, setting the vivid *Iron Curtain* separating the communism from the free world. Armed border guards with vicious German Shepherds patrolled the boundary line, preventing any escape attempts of East European citizens to Turkey.

A filthy and crowded Turkish station and border checkpoint gradually emerged as confirmation that we had entered a different world. A smiling, long mustached Turkish officer, guarded by a soldier with an American M16 rifle, repeated the documents inspection procedure.

Although my silent *Cold War* against the totalitarian communism had not yet been won, my successful exfiltration was more or less a new promising reality. Momentously daydreaming, I saw Turkey eight years earlier, during my first foreign intelligence assignment.

TURKEY 1976

In the thrilling world of intelligence and espionage operations, it is seldom that a spy is active on two continents within the time span of an hour. The imagination may envision fast supersonic jets, signal intelligence by satellites far in the sky, or perhaps super-fast speedboats, which are all the common requisites of modern narcotics-smuggling barons, and nonetheless the latest novelties of the James Bond movies.

However, the bona fide prospects of such pan continental action in the 20th century were only two, flanking the Mediterranean Sea on the West and the East:

The Rock of Gibraltar and mount Abila in Morocco form the classical *"Pillars of Hercules,"* characteristically separating Europe and Africa. Gibraltar, also well known as *Jabal Tariq,* for centuries monitored the water passages of the Atlantic Ocean and the Mediterranean Sea under Spanish, French, Portuguese and British flags. After the brutal sacking of Gibraltar in the early 16th century by the corsair *Barbarosa II,* the majestic Rock was furnished with strong defenses by the great Roman Emperor Charles V, mighty fortifications evident even today.

Far northeast in the Mediterranean, the *Bosphorus Tracius* strait between the Black and Marmora Sea in Turkey separates Europe from Asia. This strategic geographic strait should be attributed to some of the most destructive and devilish happenings of the 20th century.

* * *

In early August 1976, General Grigor Shopov approved my travel to Turkey, the utmost archenemy of communist Bulgaria. Under the cover of a deputy director of the Bulgarian volleyball federation, I visited Istanbul, Turkey, for a few friendly games with the Turkish national champion *Ekzashibashi*. It was one of the rare forms of cooperation between the two greatly polarized nations.

Bulgarian coach Costa Shopov successfully trained the Turkish team for almost two years, achieving prominence by capturing the national championship in 1975. My boss, Colonel Ivan Diankov, maintained a close relationship with Shopov that dated back to the time of his recruitment as a State Security secret agent. Working in Istanbul, Shopov had become a priceless foreign intelligence source.

The largest pharmaceuticals corporation in the Middle East—Chem Pharma was owner of *Ekzashibashi*. State Security and KGB had classified the industrial conglomerate as a major intelligence and military target. Besides legitimate pharmaceutical production, the company was developing chemical and biological agents for weapons of mass destruction. Numerous processing facilities across the country and secret R&D medical and scientific centers became of strategic concern to the Bulgarian and the Soviet Union's national security and the Warsaw Pact's command.

Turkey was the Southeast European stronghold of the USA's and NATO's geo-political and military interests in the region. Without the knowledge of the USA and to the great irritation of the West European Community strategists (State Security analytical assessment—10/1975), Turkey had utilized in numerous instances bio-chemical and bacteriological weapons in suppressing the separatist and pro-socialist Kurdish minorities. Notwithstanding, the region separates Europe from Asia, and most importantly the *Bosphorus* and *Dardaneles* straits that link the Black Sea and Danube River with the navigational channels of the world.

*   *   *

Two months of preparation for the Turkish assignment gradually blended me in with the national volleyball team and officials. I recruited an agent and received for temporary control two others, a player and the team's doctor.

With an FCD team, we developed a plan for the secure delivery of a package to a specific Istanbul location. Colonel Vlado Yankulov hesitantly told me that the package would hold a $50,000 payment to a renowned Turkish journalist for publishing a sequence of active disinformation through his newspaper. The program was surprisingly elaborate to be a hoax or ingenious check of my integrity.

Istanbul was the most vital link of Asia to the European continent and the Balkans. The Russians blame it for the Crimean War, the surrender of Sevastopol and General Wrangell's White Russian intervention. As Vienna has been declared the eminent European capital of the intrigues, espionage and shady financial dealings; similarly, Istanbul has been living with the incomparable clouts as the global capital of international commerce, smuggling and devious treacheries. Veiled in the mystiques of the Orient, riddled by the deceit of the Byzantines, and greatly appreciated through the jurisprudence of the Romans, Constantinople nonetheless scrupulously had preserved the democratic principles set forth by the ancient Greeks.

The USA and NATO maintained large naval, military and air force facilities on Turkish soil, thereby controlling and monitoring the overall movement of Warsaw Pact navy and merchant ships throughout the Black Sea and the Mediterranean.

The geo-political antagonism of Turkey and Bulgaria was catalyzed by the Bulgarian survival of five centuries of gruesome Turkish oppression and Stalin's decision that the southern flange of Eastern Europe would be represented exclusively by the Bulgarian military, security and intelligence agencies.

With General Alexey Bureniok, we become privileged in 1973-1974 to learn the most sinister geo-political role of the region for the outcome of the devastating Second World War: During a 1974 dinner at the Sunny Beach resort restaurant *"Neptune"*, the notorious Briton turned KGB communist spy Kim Philby disclosed to us that British and American intelligence had identified Turkey and the *Bosphorus* strait as the main "Achilles heel" of the Soviet Union prior to the Second World War.

Philby believed that by promptly relating specific secret American and British intelligence to Joseph Stalin, he had personally prevented the destructive British bombings of the largest Soviet oil-refining complex in Baku, thus saving the Soviet Union's strategic oil reserves for the upcoming war. However, the *Bosphorus* straits have been not only of Soviet and British strategic interest in the region. In the late 1930s, Hitler's Third German Reich had already established a strong industrial, political and military presence on the Balkans. Germany already controlled not only the vast Romanian oil refineries and ports, but also the fascist Bulgaria of Boris III Saxe-Coburg Gotha and the navigational channels of the largest European river, the Danube, which strategically linked Europe with the Black Sea and the Mediterranean. Furthermore, I vividly remember Philby's confidential information on the British interception of Hitler's negotiations with Stalin and the diplomatic innuendoes of Molotov and Ribbenthrop during their stern negotiations in Munich. Philby's assessment of the beginning of the Second World War and the activation of the plan *Barbarosa**by Hitler solely as a deterrent to Stalin's communist expansion through the Balkans was startlingly accurate. In any case, the bottomless "Pandora box" of geo-political interests and intrigues known as Turkey was the stage for my impending first foreign intelligence assignment.

*   *   *

Colleagues from the military foreign intelligence asked me to deliver a few cases of duty free Scotch whisky to the Bulgarian Consulates in Edirne and

---

*   Plan "Barbarosa", the German codename plan for the beginning of the Second World War.

Istanbul. After a few hours of driving through the countryside, our modern Mercedes-Benz bus crossed into Turkey. Major Vulchev, the Edirne consul, graciously offered me two bottles of whiskey with the advice to have them handy in case we have problems with the notoriously corrupt Turkish police.

Perhaps he knew of a well-established policeman routine, because for no apparent reason, 30 miles out of town a police car pulled us off. A barrage of seemingly angry Turkish words disturbed and intimidated us as the police officer took away the documents of our driver. Having no other choice, I had to intervene and smilingly approached the police car. The unflinching demand of a 500 liras bribe or the payment of a 750 liras ticket fine (an equivalent of $25) at the nearby police station was our only option. Exchanging few limited words in Turkish and English, I expressed a notion of good faith and one of the Scotch bottles played a pivotal role in our negotiations. Controlling the situation, I exchanged the plastic bag with the aged scotch for our driver's documents and unwittingly became the savior of the driver and the national volleyball team's mission.

Our accommodations at the Opera Hotel, a block away from the Sheraton International on *Taxim Meydani*, were superb. My room faced the monumental statue of Kemal Attaturk, the father of the Turkish Republic.

The city, however, was loud and never slept. The offensive Turks' driving, in which streetlights were ignored, contributed to unbearable traffic noise and nuisance. It was an imposing environment taken over by human madness.

Upon our arrival, I called Plamen Georgiev, a RUMNO intelligence officer working under cover as a Second secretary at the Bulgarian Consulate in Istanbul, and arranged a meeting at the hotel for delivering the whisky. He arrived at the hotel lobby after dinner, accompanied by Colonel Dimitur Vandov, Istanbul's chief of station and my FCD contact. Transferring the two cases to Vandov's *Opel*, we agree to meet for a drink at the nearby Sheraton's sky bar in an hour.

Vandov possessed the charm of an academician and the manners of a filthy banker, though composed and courteous. His son Svilen, after graduation from the State Security academy, became a member of our team of operational officers responsible for the recruitment and running of foreign students as secret communist agents. Colonel Vandov had already completed few assignments in France and Belgium, where he had successfully managed to recruit among others, Turkish military, MIT (Turkish Intelligence) and security officials. One of his recruits had become ranking general at the Istanbul Military Garrison. As a result and consequence of this covert liaison, however, Vandov was exposed by MIT a year later and expelled as *"persona non grata"* by the Turkish government.

In the Balkans, State Security and RUMNO were the ultimate Warsaw Pact and KGB strong arms, responsible for the recruitment and running of Albanian,

Yugoslavian, Greek, Arab, Kurdish and Turkish political, military, government and intelligence officials. However, this historically tagged "*powder keg*" region became ethnically intolerable and exceedingly politically intricate to operate within. Unbalanced political inclinations, anti-American and anti-communist tendencies were met head-on by burly leftists, deeply rooted religious fundamentalism and nonetheless staggering corruption. Ever-growing narcotics trafficking and terrorism proliferation deeply tainted the region as the "*Black antechamber of Europe*". Though a strategic geo-political locale, Turkey was associated with numerous military and political alliances.

Walking around Sheraton International, I recognized a broad spectrum of surveillance layouts. Through the main lobby, the elevator catapulted me to the splendid sky restaurant & bar. The city lights below mesmerized me as condensed lines of red and white lights indicative of the major arteries dissected the European enclaves. Illuminated fortresses and palaces contrasted the night, faithfully guarding the *Bosphorus'* darkness. An arching bow of lights further northeast charted the new modern suspension bridge connecting Europe with Asia.

While offering promising glances, seductive *Playboy* bunnies delivered drinks in the high scale bar. The pleasant ambiance was complemented by surround sound music and an exotic belly dancer. Chicly dressed Arab men, displaying affluence and riches, entertained few *à la mode* blonde prostituts in one of the main booths. At a nearby table, my company was already seated.

Our conversation evolved around the greatness and the diversity of the country and the Young Turks movement of Attaturk, instrumental for the formation and the establishment of the new democratic Turkish Republic. Vandov professionally toggled the dialogue around sports events and the impending competition with the Turkish national team. The conversation shifted on the beautiful entourage of the Arab patrons and I learned with surprise that strong underground Russian organizations have for years been providing Istanbul with common prostitutes and super expensive cover girls. The local tabloids became busy exposing the secret life of the ultra rich Arab Sheikhs and petrol-dollar-loaded Bedouins. They have transformed Istanbul into a private congenial *Mecca* and *Medina* that circumvented the usually strict Arab religious precincts.

Enjoying the unusually warm for the season evening, I received a tour of the illuminated city of Istanbul on the terrace. There our dialogue was craftily intermingled with specific operational details. On the way out, Vandov laconically stated that the operational environment in Istanbul has become very thorny and we should split in the hotel's mezzanine, alleviating the lobby's surveillance ground *hogs*. Unnoticed, I exit the hotel through the cafe's terrace, prudently avoiding becoming an early target of the notorious MIT.

Costa Shopov was at our hotel's bar, immersed in superficial globetrotting. Indisputably a sinister manipulator, he promptly eliminated my initial mistrust. Besides setting the training plan and the calendar for the control games, our chat trivially revolved around the history of the old metropolis.

On October 17, during the team's practice at the sports center, Georgiev and Vandov delivered to the players a few cases with vitamin-enriched drinks and gift packages with Turkish locums for the management. Vandov personally handed the plastic bags to four of us. The brown package in my bag however, instead of locum contained the cash equivalent of two, perhaps three truckloads of the popular sweets.

After lunch, I informed the coach that I would be slightly late for the afternoon practice, for I intended to visit the *Topcapi* Palace museum. Securing the precious package in my inside pocket, I leisurely walked out of the hotel through the convenient side door. All of a sudden, I was alone, *out in the cold* with pocket full with cash, ready for my first intricate intelligence assignment. The windy and chilly day was not pleasant for sightseeing. Thus, a legitimate visit to Istanbul University's admissions office, and a walk down the Dolmabahce Cadezi and Kabatash district made certain that I did not have a tail. In the far end of the park, a man resembling Vandov was walking a dog. To consider the finding a legitimate forewarning, however, I had to cross the individual once again. Drizzle and fog pushed up the Marmora, completely veiling the coastline.

Thinning any interests, with my leather coat I looked like local. At the ferry landing, the gatekeeper soon started accepting the small waiting line of cars, followed by the passengers. Nonchalantly crunching a waffle at the bakery across the street, I diligently assured my clear getaway to the ferry. A car with diplomatic license plates stopped in front of the terminal and a tourist hurriedly boarded the ferry. With the drizzle, the ferry's tarmac became practically deserted. The gatekeeper pulled a long black windbreaker from a storage cooler, and covering his shoulders, annoyingly rang the gate bell in an ill-destined attempt to attract passengers.

I hurriedly crossed the street, boarding the ferry seconds from departure. Soon the powerful diesels shook the vessel shooting clouds of dark exhaust into the air, as the nose effortlessly rose, splitting the waterways. The deck bell and repeated horns went off through the fog in a few minutes, and the ferry suddenly diminished speed. Perceiving danger, I intuitively exited the main cabin and glanced back, nervously anticipating a boat to be following us.

How naïve of me! Dispersing the fog, a massive grayish wall emerged in front of us instead. Almost foolishly, the captain announced that he would give the *"right of way"* to the mighty Soviet aircraft carrier "Admiral Nakhimov" that was moving to the Mediterranean.

Armed sailors looked at us from the decks and the sterns high above as the Captain's narrative become a shivering reminder of the mercilessness of totalitarianism. According to the grapevine, it had become routine for Soviet sailors to shoot "*to kill*" comrades that jumped ship in more or less suicidal attempts to reach freedom. The startling reflection made me realize that I was a freeman, able to do as I wished with my own destiny and perhaps with the hefty sum of cash in my pocket. Shuddering away the deceitful thought, I looked around while the sun unexpectedly emerged through the clouds, beautifying the uneventful and sooty Asian coastline.

The tourist from the diplomatic car was nearby taking pictures. Much later, I learned from Colonel Vandov that a counter-intelligence squad had been dispatched to assure that the precious package was delivered and collected. In the KGB's tradecraft of intelligence and espionage, security procedures are always incorporated and never ignored.

Small businesses and industrial warehouses dominated the neighborhood of Uskudar ferry landing at Pasa Limani Cadesi. The confirmation mark to proceed with the operation, a small undistinguishable Marlboro sticker, was permanently attached on an electric pole at the busy intersection of Bulbuldere and Baglarbasi Caddesi. Anyone casually waiting to cross the street could easily attach the signal to the pole, unnoticed to anyone, even if closely monitored. Two blocks up the street, I entered a large automotive parts store and while nonchalantly looking around selected an impending purchase. The auto tires section was secluded in the right half of the premises and I easily noticed the Michelin sticker attached inside one of the tires on the last row. This was the indicated drop sight for the delivery of my package. I carefully took the sticker between my two bent left fingers (eliminating the possibility of leaving any fingerprints), easily replaced it with my package with my right hand and on the way to the register as I prepared my cash, I hid the sticker in my wallet. The purchase of a set of disk brake pads legitimized my store visit and the mission was completed.

I left the *Auto Mart* store and casually walked down the street until curiosity forced me to glance back through the window displays of the store. Almost like in a movie, I observed a heavyset, grayish and mustached man with thick corrective spectacles approaching my drop site. The man had obviously been in the store when I walked in. Waiting for a green light two blocks further, I casually wiped away the drizzle's wetness and in a single motion affixed the Michelin sticker on the sidewalk electric pole.

Only twenty-six minutes of the estimated maximum of 30 elapsed from when I landed in Asia until I returned to the ferry landing. Grayish clouds erased the remote silhouettes as we moved back across the *Bosphorus*. In the due course of hopping two continents, I eventually received my first foreign espionage "communion", regrettably at that time in favor of the global communist fraternity. Back in Sofia, I learned that if the Turkish security had identified me as a State Security NOC officer and had traced me to the delivery spot and exposed me, I would have lost 20 gruesome years in a prison. The "go between" operation was apparently an absolute necessity, for Soviet and Bulgarian diplomats had recently been under forceful (virtually total) surveillance by the Turkish security forces.

The return ferry was uneventful and much shorter. I took a taxicab to the Ataturk memorial and casually walked across the street. Relaxing in the room, I called the consulate and invited the staff to attend the first friendly game of our team. This invitation was a preset message that confirmed the successful completion of my mission.

Another cab within minutes whisked me to the front of the sports center. The driver, showing skillful traffic navigation, dreadfully crossed a few intersections on red lights. At the sports center, he boldly charged me double fare and thwarting my protest opened his jacket, flashing a police badge and gun. He was moonlighting unashamed during his official duties.

A cheering group of Bulgarian and Soviet diplomats and officials joined us for the first game in the surprisingly crowded sports arena. Our team management greeted the group, and as I shook hands with Colonel Vandov, he conspiratorially acknowledged my flawless work. For a week, we enjoyed the hospitality of *Exashibashi* and Chem-Pharma Corporation and our host Costa Shopov. In the end of the sports camp, Shopov gave me the sum of $12,200, proceeds from tickets sold to the public, which I delivered back to the Sports federation.

A month later Colonel Yankulov showed me few "*Jum Huriet*" editorials. The articles grossly compromised and publicly exposed the *Exzashibashi's Chem-Pharma* Corporation as a malevolent manufacturer of biological substances in violation of international laws and multinational agreements. From two small pictures annotating the investigative journalist, I recognized the grayish, mustached man from the *Auto Mart*.

Soon thereafter, the KGB and State Security received reliable military information that incriminated Turkey of the creation of a 40 kilometers long anti-tank minefield along the Bulgarian-Turkish border, consisting of conventional and deadly biological charges. The information was eventually circumspectly disseminated through the Turkish press and leftist and communist newspapers in France, Spain and Italy, setting off an international scandal, public protests and even a UN Security Council investigation. Following UN actions, the Soviet Union, a Permanent Member of the Security Council, launched an official protest and demanded independent international inspection of the Turkish border with the Soviet Union's Georgia, Armenia and Azerbaijan, grossly undermining some NATO and USA interests within the region.

The Bulgarian and most of the Soviet Moslem population were perceived as enemies of the socialist fraternity and treated as a stealthy and subversive Islamic *"fifth column"*. Brutal campaigns of destruction of mosques, Islamic ethnic centers and literature was initiated, resulting in the banning of the official observation of most sacred Muslim traditions. By the mid 1980s, for example, most Muslim names were forcefully changed to Bulgarian and Soviet ones, triggering one of the most complicated diplomatic standoffs between Bulgaria and Turkey. Protests and disagreements with the ethnically discriminatory policies of the totalitarian dictator Todor Zhivkov hurled more than 350,000 Bulgarian Muslims into exile to Turkey.

THE TRAIN TO HEAVEN

A pleasant man in his forties slid the door open and politely asked for a seat in Bulgarian. I gestured invitingly and then continued reading my book, albeit slightly alarmed. It was passenger from my wagon, and we had walked in front of each other's compartments during the trip through Bulgaria. I embraced my backpack and bluntly discouraging conversation, closed my eyes. My left hand expediently took hold of an inconspicuous ballpoint pen, a crafty immobilizing projectile invention of the Technology Directorate (OTS).

The passenger's clothes were western, although more casual than European, his blond hair and blue eyes made him notably of Germanic or Nordic heredity. Traveling internationally with only a duffel bag and a briefcase was unusual; I instantaneously envisioned danger.

While reviewing documents inside his briefcase, the passenger exchanged a barely discernible sign with a man from the adjoining compartment that was standing in the corridor.

"You should set aside your mighty pen and see these materials, comrade," nonchalantly stated the newcomer in slightly accented Bulgarian, cautiously putting an edition of National Geographic magazine on the table in front of the window.

I opened my eyes, coolly glimpsed at the glossy magazine without touching it, and in English kindly rebutted the offer.

"Not interested, thank you!"

My brain worked fast, and although well composed, I was ready to harm anyone if approached. Already envisioning the deadly trap, I stretched and moved closer to the door, ready to obstruct any incoming perpetrators.

"I did not know that you speak English." "I am John Martin, from the American consulate in Istanbul, and some of your good friends are sending you this package. You should look inside the magazine!" His voice was forthcoming and kind.

"I have been with you since you boarded the train and you are secure in friendly hands." John took the magazine, and standing in front of the door removed a yellow envelope from inside and handed it to me.

In the envelope was a set of travel documents with my real photo and a leather wallet containing a variety of identification papers, cash and even credit cards, all on an alias name. John glimpsed at the corridor, where just in front of the door my neighbor unceremoniously controlled the situation.

Tears overwhelmingly filled my eyes as I stood and mumbled gratitude, and then firmly hugged my savior. The outer man opened the door and greeted me with a firm handshake.

"Alan Pace. Welcome to our business!" He smiled pleasantly.

"Thank you gentlemen! Thank you!" My gratitude overcame my emotions. The exfiltration team had pulled off a most terrific professional job, craftily masterminding the complicated operation from inception until completion.

At the crowded Edirne railway station, we disembarked the train inconspicuously and swiftly melted into the dark refuge of a shop across the street. Exiting on a back street, two waiting cars speedily whisked us away. Within an hour we entered the secured courtyard of a luxurious villa overlooking the *Bosphorus*.

In a matter of days I was thousands of miles away, a free and proud person, and a never yielding fighter against the totalitarian malevolence.

DEMOCRACY OF
TOTALITARIANISM

MISANTHROPY

S oviet and East European intelligence officers, diplomats and party officials incessantly escaped to the West. As well-educated, professional individuals, they belonged to the most privileged and affluent communist strata of the society. However at this level they discovered the misanthropy of the utopian socialist reality. Others were cunningly recruited by western intelligence and worked for years against the communist establishments. Through courageous and dangerous endeavors these individuals provided invaluable information that helped to curb the destructive role of totalitarianism.

The ever-lapsing socialist paradigm of human and industrial prosperity became a transparent melodrama behind the secrecy of the shabby *Iron Curtain*. The crumbling centrally planned East European socialism eventually led to the ultimate moral, ideological and economic annihilation of the Soviet Union and the Warsaw pact. An astounding *"Velvet Revolution"* imploded, making it possible to preserve the world's peaceful coexistence and chart new democratic opportunities.

The Cold War, potentially the most devastating war of the 20th century, was extraordinarily won peacefully. Many factors contributed to this phenomenon, including but not limited to the silent and perilously dedicated work of a few faceless individuals who risked their personal and their family's lives for the future well being of the global community. Similar to what I have selflessly accomplished, these nameless heroes today deserve special acknowledgment:

Silent Cold War warriors, who upon special circumstances succeeded to reach the United States of America, sadly often became more or less victims of American intelligence blunders and negligence. The CIA truly lacked the understanding of key cross cultural matters and human motivational development. Because of missing guidelines and visionary policies in the mid 1970s, Capitol Hill legislators inflicted serious and lasting damage to the overall intelligence process. McCarthy's rather paranoiac legacy, combined with the tumultuous suspicions of communists' "double play" and deep penetrations of vital American institutions gravely eroded American intelligence. The dubious CIA policy of *"Squeeze then discard the lemons . . ."* that was prevalent during the 1970s and 1980s should be professed as an ultimately destructive tumor to the world's best intelligence agency. Today and for generations to come, the USA owes great respect, faith and recognition to the few silent and dyed-in-the-wool individuals who selflessly helped the United States government interests to materialize during the Cold War.

*   *   *

I should outline the case of Vitaly Yurchenko, for he defected to the United States at a time when I was deeply involved in grinding down the totalitarian Soviet system. In late July 1985 Yurchenko defected to the United States embassy in Rome after becoming greatly disillusioned by the Soviet society. Months earlier, he had become deputy chief of the KGB's foreign intelligence First department. Yurchenko supervised the North American residencies and managed the worldwide operations against the USA. This included all coordinated operations by the Bulgarian State Security and the East European fraternal security and intelligence services, including Mongolia, Cuba and Angola.

Between 1975 and 1980, Vitaly Yurchenko worked in the United States as the KGB's counterintelligence representative. Back in Moscow however, he had grown disillusioned by the almost forgotten meager socio-economic reality of the communist motherland. Vitaly plainly and frankly had delineated the truly *"gloomy Soviet realities"* in 1978 to his official FBI liaison J.M. Brannigan. Prior to the undertaking of his new assignment, Yurchenko spent four years as chief of the counterintelligence's Fifth department of the KGB. He worked at investigating any espionage activities inside the KGB, defections by KGB officers and tracking down their whereabouts in the west, debriefing and utilizing intelligence gathered from western defectors to the Soviet fraternity, and nonetheless assassinating human targets worldwide.

By asking for asylum in the United States, Yurchenko adamantly had tarnished the Soviet Union's communism and stoically defenestrated the KGB's internal oppressive and global intelligence operations. Loaded with invaluable intelligence, he promptly incriminated western moles and revealed the most sensitive communist operations against the United States. Yurchenko's timeless information should be credited for saving from a firing squad the indispensable British spy and Soviet intelligence resident in London, Oleg Gordievsky. The CIA prudently and promptly shared information with the British MI6, who then craftily snatched Gordievsky from under the watchful KGB surveillance and smuggled him across Soviet borders to London*.

Much more, including but not limited to Walker's and Howard's devious betrayals, helped the United States government to eradicate some of the most destructive Soviet espionage operations against North America.

---

*   The British government announced Gordievsky's defection and expelled more than two dozen Soviet diplomats.

For three months CIA, NSA and FBI experts debriefed Yurchenko from 8 AM until 2 PM five days a week. Numerous classy restaurants in Mc Lean, Falls Church and Vienna, even far out at Middleburg often concluded the grueling daily debriefings.

Vitali's safe house was adjacent to a Fairfax golf course and the naturally athletic Yurchenko immersed himself in the game of his American dreams. Unnoticed by his handlers however, Yurchenko grew despondent and irritated by the sloppy job of the CIA's resettlement group. Instead of dignity, respect and attention, the CIA insensitively was suggesting to him that he was just another outsider. The top CIA executives and senior case officers handling Yurchenko, such as, but not limited to Aldridge Ames, started to show him rather peculiarly that he was nothing more than a lousy KGB defector who, having been squeezed dry of information, was soon to be discarded. Under these circumstances, it was no wonder that Yurchenko craftily elected to re-defect to the Soviet Union, ferociously implicating the CIA of his kidnapping in Rome.

COMMUNIST ASSASSINS

D uring 1987, State Security eventually learned from the KGB my whereabouts in the USA. The same year, disguised as a Fulbright scholar, the FCD officer Nedelcho Penev promptly traveled to the USA, inconspicuously visiting the American Graduate School of International Management *"Thunderbird"* in Phoenix, Arizona. His mission in the USA, however, was much more sinister than obtaining graduate education. Penev was dispatched with specific instructions to gather information on my location, life, connections and the best ways a team from Canada to eliminate or incapacitate me.

Based on Aldridge Ames' information, a sealed KGB disclosure had allowed the Bulgarian Military Court to sentence me to death by a firing squad "in absentia", effective September 16, 1987. In essence, the outraged General Secretary Todor Zhivkov had sanctioned the prompt verdict, warranting my worldwide search and assassination. Miroslav Janev, a former member of a special Fourth directorate team, revealed in late 2000 his involvement in the preparations undertaken by the KGB and State Security for my physical elimination in the USA, or during my impending visits to Antwerp, Belgium, the hometown of my wife.

Perhaps, it may be very disturbing to the readers to learn the truth behind the extended tentacles capabilities of the KGB and State Security. Even long after the shocking assassination of George Markov in London, and the ignominious attempt on the life of Vladimir Kostov in Paris, the totalitarian Soviet leadership relied on the trusted hands of KGB trained assassins.

The Soviet Consulate General in Antwerp, Belgium is located in the affluent neighborhood of Wilrijk, bordering Den Brandt castle's *"Nahtegalen"* park. For many years, the bulky red brick building tantamount with the Kremlin wall had been one of the Soviet Union's key foreign intelligence residences in Western Europe. From this inconspicuous high security building, the KGB and State Security perpetrated industrial, political and commercial espionage against the West.

Since early 1960, when my father-in-law, the Honorable James Edward Van de Velde built the imposing family residence on "Pierebeek straat" in the lovely Wilrijk, the neighborhood has steadily grown to prominence, lightheartedly called today the "Beverly Hills" of Belgium. Rich merchants, diamond traders, industrialists and bankers developed astonishing mansions and villas contending even with the American glitz. In this pristine, priceless and chic neighborhood, Moscow and Sofia masterminded an attempt to carry out my physical elimination on direct orders of the Bulgarian totalitarian dictator Todor Zhivkov and a group of vengeful senior KGB operatives.

In preparation of our wedding, I uncovered with concern that our outings and our Wilrijk home were under surveillance. Although circumstantial observations revealed an unambiguous American derivation, other conclusive evidences pointed towards the Soviet consulate.

Senior CIA officials were invited and had confirmed their attending our wedding. Thus, I immediately warned Langley. I was more than bewildered when I was informed that a special team had been dispatched for the time being. Tipped by the Belgium and Holland authorities, the CIA had unraveled a peculiar Soviet and Bulgarian intelligence build up in Antwerp and Amsterdam. Combined American and Benelux efforts linked the unusual KGB activities with our impending wedding and the whereabouts of an individual in Holland. The totalitarian intent to harm and perhaps silence me unequivocally implicated the Bulgarian intelligence officer and Soviet educated Nedelcho Penev with his abnormal trip to the USA few months earlier.

Thwarting any craven Soviet or Bulgarian dealings, the United States government promptly installed a permanent 24-hour security detail, explicitly sending an unyielding message to the would-be perpetrators.

Although my wonderful fiancée Dominique was consumed with the forthcoming wedding, her diligent and observant mind instantaneously noticed the unmistakable display of security measures; however, she understood little to none of the complex and dangerous situation. To my professional colleagues and me it was clear and present that a communist assassination team was attempting to silence my voice, perhaps to set a precedent to future would be renegades about their indisputable destiny. The orders had come from the highest echelon of the Soviet and the Bulgarian communist government. For long time, I had been not only a hunting partner of Zhivkov, but had also been considered a strict and ideal KGB asset.

Predictably, as soon as the American and Belgium elaborate security measures were displayed, the would-be perpetrators swiftly pulled off the stage. They had however grossly compromised a few Soviet covert intelligence links with an international transportation office in Zeebrugge, Belgium, and a sea merchant and Danish antiquity dealer in Amsterdam. This allowed the European authorities and the CIA to uncover a stealthy Soviet/Bulgarian/East German smuggling center for high technology and embargoed industrial products.

Today, the peaceful and industrious Benelux people and perhaps Belgium's authorities would be perplexed to learn details about the devious preparations of the KGB and State Security that were set off on their soil in order to silence an upright anti-Communist. Under these circumstances, the American authorities a few months earlier had prompted my fiancée Dominique's and my move away from Phoenix, Arizona to the lovely earthly paradise of California.

The elaborate totalitarian plot was successfully thwarted, undermining the gruesome continuations of the Soviet's *"Trotsky"* era of revenge, brutality and assassinations.

TOTALITARIAN SINS

G reen rolling hills gradually replaced the uncultivated and lackluster farmland and snow capped mountains to the southwest, clearly visible from our plane window. Dark clouds steadily dissipated and the sun shaped the industrial and urban contours of a forthcoming city. The shaded slopes sharply contrasted with the clusters of residential buildings, brightly lit by the descending sun. A colorful rainbow arched the valley, completing the first impressions of Sofia, the capital of Bulgaria.

With my wife Dominique, we were the only business class passengers on the *Sabena* flight from Brussels. The plane was practically empty, with no more than thirty other passengers in the main cabin of the modern Airbus jet. We made it quickly and easily through passport and customs control. Our American passports were more than *Cartes Blanche*; they were of recognizable and respectable status and promptly opened many doors. A *Hertz* rental car was readily waiting for us and within minutes we were on the way to the capital, virtually alone on the nearly barren highway.

It was May 2002, and we had arrived in Sofia for the tenth anniversary of my father's tragic death in the hands of the communist satraps. I had been gone from my motherland for almost twenty years.

General-Colonel Atanas Semerdzhiev, former Chairman of the General Staff of the Bulgarian Peoples Army, former Minister of Internal Affairs and Vice Prime Minister of the new Bulgarian government, was eventually the first government official to disclose to members of my family during 1991 that State Security and KGB had obtained operational intelligence on my work for the American government since 1987, when through KGB sources they had learned of my whereabouts in the USA.* General Semerdzhiev was the sole government official in December 1990 to authorize the destruction of my operational and investigation file consisting of countless evil details, such as, but not limited to:

---

* By July 1987, the CIA mole Aldridge Ames had disclosed to the KGB my whereabouts in the USA. The CIA renegade Ed Lee Howard had tipped the KGB in December 1986 about a *nameless*, well-informed State Security defector to the USA. O. Kalugin, L. Shebarshin 2001.

251

—KGB and State Security planning of my assassination in the USA and Belgium.
—Sixth directorate operational planning and details of my father's lengthy and inhumane exposure to addictive and brain influencing substances.
—Interrogations and investigative techniques employed against my wife, family and children.

Details abounded about the psycho-dependence programs experimented in the late 1980s on my son Panko who was intentionally and steadily developed into a drug and alcohol addicted high school student. These programs and especially his chronic alcoholism had led him to attempt suicide twice.

Tragically, my former wife Svetla Panova—Halatcheva was not only intentionally addicted to psychotropic drugs and substances by State Security doctors and agents, but was also intentionally pushed to almost total mental incapacitation. So far manipulated was she, as to even confess killing me in a moment of jealousy. She was almost forcefully committed to psychiatry.

Around June 1988 the State Security and KGB had initiated an aggressive active measures operation under the code name *"Red Wind"**. It was designed and aimed at disseminating through covert East European intelligence channels, specific misleading information to the West. The stint corroborated that the KGB had sent me to the West as an illegal operational officer, specifically trained to penetrate the American CIA and FBI**.

Another plausible insinuation was invented by the Sixth directorate, associating me with the Chairman of the General Staff of the Peoples Army, General-Colonel Atanas Semerdzhiev. Eventually I had changed jobs through my hunting and social connections with the general, and as an intelligence officer of the military intelligence directorate RUMNO, was trained by the Soviet GRU and sent to the West as a double agent***.

Perhaps the most damaging testimony about the State Security and KGB malice and incompetence was the fact that they did not have any indications or data leading them to conclude my whereabouts from 1983 until late 1986. They relentlessly had dug through thousands of tons of rocks in the Rodopa Mountains' collapsed mine shaft and even in September 1986 officially disclosed to my family and the police Investigative directorate that my skeletal remains had been found. The Ministry of Internal Affairs issued a formal notification to my family and a Fifth District Court of Sofia officially had

---

*   During 2001 meeting in Sofia, Colonel Vladimir Nikolov, a former Sixth directorate officer disclosed details to the author.

**   G. Kuzov, a former senior foreign intelligence officer disclosed details in 2002.

***   V. Dinev, a former Sixth directorate officer corroborated the disinformation in 2002.

declared me as deceased. A dead certificate #011369 was issued on August 08, 1986.

By September 1987, all my police investigative files and documents were transferred to the State Security's HQ on the orders of General-Colonel Grigor Shopov*. This unusual move flabbergasted the police's incompetent management, for they had developed an indictment against my wife for my murder.

After the collapse of the totalitarian rule in Bulgaria, Colonel Katzamunski and his deputy Colonel Tuparov initiated public complaints against the State Security administration, greatly emphasizing my case. Two major TV shows described details of my murder and cover up by the State Security administration**. State Security and the KGB, in a bold move to control any further developments, even misled their own investigative directorate.

---

* Grigor Shopov had authorized operation *'Justice'* against me, including my physical elimination.

** Two TV interviews with Colonels: Katzamunsky and Tuparov in early 1990 have disclosed my name, and details of my "apparent" murder. The news had generated hundreds of condolences to members of my family.

"CONNOISSEUR"

P eter Uvaliev a.k.a. Pierre Ruff, a naturalized British citizen and former Bulgarian diplomat, was an avid writer, movie director and art connoisseur. In London, Uvaliev maintained intricate relationship with government officials and intellectuals from both countries. He developed trustworthy relationships with representatives of the Bulgarian embassy in London, prominent politicians, intellectuals and even with the Bulgarian Minister of Culture Ludmila Zhivkova. Uvaliev graciously and eloquently assisted Ludmila during her studies in Oxford and thereafter entertained her during visits to Western Europe.

Sophisticated, aristocratically mannered and scholarly, Uvaliev helped visiting Bulgarian and Soviet intellectuals and politicians with daily occurrences. Well erudite and highly connected through his stealthy exploits with John Cairncross and even with the Buckingham Palace, Uvaliev offered his sentimental and moral support to the efforts for Bulgaria to be recognized as a world leader in culture and children's education. Under the banner of the *"Flag of Peace"* that was resourcefully introduced by Ludmila Zhivkova at the annual UNESCO Assembly in 1974, Bulgaria gained remarkable positioning throughout the world.

Although Uvaliev was a familiar face to the KGB and State Security through his critical BBC commentaries against Stalin's communist totalitarianism, he was eventually positively appraised by foreign intelligence as a promising *"contact of authority"*. His willingness to help Eastern Europe and his motherland in particular was greatly exploited by the communist foreign intelligence and the London residencies of the KGB and State Security. I should also not withhold Kim Philby's 1974 information relevant to Pierre Ruff's stealthy connections on behalf of the KGB with John Cairncross.

With Zhivkova's approval from the Central Committee of the Communist Party, FCD-foreign intelligence and Sixth directorate's cultural heritage, he developed a special program. It was secretly aimed at the location and recovery of lost, stolen or illegally traded treasures by museums or private collectors relevant to the Bulgarian ancient, middle ages and modern cultural and historic legacy. Thus, any possessions that remotely represented Bulgarian national, cultural, religious or historic riches had to be identified. The vast program encompassed covert operations on Bulgarian and other European territories as well. Teams of leading historians, archeologists, ethnologists, artists, sculptors, religious leaders and art connoisseurs were employed and in many instances recruited as State Security agents in order to loyally work in building and rebuilding the grand maniac Bulgarian and Slavic identity. Bulgarian foreign ministry cultural attachés in major European capitals were recalled and replaced by stealthily intelligent officers from the "Cultural and historic heritage" department of FCD managed by Colonel Emil Alexandrov.

In effect, a foremost Pan-Bulgarian nationalistic and chauvinistic agenda was in the making. Certain rootless megalomaniac apparitions and historic insinuations started to intentionally curtail the growing discontent and divergence with Yugoslavia on the ominously dubious "*Macedonian question*". Lasting issues about language origin, territorial dimensions and varying Slavic nations influence on pertinent historic, religious and literary heritage of the Balkans were polarizing and aggravating supposed good-neighborly relations. However, it was not only a crafty active measures program aimed at recruiting and manipulating influential politicians, journalists, historians, cultural and art experts in order to promote the Grand Bulgarian heritage (in conjunction with the celebration and propaganda around "*The 1300 years Bulgaria*"); it was also an aggressive program, aimed through the utilization of varying covert methods, to allow authentic documents, historic manuscripts and records, art and precious objects to be undetectably replaced by fake and in many instances content falsified copies. Thus the Bulgarian government maliciously blessed a plentitude of stealthy intelligence activities that were shrewdly projected to change historic, religious and ethnic facts and events.

The General Secretary Todor Zhivkov compellingly supported Ludmila Zhivkova's goals, visions and initiatives. The foundation of a world cultural forum aimed at directly popularizing, promoting and virtually imposing the "Grand" Bulgarian heritage and national identity, became more or less a self-centered attempt at national chauvinism and jingoism. Hidden to the public and the world's intellectual bodies, including, but not limited to UNESCO, was the fact that documents at major international institutions, archives, government and private collections and libraries had been meticulously combed by experts and foreign intelligence officers. Many precious authentic archives and manuscripts had been replaced by ingenious fabrications; others had been stolen, or in few instances even maliciously destroyed in order to promote, preserve, impose or verify the bogus validity of the "Grand" Bulgarian legacy.

With the help of Uvaliev in England for example; State Security officers and leading Bulgarian historians received virtually unsupervised access to archives and historical artifacts at British museums, universities and prestigious private collections and colleges. Despite the professionalism and the prudence of British curators and history experts, major documents and historic artifacts were sumptuously replaced by fake ones, allowing the totalitarian Bulgaria to build up, accumulate and preserve vast invaluable treasures relevant to the world's history and the heritage of the Slavs*.

Even today people strolling through The British Museum unsuspectingly often gaze in wonder at fake reproductions of the *Manasievv* manuscript and St. Cyril and Methodius triptychs created by iconoclastic Slavs.

State Security perpetrated similar devious milieus in France, Italy, Greece, Turkey, Yugoslavia, Austria, West Germany, Albania, the United States of America, reaching even far out to Norway and Denmark. Well placed high ranking government officials and leading intellectuals that were recruited as devious KGB and State Security agents provided not only political, military, economic and scientific information to their communist masters, but also assisted in active disinformation, ranging from misleading interpretations of the "*Macedonian Question*" to grand scale propaganda and acclaims of the "Slavic Cultural and Historic heritage".

One individual with significant contributions was the Chief of Station at the Bulgarian Embassy in Paris, Colonel Raiko Nikolov, who among many affluent agents controlled for the KGB and State Security one of the highest ranking government officials of France, the French Minister of Internal Affairs**.

Ironically, the French judicial authorities would rebut the CIA's unambiguous leads to the communist spook's whereabouts for years as unsubstantiated, in the end to be grossly deceived by one of their favorites.

In the late 1970s Ludmila Zhivkova relinquished her duties as Minister of Education to an old friend and colleague, Professor Alexander Fol. Many of the historical, cultural, folklore, educational, artistic and political activities of the colossal undertakings "*1300 Years Bulgaria*" and "*Cultural and Historic Heritage*" were persistently developed by Ludmila Zhivkova and her deputy Emil Alexandrov, George Jordanov and Professor Alexander Fol, Zhivko Popov and Kosta Chakurov. Although strongly predestined by the Soviet leadership, all programs were carried on by a group of trusted Communist Party apparatchiks and State Security officers.

During the same period, Peter Uvaliev was perceived as a secret collaborator of the British intelligence services and was placed under intense surveillance while visiting Bulgaria. Even though the former FCD officers in London, Colonels Hristo Totev, Peter Chernev and Dimo Stankov had decisively vetted Uvaliev as a leading pro-Bulgarian patriot and intellectual, the KGB and State Security's counterintelligence had different points of view. As a result of the new mounting counterintelligence convictions, the Fourth directorate eventually succeeded to

---

*   Information by L-Colonel Milcho Zdravkov and Major Rumen Spasov in 1980 and 1981.

**   French resistance fighter and a long-standing covert communist.

electronically monitor most of Uvaliev's conversations, his dialogues and meetings in Bulgaria. Not surprisingly, some of the perceptive communist leaders and counterintelligence officials had professed behind Ludmila Zhivkova's back that Peter Uvaliev was a western stool pigeon and a turncoat that was cunningly controlled by the British intelligence services.

On these assumptions or perhaps judiciously professional, Fourth department technical wizards craftily transformed Uvaliev's infamous fur coat's shoulder pads in the late 1970s into a modern eavesdropping electronics center. Pier Ruff's questionable acquaintances in England warranted the special technical and electronic monitoring programs expansion far across the Channel, into the heart of London. An especially crafty team was dispatched and has been able to monitor for months Uvaliev activities and contacts, eavesdropping his conversations throughout London and the outskirts of the city.

Uvaliev's fondness for his rusty Siberian lynx coat eventually turned out to be of enormous value to the KGB and State Security initiative. In due time, the electronic monitoring compromised not only the deceitful character of Uvaliev, but also undoubtedly exposed his covert affiliation with the British secret services. Perhaps the most detrimental information gathered about Uvaliev was his obsession with the apparent secret work of the Bulgarian *"emigrant"* writer George Markov for State Security and KGB in London. Information gathered by the stealthy operatives in London, plainly identified Peter Uvaliev as the main originator of the secret information submitted to the British intelligence that grossly had implicated George Markov as a KGB and State Security agent in England. Uvaliev's sinister inspirations could be justified or perhaps elucidated with Markov's egotistical and glitzy character, including but not limited to his sexual seduction of Uvaliev's long-standing vivacious secretary and lover.

Once again in the historical annals of espionage: sexual imprudence, political intrigues and gluttonous business interests did not harmonize, but rather lethally divided.

*   *   *

In the late 1970s I worked with Minister Alexander Fol, one of my favorite professors at Sofia State University, especially since his appointment to the ministry of education. My official legend was that I was one of his students and we often overtly gathered at his office, conveniently and justifiably discussing the international exchange of scholars, among a vast spectrum of topics and even gossips. Minister Fol knew about my association with Ludmila Zhivkova and managed to be perfidiously delicate, if not even exceedingly precautious not to cross the lines of political and ethical indiscretions. He was indifferent to the traditional and constant fear of the communist nomenclature from the notorious

State Security and especially from the *"Ideological Police"* of Sixth directorate. Maintaining a working relationship with Emil Alexandrov, he had learned to stay craftily above the treacherous shallow waters of political intrigues.

The Sixth department eventually became puzzled by my contacts with Minister Fol, for the soon to become general, Colonel Boian Velinov, was bowled over by his inability to recruit Minister Fol as agent. Reading some of my analytical reports on trends and ideological predispositions within the Bulgarian cultural cream of the crop, Colonels Velinov and Anton Musakov envisioned danger for several of their complex operations, and I one day received a summons to the office of General Peter Stoianov.

Walking through the cool marble corridor of the second floor I grew apprehensive. Days earlier, during my security duty at the directorate, I penetrated General Stoianov's office and with keys (managed by the duty officer's desk), I had craftily opened his personal safe and photographed virtually all documents inside. Two secret reports; one from a former partisan and another from a member of the underground communist party resistance group of Panagurishte plainly charged General Savov with treason and collaboration with the fascist Bulgarian government.

The reports straightforwardly held Stoian Savov responsible for the gruesome and murderous betrayal of few antifascists*.

In General Stoianov's office were Colonels Velinov and Musackov. Almost from the door Petar Stoianov laconically explained that Fol's secretary was Colonel Velinov's secret agent, providing some conflicting information about our meetings. He was convinced that professor Fol cooperated with me, not from a camaraderie standpoint, but because I was a State Security officer. General Stoianov resolutely stated that my meetings with Minister Fol were to stop immediately in order to prevent compromising some ongoing investigations.

At previous meetings, Alexander Fol provided me with unambiguous and provocative information about the peculiar relationship of the Political Bureau member, Alexander Lilov and the CC member Andrey Lucanov with Ludmila Zhivkova. Although Lucanov had been a close personal and professional acquaintance of Todor Zhivkov for some time, under unmistakable strong influence from the Soviet Union, rumors had it that he had become critic of Ludmila Zhivkova's ostentatious and portentous "Art, History and Culture

---

* General Stoian Savov, Chief of foreign intelligence, committed suicide after the communism collapse in Bulgaria. By pulling the trigger of his resistance pistol Savov had evaded responsibility for old devious sins. Imprudently Savov had anticipated that his stealthy double crossings and collaboration with the CIA would never been discovered.

without Boundaries" concepts. The powerful, unorthodox Soviet complaints had made the Zhivkovs distrustfull of the secret messenger Andrey Lucanov.

Ultimately, Fol played a morbid political gambit with Ludmila Zhivkova's xenophobic, historic and cultural heritage programs celebrating the *"1300 Years Bulgaria"*. The Soviet political, cultural and intellectual elite had foreseen diminished Russian historical prestige and eroded cultural heritage as a result of the aggressive pro-Bulgarian and pan-Slavic ethnic, folklore and global cultural and art crusade of Ludmila Zhivkova. Her visualization of how culture, art and education could evolve into universal forms of diplomacy and lasting harmony were harshly criticized by the Secretary of the Central Committee of the Communist Party of the Soviet Union, Leonid Zamiatin, during 1980 and 1981.

Alexander Fol shared the controversial developments in Moscow, confidentially mentioning that Ludmila was emotionally devastated by the facts. She had slowly developed a sincere repugnance towards the Soviet position, not to mention her degrading standing with most of the old Bolshevik apparatchiks, who had become spiteful towards her father. Fol was genuinely concerned about Ludmila's state of health and mind and illuminated her rejection of friendly contacts.

During the opening of the Bulgarian Cultural Center in Mexico City, Ludmila Zhivkova showed bizarre behavior. Two serious nervous breakdowns rapidly changed her mental state, to the extent that Colonel Naiden Petrov called her husband Ivan Slavkov. He flew to Mexico City with Dr. Gerasimov on a government jet and succeeded to calm Zhivkova, in essence sedating her to an incoherent bundle of nerves inside a body.

Suffering from a progressive and degenerative psychosomatic depression and a persistently painful traumatic head injury sustained in a 1973 car accident, Ludmila Zhivkova eventually overdosed with anti-depressant drugs and drowned in her bathtub one night in 1981*.

Her death triggered an avalanche of gossips and lasting details of mysteries and speculations. It should be clearly stated, however, that Ludmila was very disturbed by the Soviet communist leadership insinuations and the lack of support for her sincere international efforts to promote not only the Bulgarian cultural and historic heritage but also to unite children, students, teachers, intellectuals, artists and their respected governments around the globe under the pro-socialist banner *"Flag of Peace"*. From UNESCO to the United Nations and many developing and developed countries, Ludmila Zhivkova's initiatives were embraced with enthusiasm, hope, vision and promises for cooperation and peaceful global unity

---

*   Colonel Dimitur Murdzhev, (Zhivkova's UBO bodyguard) should be investigated for complicity with her dead. Uncorroborated KGB lead in 1981-2 convinced me of Murdzhev's secret cooperation with the KGB since 1956.

and understanding. On the other hand, overtaken by her grand-maniac visions, Zhivkova had forgotten an important and fundamental rule, imposed on the Eastern European communist fraternity already by Joseph Stalin years before:

"...*All cardinal national and international events by the East European countries, should be coordinated with Kremlin, and their main purposes should be to promote the credibility, the strength and the supremacy solely of the Soviet Union!*"

Soon thereafter, I found that Alexander Fol was under State Security investigation DOR *"Zeus"* by the Sixth department, and was implicated in an apparent extramarital affair with Zhivkova and complicity in her suspicious death. Even her unsubstantiated anti-communist standing and even stealthy ideological subversion activities were related to him. Fol made another mistake that was surreptitiously discovered by State Security during a secret search of his home: he had exploited his position to amass old artifacts, manuscripts and a collection of rare old Greek, Roman and Byzantium coins.

COURTESY TO LUDMILA

I contacted Ludmila Zhivkova in June 1976. I had grown up together with her and Vladimir during our early childhood summers in Pravetz. Later on Vovata was one of my junior classmates in the Russian school. Ludmila initially accepted me with very cordial and professional attitude, despite the fact that I blatantly used my State Security acumen and credentials to reach her office and to annoyingly surpass even her bodyguard *"Murdzho"**. We discussed the international exchange of students and academicians, and opportunities for Bulgarian artists, intellectuals and actors visiting and performing abroad. My early acquaintance was more or less nerve-racking, for Ludmila was a superbly versed intellectual and academician. Gradually, however, I adapted to her demeanor and soon she began providing me with continuous information on foundations in Western Europe, the United States of America and Latin America, that represented certain interests to her own goals as well.

On many occasions, Ludmila asked me for special help and assistance. Although her assistant Kosta Chakurov, an intelligent and politically perceptive former Commsomol careerist, or even her Secret service bodyguard Colonel Mitko Murdzhev could have offered immediate help and even better solutions, she demanded my aid. It was perplexing to me that Ludmila started soliciting my assistance, some times even for trivial tasks, such as, but not limited to approving someone's foreign passport file, or obtaining the State Security archive information on a specific individual. For some private matters Ludmila utilized the help of Emil Alexandrov, her deputy chairman and a State Security Colonel, director of FCD-foreign intelligence's cultural heritage department.

Besides her intellectual brilliance and almost unilateral separation from the earth's destiny, it was fascinating that Ludmila possessed a unique sense of conspiracy. Due to the fact that she used always her HF-VC (secure telephone line) to call me on my direct secure State Security phone, our Sixth department and Colonel Velinov's operatives did not intercept our contacts. Later I realized that perhaps I was wrong, for all of Zhivkova phone calls had been connected through a secure Secret service switchboard!

---

* Synonym for a friendly dog

Day after day, I noticed Ludmila's growing solitude, deepening narcissism and almost nascent obsessions. She grew adamantly fearful of KGB and State Security, believing that they listened to her and her father's conversations. She constantly envisioned clandestine surveillance. Strangely enough, she started to treat me as a dependable and trustworthy conspirator. When she asked me almost naively if State Security was listening to her visitors, I was perplexed and already foresaw retribution from my senior management. Extremely cautious, I assured her that it would be impossible for me to know the State Security's operational procedures. However, I remember her semi-angry jagged response: "Obviously you do not know everything!" "How do you think we found the truth about Marusia's affairs?"*

I was surprised that she initiated and then almost intentionally aggravated the dialogue. Conceivably, during some of our meetings, I became apprehensive and uncertain of Ludmila's rationality. Steadily the frequency of our visits diminished. It was normal, considering Zhivkova's increasing state and especially political responsibilities; nevertheless, in due course I was not forgotten, as I was always available to assist and support.

Markedly Ludmila disliked the Chairman of the National Assembly, Vladimir Bonev and subtly declared him in few instances as an imposed Muscovite *"jester"*. As soon as Grisha Filipov replaced the pro-Zhivkov Stanko Todorov by a blunt Kremlin move, Ludmila cautiously asked me to find if he was a Soviet citizen, for he was born and had grown in the Soviet Union. Ludmila was astutely fishing for clues to implicate the monstrous KGB in complicity and even subversive activities against her and her father. She perceptibly envisioned the forthcoming socialist manipulation and harsh reality. Sometimes, I was not certain if Ludmila was attempting to discretely stage manage our conversation, or perhaps was attempting to learn more about the functionality of the State Security, KGB and the security surrounding her office.

General Ilia Kashev, the Secret service chief, was very close to Todor Zhivkov and his family, offering lasting loyalty, unquestionable protection and professional support to them. In late 1986 he committed suicide after being callously grinded down and demoted by Zhivkov for allowing a *"mortal enemy of communism"** to hunt with him. Not surprisingly, Todor Zhivkov personally authorized my physical elimination in the United States or Europe during 1987-1988; the communist tyrant grew more than vengeful, for I was a close associate of Ludmila and a friend

---

* The Sixth directorate exposed the first wife of Vladimir Zhivkov in an extra marital affair with a family friend.

** KGB had perplexed Zhivkov in late 1986 with Aldridge Ames' information on my whereabouts in the USA.

of Vovata, his hunting partner (more of a hunting dog), and my wife Svetla had developed his personal legacy museum in Pravez.

How erroneous! The mighty totalitarian tyrant was deceived!

In early 1980, Ludmila started envisioning enemies among her staff, friends and colleagues; a classic example was Colonel Murdzhev, whom she deeply mistrusted for he had investigated Todor Zhivkov twice during the 1950s and 1960s for alleged collaboration with the fascist police director Geshev. However, to thwart any rumors, or perhaps to keep a closer control on him, Zhivkov made him the personal guard of Ludmila. On one occasion, Ludmila revealed to me that she had observed Murdzhev to be in contact with a known senior KGB official during a trip to UNESCO in Paris, thus she assumed a grand scale KGB conspiracy.

Ludmila personally selected her driver Kircho to be close to her age and thought highly of his loyalty. However, very similar to her father, she started to suspect him of spying on her under Colonel Murdzhev's guidelines and control. In reality, Kiril Dragnev was a secret agent of Sixth directorate who diligently reported on Ludmila's activities, conversations and contacts.

Ludmila Zhivkova's painful and malignant obsessions should be ascribed to the deceitfulness of her highly politicized social and government environment. Political doctrines, devious colleagues, overall imperceptions and criticism of her "cultural" diplomacy and intellectual vision, relentlessly grinded down her genteel demeanor. Not surprisingly, she lived in a few different worlds; one was the world of deception, treachery and intrigues, consistently catalyzed by the primitivism of the socialist environment.

My brother-in-law Dr. Dimitar Popov was one of the favorite personal doctors of the legendary psychic Vanga in Petrich. Through this virtue, Dr. Popov became aware of the secretive visits of Ludmila Zhivkova with Vanga from 1977 till 1981. Besides Vanga, Ludmila entertained a renowned Russian friend, Sasha, (Alex Lubimov) truly one of the gifted supernatural clairvoyants of Moscow. Both extra sensual spiritualists independently professed to Ludmila the inevitable cataclysm of socialism.

The other world was a very exigent, though gratifying one: Ludmila's world of intellect, culture, music and lucid visualization of humanity's potential through history, art and education, global cooperation, peaceful coexistence and understanding.

I should knowingly emphasize Ludmila's deepening interests with the ancient Buddhist traditions of trans-meditation and even with the measured martial arts movement of Tai chi. In reality, Ludmila Zhivkova's upbringing was a gradual deception from her family roots, her career was set forth against her will, and her personal life was in a real muddle. She was rather reticent, and even in her very personal settings would often become far-flung and unemotional. Ludmila's eyes would quickly flash across the paintings on the wall, glaze over, and without noticing colors and nuances her mind would flow through the windows and far over the ridges of Vitosha or Rila mountains without saying a word. Perhaps she was getting used to overdosing with amphetamines and medications, which she took in quantities, often replacing regular meals with a handful of tablets and a cup of herbal tea. Her increasing devotion to the Buddhist occultism made her surprisingly obsessed with spiritual trans-meditation, and I should be greatly creditet for helping her to develop something virtually unknoun in Bulgaria—the inner energy transformation of Chan's Ian and tui. She ate specialized meals and possessed a very fragile and physically delicate body.

In a private setting Ludmila once closed eyes and with her head firmly extended backward, started stretching hands high above her head and in a moment of a deep transfixion moaned, falling back cataleptical on her bed. For few seconds (it was like an eternity) Ludmila was utterly motionless. Slowly recovering from the incoherent impetus stage, she placidly affirmed: *". . . my personal life is never genuine and pleasing, however my inner meditation makes me feel as a Goddess . . . The feelings of immense power, internal peace, balance and tranquility are a mesmerizing and prevailing blessing . . . Something potent and distant in my brain drags me and submerges me in a wonderfully peaceful, comforting and painless steaming pond . . ."* (Audiotape of LZ's voice #11/80)

Ludmila's latest husband, Ivan Slavkov, was more than an executive of the Bulgarian Television and functionary of the Olympic Committee; he was, as the public had put it openly, an Olympic champion of womanizing, living the gregarious life of a semi-decadent tramp and a licentious playboy. Years later Slavkov ironically become Chairman of the Bulgarian Olympic Committee and a member of the International Olympic Committee.

However, his credentials were suspended due to corruption allegations by the IOC President Jack Rogh just before the Athens '04 Olympic Games, and soon thereafter in 2005 Slavkov was disgracefully expelled from one of the most esteemed world's body, as well as from the BOC.

Although never discussed with Ludmila, from her own accounts it became understandable to me that as of March 23, 1981 she had not had sex with Ivan Slavkov for a long period of time. A few months later her extraordinary life ended peacefully, although not without the help of a devious hidden hand.

NEPOTISM AND PERKS

As State Security officers, we received silently perquisites, even without asking for them. It took me time and even valor however, until I discreetly asked Ludmila Zhivkova to assist my wife with her professional career. With Zhivkova's approval, my former wife Svetla Panova became director of the cultural and historic department of Sofia county (oblast). Among different projects since 1978, she developed the historic museum of Mara Maleeva and Todor Zhivkov family in Pravetz, near Sofia. The traditional Bulgarian architecture building with advanced western audio-visual systems and displays opened to the public in 1979 with fanfares and great festivities. It revolutionized the obsolete exhibition venues of Bulgaria, although the utilization of western technology justifiably set off criticism for excessive use of national resources.

The diligent process of collecting relevant information about Zhivkov's life and governing required in the due course cooperation and constant contacts with his family. Svetla eventually developed a close relationship with the General Secretary. After the death of Dr. Mara Maleeva, Zhivkov's wife, he developed a perplexing urge of surrounding himself with discrete women, ranging from his personal medical adviser Major Anny Mladenova who in essence lived with Zhivkov, to his personal assistant and others. Persistent rumors abounded about the General Secretary's relationship with his personal secretary Angelina Gorinova, whose son was propelled to a diplomatic assignment to Luxembourg in the early 1980s by Zhivkov.

During the same time, I learned with astonishment of Todor Zhivkov's personal affections and the resulting promotions into the roster of the Young Communists Organization of his latest secret lover Sashka Shopova. It was a deplorable finding, for I knew Sashka well, becoming in reality her first lover while vacationing at the Black Sea resort of Nesebar with Kim Philby and the KGB General Alexey Bureniok in 1973. Envisaging Shopova's beautiful body in the dirty hands of the old beefed up peasant turned communist tyrant was unbearable. However, Sashka's personal aspirations were perceptibly much greater than the repugnance of being soiled by an aged autocrat.

Zhivkov's frequent planning meetings with my wife started to hassle me personally. My uneasy feelings were strongly aggravated once, as Boncho Halhulov, Zhivkov's personal bodyguard (a Secret service officer, friend and member of my Judo team) cynically suggested: *"Hey . . . I'd rather have the First banging my wife . . . instead of any filthy stud from the street . . ."*

Instead of getting aggravated by jealousy, I entrusted confidence in my wife's decency. During the traditional Pravetz evening dinner in 1980 at Grand Hotel Sofia, I was one of the first to shake hands with Zhivkov upon his arrival. With his habitual smile, he turned to me and requested to open the dance floor later in the night with my wife. I related the message with deep repugnance, and later the General Secretary opened the festivities with my wife, to the overall applauses of the guests.

* * *

Adjacent to Todor Zhivkov's residence on "Oborishte" 17 Street in Sofia was the former residence of Alexander Bathenberg. Secluded and well hidden behind a meticulously maintained high iron fence the Viennese Baroque guesthouse has entertained important international dignitaries and European royalties in the beginning of the 20th century. In the mid 1970s this exclusive architectural marvel become protected with advanced video surveillance and electronic sensors and silently transformed into the secret treasure vault of the Bulgarian national *"Cultural and Historic Heritage"*.

At a building behind the King's Palace (The National Art Gallery) was established the operational center of "Cultural and Historic Heritage", with directors Colonels Milcho Zdravkov aka Muti, Petko Kovachev and Ivan Ivanov. Muti was a well-known State Security officer, a flamboyant and egotistical man strongly associated with the family of General-Colonel Mircho Spasov and his clique. Mircho Spasov's son Rumen, a FCD intelligence officer, in late 1970s became the exclusive representative of the group in London. Working under diplomatic cover as First secretary of the Bulgarian embassy, he controlled, guided and exploited highly placed intellectuals such as Peter Uvaliev, George Markov and British politicians and communist spies. In the late 1990s, however, Rumen Spasov escaped to Moscow and then to South Africa* with millions of dollars swindled by him and his wife Veska Medzhedzhieva. Their elaborate banking fraud was facilitated through the infamous business group *"Orion"*, a proprietary cover for the management of hard currency reserves of the former communist party. Rumen Spasov was indicted in 2000 by the Bulgarian magistrate Ivan Tatarchev as one of the organizers of the Russian mafia murder-for-hire of the former PM Andrey Lucanov.

---

* Since 1999 the Spasovs were fugitives from the Bulgarian justice, comfortably living in Johannesburg, South Africa.

The Cultural Herritage operational management was delegated to Colonel Zhivko Popov, deputy minister of Foreign affairs and the deputy chairman of the Committee of Culture, Colonel Emil Alexandrov. Both individuals were investigated in early 1980s by the Sixth directorate and convicted thereafter of multiple crimes and gross mismanagement of millions of dollars.

A well-known Olympian shrewdly benefited however from the activities under the Bulgarian *Cultural and Historic Heritage* banners. The legendary Greco-Roman wrestler Boian Radev, holder of numerous Olympic and World titles, a decorated Hero of the Socialist Works, diligently amassed a vast collection of priceless art and ancient artifacts. Maintaining a close relationship with Milcho Zdravcov, Mircho Spasovs' clan and other high-ranking government and communist party officials and intellectuals, in the due course of his hobby, Boian Radev stockpiled a priceless collection of art and historic treasures with national and regional significance.

This charismatic man of willpower and Bulgarian spirit not only loudly had announced to the world the name of the Balkan nation, many times with his convincing sports victories, but also has offered his antiquity and art collections for open viewing by Bulgarian and foreign visitors. His strong national and patriotic sentiments allowed him to create public displays for the appreciation of the Balkan's cultural and historic heritage. Boian Radev opened to the world something that was strictly hidden under a veil of secrecy during the totalitarian regime of Todor Zhivkov. He grew within the years to become the Bulgarian most credible messenger of global peace, cooperation and human understanding.

THE GENERAL SECRETARY

With my wife in charge of the development of Todor Zhivkov's museum in Pravetz and the anti-fascist partisan brigade "Chavdar" memorial and museum near Sofia, my family gradually entered the inner sanctum of the first family. Todor Zhivkov invited me to go hunting during the season with his hunting group and for four years I hunted at national preserves, such as "Voden", "King's Bistriza", the Balkan Range and the Simitli Mountains with some of his closest comrades.

General Ilia Kashev, Chief of the Secret service (UBO) and Boncho Halhulob were always present during these hunting outings. General Kashev had a strong bonding relationship with Zhivkov. Perhaps my judgment was overstated; however, I overheard both of them constantly discussing government and personnel issues during these trips.

In a few instances, I hunted with Vladimir (Vovata) Zhivkov and his bodyguard, former wrestler Stoian Bimbalov. Once at the Koprivshtiza Mountains, we opened the hunting season for wild boars. Disheartened from the lack of success for hours, finally we encountered a stack of deer, and Vovata followed by our hosts Maxim, son of Ivan Vrachev, member of the Central Committee of the Communist Party, opened fire at the forbidden to be hunted animals. Two deer were taken, while four or five escaped in the shrubbery perhaps mortally wounded.

The same evening our exultant group settled at the *Koprivshtenska Mechana* restaurant and after a solid drinking binge a bizarre contest took place: Vovata Zhivkov pulled his 9 mm "Beretta" pistol and aimed at the eyes of an elk trophy on the far wall of the restaurant. As he missed the target, Maxim Vrachev aimed his father's 45 calibers "Colt" and fired, hitting the elk straight in the forehead. Screaming restaurant patrons ran for cover, some hysterically diving for safety under the tables. The powerful handgun shots were overwhelming in the enclosed space. At this instance, the agitated and drunk Vladimir, disregarding the commotion, stood up and emptied his clip of 12 or 13 cartridges, completely destroying the trophy. The dreadful setting was impossible to understand in any literary sketch, for trophy, empty shells, and fractured wall particles flew in all directions. The restaurant was filled with dust and the burned stench of gunpowder. Bimbalov, the Secret service officer, took the matter of the damages in his hands and precluded the promptly arrived local militia to intervene. Shamefully, ". . . the laws of the jungle seemed to be the governing laws of the totalitarian elite . . ." and disgracefully for me personally, I was part of this tribulation.

For most Bulgarians, the General Secretary Todor Zhivkov was an unreachable tyrant, a treacherous, harsh and mighty "Balkan God". In reality, for the people around him, Zhivkov was capable to play well the artsy role of a down to earth, considerate human being, with good sense of humor and gracious kindness. He demonstrated simplistic personal style and life, although lavishly spending government funds on his children and grandchildren. Besides the hunting, Zhivkov was a loner, who, next to young and mighty women was not capable of hiding his devilishly sparkling eyes, emotional excitement and primitive manly desires. With certainty, some of his personal nurses, assistants and some unscrupulous political cronies and affiliates gained personally from discreet and dedicated time spent with the tormenter.

Zhivkov was not admirer of any material possessions or extravagant habits, mainly due to the constant and excessive government benefits and the never ending gifts from ranking and senior communist and government officials and international dignitaries. However, it should be known that behind the common peasant propensity of Todor Zhivkov, was hidden an astoundingly astute, prudent and greedy financier. Through a reliable and trusted FCD (foreign intelligence) source, I learned about Todor Zhivkov and Ludmila's secret bank accounts set in Switzerland and England. In fact, Zhivkov's son-in-law Ivan Slavkov maintained a particular relationship with the prominent Swiss lawyer Jhan Ziclunow in order to facilitate the First family's legal and financial transactions. Ognian Doinov's clever money management strategies led Zhivkov to authorize substantial proceeds from sales to Western Europe of machines, gas and petroleum derivates to be deposited in bank accounts in Switzerland, West Germany and United Kingdom. Elaborate escrow deposits and trust accounts were wisely utilized as guarantees for Bulgaria or specific designated judicial entities to obtain substantial western bank credits guarantied by the Bulgarian National Bank. Specific transfers to the "*Zinovia Katzarova*" foundation in Switzerland and "*Wittgenstein*" in Austria were entered into the books of the non-for-profit institutions with special contingency attachments aimed at providing virtually unlimited educational, room and board funds and expenses to Zhivkov's children and grand-children.

In essence, Todor Zhivkov was a street-smart, common-sensed, underground communist conspirator with some very questionable fascist police affiliations and even records.

During my preparation of a classified thesis for the Communist Party leadership conference in 1979 on the key role of George Dimitrov for the formation of the Bulgarian State Security and the Ministry of Internal Affairs, I received authorization by Minister Dimitar Stoianov to work with the country's most secretive archives, including, but not limited the secret archives of the communist party. Digging through files, not opened for more than 35 years, I found "forgotten" police documents from the secret archives of the fascist police director Geshev. Dated 1938-42, neatly hand written and faded typed pages described the police's successful operations in penetrating the underground Bulgarian Communist Party. Some of the staggering materials undoubtedly implicated Pencho Zlatev, Nikola Stoev, Todor Zhivkov, Boris Velchev, Milko Balev, G.M. Dimitrov, Nako Boiadzhiiski and others as fascist police assets and collaborators.

Whit the joyful sense that I was unearthing distrust within the party's leadership, I related the findings promptly to General Peter Stoianov, Chief of Sixth directorate. Sure enough his deputy Colonel Anton Musakov, urgently summoned me to his office the following day. Calml and composed he asked details about my findings and avowed me to strict silence on the "speculative and uncorroborated" matters.

Fundamentally, I had unearthed some of the fascist records of the police chief Geshev and eventually have set the beginning of an unprecedented secret stage-control of Todor Zhivkov by a small and powerful State Security clique*. Unfortunately, Todor Zhivkov grew to become an ideological follower of a system that was doomed to failure virtually since its inception. He went into his last journey in disgrace and humiliation as a notorious Bulgarian tyrant and vicious communist oppressor.

Zhivkov was an uneducated government apparatchik who often, even in official settings, used slang peasant words and weird gestures, inevitably offering reasons for denigration, jokes and doubts of his intellectual veracity. All were consequence of Zhivkov's understanding of Stalin's merciless strategy of sustaining power and keeping in check not only enemies and friends, but also all of his high-ranking communist party and government apparatchiks.

Todor Zhivkov, whom I had the privilege of knowing personally, was a vengeful and treacherous principal who incited and provoked dialogues, gossips and actions, thereafter sinisterly using them as reasons for reprimand, demotion and even cruel elimination of his personal and party opponents, even some of his personal friends. A typical example was the member of our hunting group in Velingrad, Constantine Giaurov "Kocho". He became victim to Zhivkov's anger over an honest criticism of the lavish annual meetings of the General Secretary with the diplomatic corps, and trumpeted charges of regional industrial and economic mismanagements in the Plovdiv region.

---

* General-Colonel Mircho Spasov was the last guardian of the original Geshev archive. In early 1990 the archive materials have been sold mysteriously to Geshev's family attorney Jose Louis Cardenas in Buenos Aires, Argentina.

As castigation, Giaurov was removed from the Central Committee of the Communist party and sent into a virtual political exile as an ambassador to Mongolia.

Venelin Kotzev, another high ranking government and party official, fell into disgrace just for openly criticizing in front of Milko Balev the development in Pravetz (Zhivkov's birth place) of a major electronics industrial enterprise. Saved by Ludmilla's intervention, Kotzev become ambassador to Italy, handling in the process some of the most controversial money spending of the secret funds of Bulgarian cultural heritage. Kotzev was a dedicated judo player and I often practiced martial arts with him.

Sometimes even gifts were misunderstood triggering Zhivkov's irrational judgements: A renowned Bulgarian politician and ambassador to West Germany gave a superb "Heckler & Koch" hunting rifle to Zhivkov as a gift in 1979. Intentionally or inadvertently, the ambassador had forgotten to remove the manufacturers suggested retails price tag of DM 13,000. The carbine was a corporate gift to the ambassador from the German industrial conglomerate and apparently, for marketing and promotional purposes, H&K has specified the (MSRP) market price. However, Todor Zhivkov became outraged by the presumed flagrant price suggestion of the gift he had been given.

Discussing the matter with General Kashev and members of the hunting group, the General Secretary became visibly agitated. A few months later, the Bulgarian ambassador to West Germany was unexpectedly recalled from his post and sent into retirement.

During his reign as General Secretary of the communist party, Todor Zhivkov received numerous expensive guns, art objects and precious jewelry as gifts. Most of the trivial gifts were meticulously inventoried by Zhivkov's office; however, the unique and expensive ones, such as jewelry and art objects, were silently appropriated by members of the First family*.

Towards the late 1970s and early 80s Todor Zhivkov became compulsively paranoid, persistently envisioning covert murder plots. A flagrant illustration of this occurred during a hunting outing in the vicinities of the Stara Planina—mountain top Baba. Boris Veltchev, a former member of the Political Bureau of the Communist Party and Zhivkov's old comrade, took care of the arrangements, although he was strained and tainted since the 1970s by an incongruous relationship with Zhivkov. General Ilia Kashev was giving us security instructions and strategy plans for the hunting, when Todor Zhivkov emerged from the Mitsubishi jeep after concluding a VCH telephone conversation.

---

*   Confidential information from Angelina Gorinova and Maria Dimitrova, former T. Zhivkov aids at the CC of BCP 2002.

Not far from our position, we heard the sudden, intense and loud barking of the hunting dogs down the gulch. The local official and his group have for weeks been tracing a rather large elk. Out of nowhere a shot echoed through the gorge and multiplied in a stunningly real effect of an automatic burst. The barrage caught Zhivkov with his left foot still inside the Jeep. As he attempted to promptly step down on the ground, he lost stability and clumsily fell forward. At the same time we heard the singing noise of a stud bullet. All this happened within milliseconds; however the unusual circumstances made it an eternity.

The semi-dry bushes and tree brunches in the beginning of the ravine violently cracked under heavy pressure and a magnificent elk with trophy antlers gracefully emerged in the open space. For a split second the stunned animal measured the group and with a powerful jump disappeared into the hilly foliage.

General Kashev and Boncho Halhulov promptly helped the General Secretary to get up from the muddy ground. In the silence Zhivkov agitatedly raised his voice: *"This is the easiest way I to be murdered . . . isn't it?"*

Although the scene was fairly humorous, we were still and motionless. My immediate inference was that no one had ever seen the General Secretary with such muddy and dirty hands and evil face.

The barking dogs came into sight, chased by their exhausted masters. They had surprised the elk in the narrow and dense foliaged gorge and as the magnificent mammal had jumped in our direction, the local hunter had decisively sent a warning shot into the air in anticipation that the General Secretary would be ready for the take. Instead of conveying one of his flavorsome peasant's jokes and pacifying his clumsiness, Zhivkov expressed a flagrant misjudgment. It was perhaps the first time I encountered him raising his voice and being visibly upset. As a result, General Kashev was not a happy man to the end of the day, for Zhivkov in a few instances agitatedly continued to grind and harass him for the incident.

"HYPOCRITE"

I n early 1960s, KGB intelligence analysts identified the symptomatic flow to the United States of America of highly secret Soviet political, economic and industrial information. During the UN General Assembly '62 in New York, KGB management prudently addressed the suspicions to State Security. Americans had exceptionally predicted the Soviet Union's position during volatile and complex multilateral negotiations. State Security would eventually discard the lead as unsubstantiated, after two years of comprehensive, though fruitless investigation jointly conducted with the KGB's General Filatov.

As the "Sixteenth" Soviet Republic, Bulgaria was considered an integral part of the Soviet Union, totally under Moscow's rule and KGB control. The arrest and imprisonment for espionage of Michail (Mick) Shipkov, translator and secretary of the American Embassy (legation), in 1949, together with the KGB orchestrated "active measures" and propaganda campaign against the USA, the Anglo-American Peace Commission and the American ambassador, during the trial of Traicho Kostov in 1947, had distanced both countries. After more than a decade of severed affairs between Bulgaria and the United States of America, new promising horizons of cooperation and understanding warranted reestablishment of diplomatic relations in the beginning of the 1960s.

The KGB assigned to counterintelligence the vital role of day-by-day operations against American diplomats and suspected intelligence officers. Operational teams of highly secretive operational officers and professional technicians specially trained by the KGB in Moscow and Leningrad maintained virtually total control and coverage of the targeted diplomats and their activities.

Even for the trained State Security and KGB operational officers, the surveillance activities and the teams' methodologies were fascinating mysteries. Young attractive women were able to change, while in motion, into old and limping seniors, or man could quickly redress from a businessman into an inconspicuous looking peasant. The team members were trained to transform from distinguished looking scholars in to mechanics, park laborers or waiters within seconds. Employing miniature Soviet made body shaped and strapped radios with changing frequency and lasting batteries, officers were capable of relating voice or signal data to each other in a complicated memorized coded forms. Surveillance activities were undetectable even for professionals, not to mention casual bystanders. Special disguises from duffel bags, blazers, packs of cigarettes, a reading book, or Borsalino type handbags camouflaged sensitive and miniature photo and movie cameras for clandestine photography and documentation. Salt, paper and napkin holders, even coffee mugs were effectively used to disguise remote radio electronics control (MRK) for secret recordings of conversations in restaurants, cafés and bars. Broad spectrums of high tech gadgets were implemented to perform similar technical operations in hotels, rooms, parks, cars or entertainment centers.

In mid 1962, a well-positioned surveillance team around the American Embassy in Sofia had noticed the suspicious and awkward behavior of the American diplomat target *"Panther"*. After numerous unjustified "cleaning and spotting" maneuvers, the Consul was spotted delivering a letter to a mailbox in front of the Central post office. Two weeks later, he was observed clandestinely mailing another letter through a mailbox near the People's library "Cyril and Methodius". State Security and KGB had already identified *"Panther"* as an intelligent officer working under the control of Robert Stolz code named *"Dragon"*, the CIA resident at the embassy. Both American diplomats spoke surprisingly good Bulgarian and had shown unusually flexible for diplomat working schedules. These symptoms had raised red flags, indicating conclusive affiliation of Panther and Dragon with the American intelligence community.

A KGB tracer had confirmed that Robert Stolz had been stationed after the Second World War in Italy as a member of the Allied Forces and had interrogated Balkan defectors in an OSS* managed refugee camp in Trieste. Stolz was instrumental in directing stealthy intelligence operations against Joseph Tito's transitional Yugoslavian government during the 1950s.

In both instances, the mailboxes' content was covertly collected by specialized postal teams and analyzed by the PK-postal control professionals and SCD-counterintelligence operatives. The scope of the suspicious recipients was soon narrowed to a single individual: Ivan-Asen Georgiev, former Chief Secretary of the Ministry of Internal Affairs, Chief Foreign Policy Adviser of the Central Committee of the Communist Party, Permanent Representative to the UN, New York and a Law professor at the Academy of Sciences. Georgiev was a member of the communist party and a close friend with leading members of the government. A vivid scholar of Hegel and a classical music aficionado, Ivan-Asen Georgiev was an intelligent academician, a bright and well-mannered diplomat, a prominent politician and a seductive womanizer.

At this juncture, the KGB and State initiated one of the most complex and secretive DOR *"Hypocrite"* on Ivan-Asen Georgiev. *"Hypocrite"* traveled extensively

---

*   Donovan managed the American SWW intelligence agency. The future CIA.

to Switzerland, France and the USA. He was placed under surveillance and his absence used for secret penetration and search of his old and new apartments and the installation of monitoring and listening devices.

Frustratingly, all these lengthy and complicated measures were worthless, for they failed to reveal any compromising materials, information, or suspicious activities of Georgiev. Analysis of *"Panther's"* activities while *"Hypocrite"* was abroad however, had revieaed surprising coincidences:

He visited the same countries as Ivan-Asen at the same times. Thus, a leading KGB theory, although a rather expensive and unusual MO for American intelligence, soon prevailed; the Americans communicated with Ivan-Asen only when he was abroad.

During one of the almost routine secret penetrations at the *"Hypocrite's"* new apartment in 1963, a finding of the operational team leader Major Ivan Dobrev* produced the long searched for incriminating clue:

Inside a portfolio with western currency, Dobrev uncovered a cipher notepad and concise radio communications instructions in English. From this moment, the case developed into one of the most serious KGB espionage allegations ever levied against a high-ranking party and government official.

At that juncture, the Committee of State Security's Chairman, General Angel Solakov, took control of the investigation. A few unsuccessful deciphering attempts of previously intercepted and recorded radio emissions as specified in the unraveled instructions would not disarm the General. Totally immersing the KGB radio intelligence directorate, he would eventually produce the needed results and the decoded meanings of a new radio communiqué, pre-ordained by a Beethoven's symphony. An elaborate CIA program had trained and furnished Ivan-Asen with variety of secret writing materials and a powerful *Hamerlund* radio receiver. He regularly received messages from *Pullah* near Munich, Germany and *Kassiotis* base near Athens, Greece. Through this relatively secure channel, *"Hypocrite"* had been instructed and guided to collect specific information and to mail it in invisible writing in common letters to fictitious addresses in France and Switzerland.

During trips abroad, *"Hypocrite"* had numerous rendezvous with CIA intelligence officers. State Security and KGB evidence gathered against Ivan-Asen in mid 1963 became overwhelming. Major Ivan Ochridsky, a government prosecutor, evaluated all relevant findings and determined a sufficient basis for legal proceedings. However, *"Hypocrite"* was in Paris, serving as an elected representative of the UN's Space Organization. State Security and KGB concluded that *"Hypocrite"* was a high-risk target for defection if a sudden trip to Bulgaria was orchestrated.

---

*   Colonel I. Dobrev becomes a trilling teacher at the State Security academy in the 1970s.

A stealthy KGB effort made it possible for Ivan-Asen to be officially invited by the UN (the Under Secretary General for Science and Technology of the UN was a KGB foreign intelligence officer) as a key guest speaker to an international conference on International and Space law in Moscow.

Neither Ivan-Asen, nor the CIA, had even the slightest clue as to the devilish trap set forth to take *"Hypocrite"* to the gallows.

Even before crossing the Soviet Union's passport control at Moscow's *Sheremetievo* International airport, KGB operational officers with official arrest warrants from Bulgarian and Soviet magistrates whisked Ivan-Asen into a private jet and flew him in the secrecy and darkness of the night to Sofia.

Under the premise that his punishment would be lessened, the State Security and KGB convinced *"Hypocrite"* to initiate a lengthy and devilish double game with the CIA. The KGB and State Security had a first hand opportunity to learn more about the intricate American goals, intelligence interests and methods of operations. In the process they expected to compromise and detain American officials in Sofia. The great KGB hope of a double operation turned out unsuccessful. The CIA's extreme caution, professionalism and early warning systems in place inadvertently tipped them off about Ivan-Asen's apprehension. Speculations exist, that for more than three years Ivan-Asen worked hard labor for 18 hours a day in the uranium mines of Southern Bulgaria, where his health deteriorated due to the silicate and radioactive poisoning of his lungs. The secret State Security records however, show that *"Hypocrite"* sentence was carried out within weeks of his conviction, in the beginning of 1964. A single shot to the back of his head in the Sofia Central Prison had ordained Ivan-Asen Georgiev's final journey to an unmarked grave.

THE DOUBLE

During 1967 an alert State Security PK (postal control) officer discovered secret writing in a letter of Dr. Radan Sarafov to his daughter Christine, a student in Switzerland. The letter was intercepted because of one of Sarafov's simple symptomatic errors: the envelope was without a sender, thus it was automatically categorized as suspicious. Making the most of new technology acquired from the west, new chemicals and new photo processing, State Security aggressively pursued spies, criminals and anonymous writers through the postal channels of communications.

Dr. Sarafov graduated from the prestigious Paris medical academy months before the beginning of the Second World War. As chief Doctor of one of Sofia's regional clinics, he was concurrently a professor at the Medical academy. His professional reputation made him well sought after for his accurate methods of medical treatments. People from all over the country scheduled appointments for visitation to his private office. As a result of his reputation and linguistic propensity, he became one of the most sought after physicians by western diplomats accredited to Bulgaria.

Under the premise that Dr. Sarafov could provide specific intelligence on his foreign clients, State Security had recruited him as secret agent in the beginning of 1960. However, Dr. Sarafov seldom had provided reliable information. Years later, his secret file was deactivated for lack of cooperation.

The State Security's PK efforts to intercept Dr. Sarafov letters, however, were inconsistent with the traditionally regular exchange of information among active spies and their control centers. The lack of results had made State Security and KGB management concerned that the *"fish was slowly swimming away"*. As a final measure, SCD-counterintelligence had imposed total control of Dr. Sarafov's office, including visually monitoring his activities and identifying all of his visitors. Through the new intelligence-gathering methods, SCD officers had succeeded to observe Dr. Safafov when he wrote secret messages and read microdots* in periodicals mailed to him from abroad with a microscope.

---

* Microdots often resemble a simple inconspicuous ink residue, incorporated in a single letter within a word, or an end of a sentence dot.

It was the first time State Security and KGB encountered the new sophisticated method of information and messages transmitted by microdots, attached on a predetermined spot on a book or periodical's page. This modern and advanced method was previously classified as a virtually unnoticeable and difficult to intercept form of spy communications.

Although, the State Security and KGB had identified and documented Dr. Sarafov's sophisticated activities, it was unknown for whom he worked and what his overall interests and goals entailed.

Sarafov daughter's involvement with the correspondence had convinced SCD that she should be arrested for espionage activities together with her father. As a result, the KGB lured Mrs. Sarafova into an elaborate, United Nations, Switzerland scam. The KGB organized a fictitious Bulgarian government delegation trip to the Middle East and a UN, Soviet representative, assigned as a head translator Sarafova.

The East German's foreign intelligence HVD (Stasi), has been training the security forces of Syria in conjunction with the KGB for years. Not surprisingly, they easily arranged for Christine Sarafova to be detained by the local security immediately upon her arrival in Damascus. Blindfolded, Sarafova was driven in secrecy to the Bulgarian Embassy compound. State Security operational officers initiated immediately interrogations of Sarafova for the duration of the night. The security around her arrest was physically diminished due to Sarafova's individual magnetism and her astutely offered collaboration. Unfortunately for the State Security officers, the erudite Sarafova had bluffed cooperation and had a different game plan in mind. Cleverly finding her way out through the embassy's restroom window, she had ran to freedom in the early morning dawn, gravely compromising the overall stealthy operation.

The interrogators had learned however, that Dr. Sarafov's main contact was the Bulgarian émigré Peter Radoev—Radly who presumably has been working for the CIA. The finding had allocated the case to the American desk of SCD and warranted the immediate arrest of Dr. Sarafov. Under skillful interrogations and high doses of psychotropic drones, Dr. Radan Sarafov acknowledge his clandestine relationship with the CIA for almost 10 years and the use of Belgian and Swiss diplomats as unwitting couriers of his secret writing letters with political, economic and military information about Bulgaria, the Soviet Union and the Warsaw Pact countries.

Dr. Sarafov was a mighty intellectual who elaborately and with dignity had justified his activities. His personal dislike and disagreement with the socialist system and the communist totalitarian dictatorship of the Soviet Union in Bulgaria has become his main irreversible credo. For his alleged spying, Dr. Radan Sarafov was sentenced to death and in the beginning of 1970 he was executed by a firing squad at the Sofia central prison.

TURNCOAT

"*Turncoat*" holds the position in my mind as the most dramatic and secretive espionage operation that I was ever involved with. This case against a First Chief Directorate—foreign intelligence officer dramatically influenced my personal and professional life, for it helped me to unambiguously comprehend the oppressive nature and inhumane principles of the totalitarian communist system and its security institutions.

During a few business trips and short intelligence assignments to Western Europe and the Middle East in early 1970s, Captain Zachary Kozarov, had become steadily exposed to the overwhelming democratic principles and prosperity of the western society. He observed in silent disbelief the undreamed-off high standards of living and enormous industrial achievements of free people. Kozarov's communist family upbringing should have precluded him from even the slightest unorthodox thinking; however, he saw hope in the west and envisioned a new way of life for his family. Marrying the daughter of a high-ranking Communist party functionary had opened unlimited opportunities to the young engineer with foreign language skills. With top party and government connections, Zachary easily obtained a prestigious job with the State Security's foreign intelligence—First Chief Directorate.

Deeply discontented with the socialist realities and idiosyncratic environment in his office, Kozarov eventually had approached American officials during a business trip to Belgrade, Yugoslavia. Although in possession of only limited compartmental secrets, he was well familiar with the overall intelligence officers training program in Moscow, the handling of illegal agents, Science and Technology Intelligence gathering, and most importantly, was in a final preparation for a four years assignment in Western Europe. He was an excellent *"agent in place"* for the CIA operations in the Balkans, and as the Belgrade residency shrewdly had calculated, he would be of greater value for American interests by staying in place, versus being assigned abroad and consequently defecting.

Satisfactorily passing a lie-detector test, Zachary Kozarov was accepted as a bona fide asset. However, his new professional masters diligently and firmly guided him to perform specific tasks and to exchange clandestine information with operational personal from the American Embassy in Sofia. According to his own submissions, Kozarov was trained by the CIA and was instructed how to perform clandestinely in Bulgaria. He was sincerely assured that his initial work in Bulgaria would be accepted as a solid guarantee and confirmation of his pledge to the American government's intelligence interests.

After an acceptable psychological and mental evaluation, instructors have been flown in from West Germany to train Kozarov in basic code ciphering and secret writing communications, code notepad use, dead drop operations, signal positioning and retrievals, and nonetheless basic surveillance detection and evasion techniques. The newly recruited American asset was informed that he would receive a monthly compensation of one thousand dollars deposited in an escrow account in the United States. Kozarov also initially had received one thousand dollars from the CIA for out of pocket expenses, and his stealthy anti-communist quests have been set off.

*　　*　　*

It was a chilly early March 1974 and the surveillance team following an American diplomat who was a suspected CIA operative had just started the second shift. The *"change in motion"* procedure however, was unable to find the diplomat's car on Javorov Boulevard as delineated by the first shift. Avoiding detection, the teams have been operating with radio transmitters off and by maintaining the target in distant visual control. The diplomat who has been following an unusual driving pattern through the city for almost an hour had vanished.

SID maintained *"flying brigades"* surveillance units, who were strategically positioned around key transportation and communication centers of the capital and were ready to help and assist. These units were considered very professional and the duty was historically awarded to the best and most masterfully performing officers.

In this early afternoon, a supplemental unit changed with the earliest shift on the parking lot of the SCD—counterintelligence, conveniently located in the suburb of *"Hladilnika"*. They faced the "Y" merge of two main arteries, leading traffic from the center of the city towards the ring road and the national park Vitosha.

Within a short time of taking the shift, the *"flying Dutchmen"* brigade received the center "Bore's" warning, that the main unit had lost visual sight of the *"Fox"*. The American diplomat was symptomatically anxious and had methodically attempted to detect surveillance. Thus, the driving pattern of *"Fox"* was highly unusual and the flying brigade was placed on high operational alert. Center analysts punctually foresaw an imminent secret operation of the target.

Two officers expediently intermingled with passengers at the nearby bus stop, nonchalantly controlling the bottlenecked intersection. Sure enough, one of the disguised hunters soon spotted the speeding Volvo with red diplomatic license plates. It appeared that the diplomat had made another tail-slipping maneuver through the neighborhood and as a result had briefly escaped any anticipated surveillance.

Passing the last tramway station, ""*Fox*"" exited the city. Less than a mile from the Ring road, not disturbed by any traffic, on a turn of the road, he diminished speed and the vigilant "*Dutchman*" observed him toss an object out of his window towards the base of a high voltage electric poll. The "*Fox*" subsequently sped away. At this instance, Captain Simeon Petkov, the unit's leader, decided to continue the pursuit of the diplomat, but not before dropping off an officer further on the road, with simple instructions: ". . . Do not approach the drop site, nor stay visible from the road, just monitor for any suspicious person or car approaching or retrieving the object . . ."

The main surveillance unit received feedback from the center about the whereabouts of "*Fox*" and soon took over the target on the Ring road. The next few hours of "*Fox's*" behavior were legitimate and justified. However, the drop site became the stage of virtually undetectable complex activities: The second "*flying brigade*" was promptly dispatched within the area, imperceptibly sealing the eventual drop site from all possible directions. An aged delivery van, hosting a specialized monitoring team soon took position far away. The meager, well-camouflaged driver with a greasy mechanics' suit leisurely was replacing a flat front tire, while in the van a team had set up advanced photo cameras aimed at the site.

Petkov's team remembered well some of the latest exercises with the highly skilled KGB trained instructors. The remote road, the right turns partially veiling the driver's activity from the following cars, and especially the permanent mark, the high voltage pole, were all suitably assessed as an almost circumstantially perfect dead drop.

At that time, the command center "*Bore*" unambiguously related to the field surveillance management that the American counterintelligence's section of SCD had requested extreme caution in handling the situation. All license plates of passing by cars were collected at both ends of the road; any walking persons near by were photographed and specialized units dispatched in order to secretly identify their identity.

Minutes past 5:00PM, a light beige popular Soviet made *Zhiguli* approached the site, stopped at the soft shoulder and a man in his early thirties retrieved an old twisted pipe, casually holding it with a napkin or a handkerchief. He was calm, although he checked the road in both directions numerous times before entering his car and driving away. A surveillance unit took the car under control, clandestinely following the target until he parked in front of a building across the Perlovetz Bridge. The driver was observed to enter with personal keys an address on Evlogi Georgiev Street, unflappably holding the old pipe, wrapped in a newspaper.

The delivery bus without a front tire was left to monitor the drop site for another 24 hours. The main unit followed the *"Fox"*, who legitimately visited *Intransmash**, an international construction and engineering company. Before returning to the Embassy, however, *"Fox"* drove by the suspect's building and at the station just across the street casually waited in line to fill up his tank with gas.

Eventually he had noticed with relief and content, a casually displayed long-necked vase with a red rose on the first floor window across the street. It was a prearranged signal that confirmed the successful recovery of the dead drop material, an almost routine procedure for *"Fox"* within the last few months.

The spirit at the American counterintelligence and surveillance departments was more than jubilant: A car registration check matched the target's address, revealing the identity of Zachary Kozarov, specialist at the State Committee for Science and Technical Progress.

A State Security archive check revealed to the astonished Nedelcho Bogdanov, chief of detachment and his deputy, Blagoi Palikarski, that Kozarov was in reality a FCD-foreign intelligence officer. The latest, verified with a personal photo of Kozarov, baffled the counterintelligence directorate. Was this a cunning FCD operation, or a flagrant betrayal? High-ranking State Security and KGB officials soon gathered in the counterintelligence's briefing room. Towards midnight, the directorate's chief, General George Anachkov, issued an urgent gag order to our small group: "... Ultimate secrecy and prevention of any leaks of information, even among any State Security officers!"

Within days, Kozarov was known only by his code name *"Traitor"* or *"Turncoat"* and was assigned to a new sumptuous office. The move was necessary for Kozarov's legend development, in line with his imminent foreign assignment. It craftily neutralized his access to secret or proprietary intelligence information. Kozarov's new office was at the Scientific Center of the State Committee for Science and Technical Progress (DCNTP) on the 4th kilometer of Boulevard Lenin.

Through two miniature holes drilled into the ceiling of the new Kozarov's office, advanced photo equipment and cameras allowed direct control of his activities. The task was very demanding to the monitoring SID officers, for they had to lay face down on two mattresses on the floor while monitoring directly through the visors of the photo camera or the movie camera the activities downstairs. Promptly installed phone taps on the target's office, home and eavesdropping "bugs" were constantly active. Active monitoring of Kozarov's home was promptly set off by urgently renting the apartment upstairs from a retired government official. Concocting a story about an ongoing major criminal

---

*   Institute for Transport and Machinery, a foreign trade consortium.

investigation of the petrol center across the street, State Security quickly moved to set a secure net around Kozarov.

During the early stage of these dynamic developments, I was summoned urgently to the office of General Ciril Neshev. With a legitimate cover and the submission of Heruvim Stoev, president of the government enterprise *"Petrol"*, I was assigned as Managing Director of the largest Sofia Petrol distribution Center *"Perlovetz"*. The center was well known as the "Diplomat's gas hub", for all foreign embassies were authorized by the Bureau for Support of the Diplomatic Corps (BODC) to use special discount coupons at this specific location's gas terminals. Similarly, cars of the Central Committee of the Communist Party, UBO-Secret service, Council of Ministers and the State Security, regularly used the center. Suddenly the petrol center became the command and coordination center for monitoring the residence of *"Traitor"* and the constant traffic of American and western diplomats. My center was responsible for the security coverage of the region in case of Kozarov's escape inclinations or extraction schemes by the western intelligence.

The new job was a respected, highly desirable and sought after business management position. It happened to be extremely demanding on my intellectual abilities in the beginning, for I had to learn the business procedures thoroughly and in the process train four new salesmen (five operational officers in total), and a new operations manager. The demanding sales/marketing functions and the strict financial management that I imposed soon become a remarkable management success, besides my never-ending counterintelligence operational duties. Virtually overnight I came in charge of controlling and managing the daily sales and distribution of almost $500,000 of petroleum products to the burgeoning diplomatic corps and selected government and public institutions. The distribution center was considered a "Gold mine" for making fast and big bucks, although through variety of combinations and semi-criminal scams. For that reason, with integrity and iron discipline I legitimized the business operations, justly replacing an affluent though greedy and corrupted retired State Security colonel. The rumor prevailed that I was a powerful "nephew" of Todor Zhivkov. Besides running the complex operational center, my new position required that I bring serious financial discipline among the existing staff of twelve and the four new additions, as well as set strict rules of engagement with diplomats and foreign nationals.

The surveillance successfully monitored *"Fox"* loading a new dead drop site with materials a few weeks later. The dead drop behind a metal heating radiator unit in the entrance to a residential building was nearby Festival Hall. Two hours later, *"Turncoat"* was observed parking his car near the exhibition hall. Casually walking across the street, he visited the building and was documented collecting a stone from behind the radiator. After few minutes of unjustifiable waiting in the darkness of the nearby tramway station, Kozarov entered his car and was followed to his home.

The technical center the same evening documented Kozarov as he used a pair of pliers and a hammer to fracture the naturally looking stone, revealing inside a bundle of $100 bills and coded instructions. Retrieving from an indiscernible pocket in the window drapes a tiny code notepad book, he deciphered the CIA message, and was observed preparing a lengthy answer on a special sheet of paper ingeniously rolled in the main console of the room's light fixture.

Four clandestine operations were successfully monitored and evidenced by State Security's SCD for four months. Everything was vigilantly and methodically documented as court evidence of Kozarov's treason and espionage activities. The "Turncoat" surreptitious activities and "Fox's" abnormal for his diplomatic status quests were diligently entered into the rostrums of the KGB success against the CIA. The KGB management soon approved "Turncoat's" apprehension and the initiation of an intricate double game with his American handlers. All gathered materials were carefully evaluated, classified in judicial files and submitted to the Investigative Directorate for professional assessment and review. Their motion was promptly submitted to a reliable state procurator.

Procurator Michail Novacov in a week determined that extensive and conclusive evidence of espionage activities of Zahary Kozarov against the State had been gathered, and he quickly issued a warrant for Kozarov and his wife's arrest for high national treason. To my enchantment, the managing magistrate Procurator Novakov was my neighbor. Not only did we live in the same building, but his wife Maria had also been a SID-surveillances department colleague that supervised the permanent control surveillance posts situated around the Doctors garden.

*   *   *

After complex preparations and heavy security measures, one early morning in May at about 7:00 AM State Security agents quietly arrested Zachary Kozarov and his wife. The arrest was carried out following the "Turncoat's" latest retrieval of dead drop materials. I was appointed by State Security management to participate in the arrest, as the only "civilian" (from the nearby business) to witness the search and recovery of incriminating evidences and the Kozarovs' arrest.

The early morning apprehension was a relatively simple, although rather merciless deed. Strict measures were taken to eliminate escape or suicide attempts and to veil any public disclosure. Zachary Kozarov turned pale and speechless when Blagoi Palikarski handcuffed him, affirming his arrest for espionage in favor of a foreign country. Observing in disbelief the accurate recovery of the hard evidence and the incriminating materials, Kozarov was asked thereafter to acknowledge in writing the validity of the findings. At this instance the *"Turncoat"* showed weakness, for he was unable to write and started trembling uncontrollable. Soon he and his wife, a short, dark haired and morbidly paled lady, together with a small baby girl were whisked to the Main Investigative Directorate on Razvigor Street in Lozenetz. We recovered from the garbage basket all of the coded messages that Kozarov had worked on the previous night, including a broken polymer case shaped in the form of a rock from the kitchen garbage been, secret note pads from the drapes and a lamp post cavity, as well as a hollow coin concealing notes, $2200 in cash from a wallet, personal possessions, stacks with secret and confidential documents from the FCD-foreign intelligence (obtained illegally and intended for delivery to the CIA), and an old vintage 6.35 mm hand gun.

Initially Kozarov refused to cooperate with the investigation. However, strongly influenced by psychologists and persuaded by the overwhelming evidence, he eventually started speaking thoroughly. Confronted by the vast collection of incriminating materials and nonetheless promises of leniency and no harm or retribution to his family, Kozarov was soon masterfully lured into a certainly deadly self-confessions.

State Security and KGB management were anxious to restore the communication process of *"Turncoat"* with *"Fox"*. However, during the days following the arrest, a prearranged and confirmed delivery of materials had passed by without exchange and inevitably had raised "red flags" within the American residency. It would have been extremely important for the American section of SCD and KGB, to get involved into a devilish, intelligent game of deception. The most sinister KGB goal, however, soon transpired: The KGB wanted to apprehend and expose the *"Fox"* and perhaps another American diplomat in the actual process of meeting and clandestinely exchanging secret information with Kozarov.

During dialogues with the procurator Novakov, I was assured that Kozarov would sooner or later face his bench and on the premise that high treason had been committed against the communist state would result in his condemnation to death: "... This will be my unquestionable, final and uncontestable ruling ..."

Eventually Novakov had received the sentence guidelines from high-ranking government officials, almost two months before the secret trail. Conversely, during this time, I often asked myself about the immeasurable, constant fear and immense risks one should constantly take and face in order to achieve an anticipated democratic freedom, to accomplish a better life and nonetheless to fulfill a decent human fate. To these questions, I years later attained answers by being a free and rational man, cunningly fulfilling anti-communist deeds similar to Kozarov's. Although Zahary Kozarov's case of communist betrayal was contained among only a few reliable State Security officers, there was serious moral impact on members of the foreign intelligence service.

Zachary Kozarov's human destiny was already transformed by his actions; from a blind communist ideology follower and satisfied government official, to the unfortunate velocities of a clear and present danger, he in the end walked into clear and certain death by communist executioners.

The KGB designed game of CIA deception was developed in the ethereal and wishful direction. Presumed legitimate exchange of post cards rejected Kozarov's second request for direct meeting. It had become indicative to the KGB and the counter-intelligence directorate that the CIA had discovered *Turncoat's*" arrest and thus terminated any forms of communication. In reality, Kozarov had cunningly cautioned the CIA by misspelling a post card word, sent to an address in Rome. Even under heavy drugs thereafter, *"Turncoat"* did not divulge his prearranged means of clandestine communications with the CIA.

Three months later, Zachary Kozarov was put on trial behind closed doors. I was one of only few State Security officials present during the court proceedings, endowed with a special pass by Procurator Novakov. The court convicted Kozarov of high national treason and sentenced him to death. Two High Court and State Council appeals were rejected and *"Turncoat a.k.a. Traitor"* was eventually executed in early 1975 at the Sofia Central Prison by a firing squad.

Soon thereafter *""Fox""* left on an ordinary TDY to West Germany, never to return to Bulgaria. Intercepted communications confirmed his new assignment to Frankfurt, Germany and his family promptly left Sofia.

Lieutenant-Colonel Nedelcho Bogdanov, as a reward, soon became the youngest Chief of State Security Regional Directorate in his native Stara Zagora oblast.

Although compartmentalization was a strict and well-enforced rule of operational security, it was amazing that as fact to the matter, the system was very susceptible from inside and from professionals with allowed access of need-to-know information. For instance, I loved to pop-up around 11:00AM in the American section's operational room at the northeast corner of the fourth floor, knowing that they had operational briefings every Monday at 10:00AM. On the wall's operational folding board, I was able to monitor the activities of all American targets identified as CIA, FBI, DOD or even NSA staff members. It was a literal synopsis, a clearly and cleverly push pinned overview of the work of many people and institutions against the American personnel, diplomats, and their connections, including but not limited to numerous pictures of individuals, dead drops, maps and suspects.

Regrettably, the *"Fox"* departure changed my duties with the American section of SCD. Soon I had to go through a complex financial and management audit of the oil distribution center in order to officially submit my resignation and announce to the staff that I had found a management job at the Ministry of Finance (my new legend).

With small, trivial discrepancies, the audit discovered that I had achieved substantial financial discipline and improved the profitability and quality of service to unprecedented level in just over seven months. This constructive and professional assessment allowed me to develop strong bond with the General Director of *Petrol*, Mr. Heruvim Stoev, for years to come.

COMMUNISM & TERRORIZM

The Palestinian Liberation Organization (PLO) in the early 1970s was granted a permanent mission status in Sofia. This mission, established on *Anton Ivanov* Boulevard, coordinated a variety of Palestinian and their factions' activities throughout Europe, the Balkans and the Middle East. With the stealthy help and assistance of the KGB and State Security, it was gradually transformed into a key secret intelligence center of Arafat's Fattah movement *Committee 77*. A mile west from the mission was located the foreign trade organization *Kintex*, proprietary organization, which PLO representatives and group of Turkish and Lebanese import/export traders have been utilizing to procure fake *Marlboro* cigarettes, pharmaceuticals, consumer goods, weapons, explosives, ammunition and military hardware.

Through eavesdropping, technical intelligence and well-placed agents, State Security and KGB received conclusive evidence of the broadening spectrum of specialized activities of the PLO and their Lebanese, Syrian, Egyptian, Kuwaiti and Jordanian factions. Substantial financial support and specialized training PLO and Fatah's Abu Jihad movement was offered to the secret network of Muslim Brotherhoods in Saudi Arabia, Syria, Kuwait and Iran. A potent under link of Fattah, the *Student Cells*, recruited the brightest students around the Middle East and Europe, even going further to the United States of America, and inducting the recruits into secret intelligence wings with extreme Islamic religious views.

One of the most ruthless and important PLO programs was to provide military and guerilla training, armament and multi purpose support to terrorist factions, conducting holy war, a soon to be named *Jihad* against Israel and major West European and American targets. These targets were proclaimed as those key affiliates that were morally supported and politically upheld by worldwide Zionism and the ruthless state of Israel. For hard currency and political considerations, PLO received advanced training in military and subversive operations by Bulgarian and Soviet military and security officials at a Berkovitza military polygon 60 km north of Sofia and a military base near Shumen (northeast Bulgaria). It was a well-coordinated KGB/GRU effort, expanding further to the Hungarian and East German (even Cuban) security officials, who conducted similar programs with representatives from Jordan, Syria, Egypt, Palestine, Afghanistan, Pakistan and other Arab countries.

Bulgarian universities and learning institutions educated and trained military, air force and navy officers, medical professionals, engineers, teachers and agricultural experts. Unknown to the PLO management however, State Security and KGB aggressively selected and recruited the most promising among the Palestinians and Arab students and graduates as secret agents and future stealthy collaborators.

By the late 1970s the PLO operational impunity in Bulgaria started to intimidate State Security and KGB. Tactful complaints were addressed to the PLO authorities, however the mission continued to run operations in a manner as such as if they were on own turf. By 1979, the PLO mission in Sofia, became not only a sinister center of international intrigues, illicit trades, weapons smugglings and terrorists gatherings, but also, against common diplomatic protocol and professional decency, it was transformed in to a sleazy brothel, where women with questionable reputation entertained diplomats and visiting Arab and Palestinian dignitaries. Many of the prostitutes were secret agents who timely reported activities, surreptitiously obtained copies of keys and even stole documents.

Technical and electronic eavesdropping by State Security revealed specific information on major PLO terrorist attacks in Western Europe, cunningly planned and perpetrated from the seedy Sofia mission. These conclusive evidences of the unorthodox PLO activities overfilled the revolutionary comradeship of the General Secretary of the Communist Party, Todor Zhivkov. He was prudent enough to maintain an atypical, nonetheless constructive relationship with Western Europe, the primary target of the PLO terror.

In October 1979, on Tano Tzolov's* recommendations, Todor Zhivkov instructed the Bulgarian Minister of Foreign Affairs Petar Mladenov to impose a strict and prohibitive status** on the PLO mission in Sofia. As a result, many ongoing and lucrative commercial PLO operations were redirected through a few new Bulgarian foreign trading companies. State Security had learned a practical lesson on how to effectively and successfully run business operations on its own. Nevertheless, they in the process cleverly utilized recruited foreign agents as business fronts. Old trading enterprises were astutely reorganized and promptly fashioned to handle lucrative international smuggling, arms trading and especially the procurement of embargoed high technologies. Turkish and Arab radicals and their extensive export/import traders were shrewdly exploited throughout the Middle East and Western Europe.

Similar to *Kintex*, the foreign trade company *Texim* was reinvented into a diverse international trading, business development and financial management/

---

*   Secretary of the Central Committee of the Communist Party.

**   One of the most disadvantageous bilateral statuses in international affairs.

banking group. Secretly set by the Central Committee of the Communist Party in early 1960s and managed by the State Security with offices in Austria, Germany, France, Italy, Lebanon and Switzerland, it was in reality an enterprise for laundering money from sales around the world of fake cigarettes, alcohol, armament, weapons, drugs, biochemical aditives and much more.

Traditionally State Security and KGB operational officers worked undercover as trade representatives guided by the KGB management to deliver not only weapons and explosives, but also hard currency to fraternal communist parties in Western Europe, leftist or radical organizations in the Middle East, revolutionary and liberation movements in Latin America, Africa and even far throughout Indo-China.

As outlined earlier, similar operational dealings were set into service in supporting radical and militant global movements, and terrorist organizations, such as but not limited to the Italian *Red Brigades*, German *Baader Meinchof*, Shining Pat's *Shindero Luminoso* and RAF the *Red Army Faction* and even Corsican, Bask and Irish prominent outlaws.

Facts to the matter were somehow documented and elaborately outlined in early 1980 by Clair Sterling in her book *The Terror Network*. With essentials, clarity and intelligent journalism she succeeded to link *Kintex, Transimpex* and *Texim* to vast networks of money laundering banking enterprises and illicit trading and smuggling of weapons and drugs throughout Europe and the Middle East. Most importantly links to the growing terrorist activities around the globe, indiscriminately supported by the Soviet KGB and State Security have been unraveled. This proliferation of illegal communist government activities should be linked with the faltering socialist economy anxious and hungry for hard cash. In the mid 1970s the greatest hard cash generating industry throughout Eastern Europe and especially in Bulgaria was the military industrial complex of companies, specialized in the manufacturing and assembly of broad spectrum of specialty military production.

NTR—Science and Technology foreign intelligence was structured on a priority basis to attain embargoed equipment and systems and metal cutting instruments for optimization. Complex cooperation was established between State Security and KGB-GRU and key industrial conglomerates of Bulgaria and the Soviet Union for the final assembly and sub assembly of modern military armament. By early 1983, prior to my departure to the West, the military industrial complex of Bulgaria was already the leading East European/Warsaw Pact manufacturer and exporter of military and communication technology, armaments, weapons, explosives and multitude of offensive weapons systems. Through secret statistics available only at the Central Committee of the Communist Party, I discovered that this sector of the economy had overgrown any other industrial sectors almost five fold. Expressed in convertible dollar value for 1983, all Bulgarian weapons systems and armament trade to the developing countries exceeded 1.2 billion dollars. This figure reached 1.7 billion dollars by the end of 1985*.

During 1977 Ognian Doinov, Deputy Chairman of the State Council introduced an intelligent proposal for aggressive development of the Bulgarian military industry in cooperation with the Soviet Union. Substantial investments in modern technology illegally obtained from the West developed the growing after market needs of the armament industry. New automated lines for manufacturing of multi million units of bullets, grenades, cartridges, anti-tank and surface to air missiles, surface to surface and conventional as well as smart mines were implemented and quickly introduced into the burgeoning markets.

Suddenly the developed Bulgarian socialist economy was thriving on the malevolence of the global conflicts: Besides the murderous and often loaded with bio-chemical agents missiles *Arrows* and *Harpoons* for Africa and the Middle East, substantial new radio communication technologies were manufactured for the armies of the Warsaw Pact as well as for many others, including Iraq, Syria, Angola, Mozambique, Libya and etc. New on demand, hydro-acoustic buoys were developed and sold around the globe for substantial hard cash amounts. The State Committee on the Military Industry with leaders Tano Tzolov and Ognian Doinov became not only the main coordinating body, but most importantly; imposed timely transitions of many existing industrial facilities towards military manufacturing and assemblies.

Through the Ministry of Foreign Trade and FCD-foreign intelligence experts, Ognian Doinov succeeded to impose compulsory and complex intergovernmental contracts with the consumer countries. Such as, but not limited to Nigeria, Zimbabwe, Angola, Congo, Mozambique and many more in Africa, Latin America, the Middle East and Asia. Boldly alleviating Western and Asian competition, Doinov shrewdly established bilateral economic and interstate associations, assuring base and incremental business growth. I should clearly delineate the feasibility of Doinov's unusual talents: A Grand master and maverick named Robert Maxwell cunningly surfaced in Doinov's life and artfully transformed the communist political and economic interests into stealthy Israeli Mossad operations of immense magnitude. Eventually Ognian Doinov learned and propagated well the revolutionary lessons of his Soviet mentors, for he established strictly enforceable and shrewdly formulated international bylaws and multilateral agreements.

Attaining strategic geo-political interests for the Soviet Union however was neither the sole purpose, nor the greedy generation of hard cash for the

---

*	The electronic tap on Ognian Doinov's office reviled these figures in April 1986. Information corroborated 15 years later by Ivan Damianov, Manager of "Kintex" in 2001.

presumed developed socialism was the ultimate goal. Astutely, Maxwell's network generated more than cash and influence. Perhaps some of the greatest Mossad operations in the Soviet Union and worldwide were perpetrated through these stealthy alliances. The same old crafts were perceptively reincarnated during the 1990s and shrewdly exploited by the Russian Red Mafia and network of Jewish entrepreneurs for enormous profits, business developments and nonetheless stealthy Mossad strategic interests.

MERCHANTS OF DEATH

During the late 1960s and early 1970s my father was assigned as the leader of a small and secretive State Security managed operational group. He was responsible to assure proper and secure transactions of the burgeoning Soviet, Czechoslovakian, East German, Hungarian and especially Bulgarian military and armament industry with international clients.

Together with a compatriot from the resistance against the fascism, Colonel Stoian Luckov, they were assigned to assess some of the presumed "damages" inflicted by George Naidenov and Hristo Milanov on *Texim* and to revitalize some of the promising business connections. Eventually they developed the new *Texim* into a viable commercial and international logistics network that controlled the European and the Middle East inland channels of heavy-duty transportation, including but not limited to restricted commodities across international borders. Many of the transactions were conducted exclusively under the auspice of the international TIR agreements governing free and transit customs passage of registered and certified vehicles. The same company already grown significantly into a multi-million dollar government enterprise few years later, SOMAT (Economic Enterprise-International Auto Transport) managed by Stoian Luckov, was implicated during the 1990s with the facilitation of endless smuggling operations and even kidnappings. The latest was based on findings of forgotten State Security secret documents about the illegal abduction and trans-border smuggling of the renowned Bulgarian dissident Boris Arsov from Denmark to Bulgaria.

The enterprise generated substantial hard cash for the Bulgarian government, State Security and KGB operations and even other fraternal communist organizations, through shrewd often semi-legitimate business and logistics practices. Stealthy shipments of weapons, ammunitions, pharmaceuticals, and government sanctioned smuggling, embargoed technology transfers and endless intelligence gathering operations characterized their overall modus operandi.

In preparation for establishing local dominance and influencing rivaling religious groups and neighboring countries, Iraqi and Iran security establishments independently approached the Bulgarian government for assistance in procuring weapons, ammunition and spare parts for their ailing and aging military and dominantly Soviet made weapons and equipment.

Although it was considered a one-way business approach, State Security and KGB offered arms and equipment for business, political and intelligence interests within the region, to both Iran and Iraq. It was a *"false flag recruitment"* intelligence tradecraft, skillfully put into practice to infiltrate both regional government structures with well-trained "*cutout*" communist agents.

Top-secret political, economic and military assessments of the local residencies and diplomatic channels identified fast budding ethnic and nationalistic tensions and amplified movements of military personnel and equipment in close proximity with the borders of both countries. The region was depicted as loaded with explosive tensions, religious fundamentalism, chauvinistic nationalism and ever-lasting territorial rivalry. The destructive ethnic hater was further justified with the deepening economic instability and regional uncertainty.

The State Security resident in Teheran, Colonel Blagoi Plachkov* and the station chief in Baghdad, General Stefan Mitev, flew to Sofia to assess the situation and to assure more or less secure channels for delivery of multi million dollar military cargos to the rivaling neighbors. After intense evaluations with the KGB center and some fraternal security representatives, General-Colonel Velko Palin** authorized the operation with the personal approval of the General Secretary Todor Zhivkov. Two of the largest weapons contracts for the Middle East were set off, although the KGB had conclusive evidence and reliable intelligence that an imminent regional and destructive war was in the making.

The substantial quantity of weapons, spare parts and ammunition had to be packaged in civilian crates, reducing the vulnerability from the Turkish authorities. Twelve eighteen wheeled Mercedes-Benz trucks were designated to travel first to Iraq. The prevailing decision was made due to the vast industrial and construction Bulgarian projects in Iraq. Most of them however, would be deliberately damaged and destroyed within months by Bulgarian made weapons, secretly delivered to Iran.

My father assessed these logistic endeavors as being of exigent and uncertain nature. The Malatia, Mus and especially Bitlis regions of Turkey, were infamous for armed tribal bandits. Furthermore the early spring season was perceived as very harsh for the heavy vehicles passing through the high elevated and poorly maintained icy roads. However, a time delivery contingency clause shrewdly attached by the Iraqis had made their deal a priority. The operation was dangerous and exceedingly illegal. Making the matter unforgiving: any arms smuggling or

---

*   Future deputy director of FCD-foreign intelligence and chief of Active measures department.

**   Chief of the Military and Administration department of the Central Committee of the Communist Party.

illegal weapons trading in Turkey was punishable by mandatory 20 years of hard labor.

Semi-legitimate TIR certificates were obtained through a reputed international logistics agency in Zeebruge, Belgium for international transit shipments. The Turkish authorities in Istanbul had approved the certification, however not without the secret cooperation of a bribed high-ranking Turkish official, soon to become an FCD-foreign intelligence agent.

Reliable and trustworthy truck operators, mostly retired security or military officers, were selected. My father was appointed as managing director of the convoy of vehicles, responsible for the overall security and success of the multi-million dollar operation.

His professionalism and cunning was to assure the harsh escapade and three purses full of $20,000 each for any needs, bribes or etcetera.

Anticipated frictions with the Turkish authorities have started almost as soon as the trucks had arrived at the Istanbul's commercial ferry district. On the way to Uskudar on the Asian side of the Bosporus, the first six heavy trucks practically prevented the ferry from departure. Concerned ferry captain had summoned the Port inspector, in order to review the shipping documents, as an apparent "good will" policy between the traditionally hostile Bulgarian and Turkish officials. The inspector's suspicions eventually had to be promptly thwarted with a case or two of Marlboro cigarettes tactfully offered as an excuse for his inconvenience. The official's cooperation was tactfully and professionally developed by my father and eventually exploited further into assistance with the port and ferry problems for the remaining six trucks. Paying symbolic additional ferry fees and flanked by the port inspector, my father had secured passage of all trucks to Asia.

The unanticipated "Rubicon" of Asia was easily taken over. The maximum load per truck allowed by Turkish law was 22 tons, while each of the twelve trucks had been loaded with close to 30 tons of merchandise. Only a very short sited, virtually blind port inspector could have accepted as a legitimate international transshipment, a cargo of so heavy agricultural machinery and Marlboro cigarettes.

Legitimizing the shipment, a clever operational officer had furnished each truck with distinguishable flags and large window stickers of the United Nations' FAO (Agricultural Organization). Permanently attached, to the radio antennas of the identical, blue painted Mercedes-Benz trucks and on the front windshields, hence they had added significant legitimacy and credibility to the overall project. The FCD active measures department successfully had disseminated an aggressive propaganda through European and Meddle Eastern TV and newspapers, providing that the European Community and International organizations had been generously providing help for the droughts devastated Iraq. The elaborate weapons smuggling operation, in grave violation of the international laws and imposed embargos, had been cunningly transformed in to a sinister, "humanitarian mission" of unknown to the world future proportions and consequences, under the auspice of the leading United Nations organization.

To show the world it's commitment to humanitarian causes, the Turkish government, in few instances had provided not only free passage through the mandatory transportation inspection centers across the country, but also had offered military and even police escorts. It would be more of a Turkish propaganda for the international media, rather than a sincere concern about the real hunger and devastation in Iraq. However, the news coverage will prove to be an excellent cover up, easily distorting and misleading the intelligence gatherings by the Iranian *Pasdaran* security and intelligence agency throughout Turkey.

On the seventh day, near Lake Van, in the Kurdistan Mountains, the convoy eventually was ambushed during the early evening hours by an armed band of Kurdish separatists. They happened to be members of the leftist Kurdish Peoples Party and after brief negotiations, as soon as their leader had learned that the convoy was Bulgarian, they apparently had vanished in the night, but not before taking away few cases with cigarettes from one of the ambushed trucks. Coincidentally, the bandleader had undergone training by the Bulgaria military, and thereafter even was identified as an RUMNO (military foreign intelligence) agent. Once at Zakhu, Iraq, the convoy was greeted by cheering residents and children, and escorted by Iraqi military police to Mosul Airport, whereas at a designated warehouse two of the trucks had been unloaded. The operation eventually had been successfully completed in Baghdad a day later.

A specially dispatched BTV—Bulgarian Television crew had filmed a highly publicized documentary. My father became overnight a celebrity at home, based on the TV reports and his 30 minutes interview with the most popular talk-show. Numerous articles and TV reports had been published and viewed all over the region and Europe in promoting the great humanitarian mission of the Bulgarian and the European governments. Only two of the truck drivers and only few privileged individuals knew that these shipments had become the final stage of the Iraq's imminent preparations for a deadly war with Iran.

Within the following 40 days, on the main highway to Erzerum in the vicinities of the secluded majestic far-east Turkish mountaintop Bagirpasha, a similar convoy safeguarded by the falling night would split unnoticed in half. Six long-hauled trucks would deliver next day substantial shipment of military hardware and ammunition to the Iraqi's archenemy—Iran. Driving without any rest through the rugged dangerously iced mountainous roads, shielded by the darkness of the night; in the early morning hours my father's restless team had crossed the Turkish-Iranian border at Bazargan. The other six trucks from the same convoy under the management of Colonel Nenko Todorov had completed successfully the second shipment to Iraq, once again masqueraded under the banners of the United Nations.

For the fallowing nine years many operations had been successfully carried out and perpetrated in astonishing secrecy all over Europe, the Middle and the Far East. The Soviet and Bulgarian communist leadership had been shortsightedly creating and sustaining a developed socialist economic prosperity through elaborate smugglings and exports of savagery.

However, despite all of the clever and shrewd totalitarian initiatives, neither the merciless internal oppressions, nor the international malevolence helped the Soviet Union, the infantile East Europe and the small global socialist fraternity to annihilate the decent human pursuits for freedom and democracy. Lenin's bloody Bolshevik revolution and the utopian communality were overtaken in the end of the 20th century by a velvet revolt, pursuing human identity, liberty and economic prosperity.

END

STATE SECURITY

First Chief Directorate—foreign intelligence: Equivalent to the CIA in the USA. It functioned as the main political, science and technology, economic, enemy emigration and cultural heritage arm of the communist governments' interests abroad. It was the directorate of the KGB's global intelligence operations, and liaison with leftists, radical terrorists and narcotics trafficking organizations.

Second Chief Directorate—counterintelligence. Similar functions to the FBI in the USA. Departments: American, British/French/Italian, Germany/Austria, Turkey, Greece, Communism revisionists—China, Romania, Albania, Yugoslavia, etc., developing countries, tourism, foreign relations and commerce, transportation, border control, state secrets, analysis and information.

Third Directorate—military counterintelligence. Functioning as FBI throughout all branches of the military, air force, navy and the army construction units.

Fourth Directorate—communications, radio and cipher counterespionage and counter intelligence. Government and intelligence secure communications with embassies, residencies and agents abroad. Monitoring and analyzing any radio and electronic waves from specific regions of the world. During the Cold War era aggressively scrambling western radio and TV emissions for the East European region (BBC, RFE, RV, etc.)

Fifth Directorate—*Secret Service.* Protection of high ranking (VIP) members of the communist party and the government.

Sixth Directorate—Internal counterintelligence

Seventh Directorate—Center for analysis and information. Prepares the daily "top-secret" operational bulletin for limited members of the communist party and the government leadership.

Independent State Security Departments:

First Department—State Security detention and investigations.

Second Independent Department—surveillance and clandestine radio/video monitoring of diplomats and State Security targets. Conducts covert investigations and background reporting on individuals through place of birth, work and residence.

Third Department—State Security archive of targets, secret agents and Ministry of Internal Affairs specialized records.

Fourth Department—Description and translation of all operational and technical operations from radio, telephone and electronic monitoring. Highly specialized section represented well-trained experts in locks /safes picking, penetration, electronic bugs' installation, tapping telephone lines and video monitoring equipment installations.

SPAR—BOOK SOURCES

I. Secret, top-secret and confidential sources:

1. The KGB-FCD* archive materials on DORs**:
   "Nemesis, Hypocrite, Turncoat, Double, Belarusian, Twin,
   Play writer, Panjandrum, Monk, Star, Vampire, Leipzig, Marat".
2. The State Security SCD*** materials on DORs:
   "Hypocrite, Double, Turncoat, Doctor, Fox, Nurse, Professor,
   Nincompoop, Lioness, Priest, Den, Castle, Club, Slammer, Carlos, Vivaldy, Geologist,
   Mazurka."
3. Archive of the Central Committee of the Communist party.(Sofia and Moscow)
4. Archive of the MIA****—State Security.
5. Archive of the MIA—Foreign Passports.
6. Archive of the KGB Center—MIA, Sofia.
7. Western technology, 1979, Ognian Doinov, Member of the Political Bureau of the CC of the CP.
8. Top-secret Bulletins of the CC of the CP (1976-1984)
9. State Security daily confidential bulletins (1972-1984)
10. Soviet Military Industrial Commission—Top-secret analytical reports: 1978-83.
11. The KGB and State Security reports on Pope John Paul II assassination attempt, August 1982.
12. Joint Resolution October 1982: The KGB and State Security fight against the Western centers of ideological subversion.
13. American and British Intelligence, 1973 KGB, A. Bureniok,
14. Who is who—Bulgaria & Soviet Union, CIA.
15. History of State Security, MIA 1982.
16. KGB & SS training manuals on Intelligence-I, Counterintelligence-II, Surveillance-IV.

II. Public, open or historic sources:

17. Court documents: Traicho Kostov—1949, Sofia.
18. Anglo-American Commission on the post WW II Balkans—1950.
19. Fascism, Dr. Z. Zhelev, 1977
20. US Justice Department, M.A. Noriega indictment 1996.
21. US Justice Department, Aldrich Ames indictment 1995.

22. The time of the Assassins, C. Sterling 1983.
23. Eclipse, Mark Perry, 1992, NY.
24. Central Intelligence, Richard Cur, 1994.
25. Milt Bearden, DDO CIA.
26. Duane Clarridge "Dewey", DDO CIA.
27. John Appel, SA FBI.
28. Frank Butino, SA FBI.
29. Inside the KGB, O. Gordievsky.
30. Political dilemma, E.Dainow 2002.
31. Corriere dela Serra (1981-84)
32. Reppublica (1981-84)
33. El Giorno (1982-86)
34. The Intelligence, R. Stolz, BEARF*****, 1994.
35. Court documents, T. Zhivkov indictment 1991-3.
36. Iz zapiski razvedchika,****** A. Polianskii, 1999, Moscow.
37. No other choice, G. Blake, 1990, NY, Simon & Schuster.
38. Fourth man, A. Boyle, 1974, NY, Dial Press.
39. Vostok-Zapad******* E. Makarevich, 2003, Moscow.
40. Enigma spy, J. Cairncross, 1997 London, Century.
41. KGB protiv MI-6, R. Krasilnikov, 2000, Moscow, Centralpoligrafia.
42. Betrayal, T. Weiner, D. Johnston, N. Lewis, 1995, NY, RH.
43. Bulgarian umbrella, V. Kostov, 1988, NY.
44. The rise and fall of the Bulgarian connection, E. Herman, F. Broadhead, 1986, NY
45. Spy Dust, A & J. Mendes, NY 2001.
46. Other side of deception, V.Ostrovski, Cn, 1999.
47. Dennis de Concini, Senate intelligence committee.
48. State Security & George Dimitrov, 1979, Sofia, MIA.
49. State Security museum—MIA, Sofia 1988.
50. Razvedka,******* P. Gromushkin, 2002, Moscow.

*Foreign Intelligence,** Case of operational investigation,*** Counterintelligence, **** Ministry of Internal Affairs,***** Intelligence forum—Sofia 1994. ****** Spy notes. ******* East-West,******* Intelligenc

INDEX

303

CPSIA information can be obtained at www.ICGtesting.com
Printed in the USA
LVOW081605190313

325017LV00005B/817/A